William Seymour

A Biography

Craig Borlase

Seymour Press
Lanham, MD

William Seymour: A Biography
Copyright © 2021 Craig Borlase.

All rights reserved. No part of this publication may be reproduced, distributed, or transmitted in any form or by any means, including photocopying, recording, or other electronic or mechanical methods, without the prior written permission of the publisher, except in the case of brief quotations embodied in critical reviews and certain other noncommercial uses permitted by copyright law. For permission requests, write to Seymour Press "Attention: Permissions Coordinator," P O Box 5544, Capitol Heights, MD 20791.

ISBN: 9781938373558
LCCN: 2021938066

Copyright © Seymour Press, Lanham, MD

Dedication

This book is dedicated to Reverend Chris Russell. Thank you for the gift of your friendship, your defiant wisdom, and your uncompromising integrity. You help me see more.

Acknowledgements

To the people who got it started. Chris Russell told me about William Seymour; Mike Pilavachi got excited about him; and David Moloney saw the value of the book. Each of you has your fingerprints on this. As does Jim Lawson, whose interest reignited my own.

The people at Relevant—Jeff Jackson, Cameron Strang, and Cara Davis—were gracious, helpful, and acted as vital links in introducing me to the good people at Strang. And, of course, without the skill, patience, and tenacity of Mark Sweeney—my literary agent, who goes beyond the call—I'd still be wondering who on earth to talk to next. Thank you, Mark, and Janet, too.

David and Jenny Rosser have always been there for crisis talks, and the fresh insight that Richard Herkes gave was a timely boost. Bishop David Pytches gave further contacts and enthusiasm, and I am grateful for his influence.

The book would not have been written without the guiding lights of those who have already written on William Seymour. In particular, the work of Douglas Nelson, James R. Goff Jr., and Vinson Synan has been vital to my research, as has the exhaustive research already carried out by Larry Martin. He has been gracious, helpful, and a true blessing. While I scratch the surface of the story in this book, Larry's eight volumes chronicle the Azusa experience in painstaking detail. If this book has whetted your appetite, his books should be your next step. Visit www.rrmi.org or www.azusastreet.org for more. Thank you, Larry, for your generosity.

Along the way, I have had the pleasure of coming into contact with some remarkable people. Members of St Mary's Episcopal Church, Franklin, Louisiana, were extremely hospitable and helpful, in particular, Fielding Lewis and Daryl Paul. Delores Stuart at Little Jerusalem Baptist Church, Ricohoc, Louisiana, also got me thinking.
In Los Angeles, I was greatly assisted by Dr. Eddie Gibbs, Dr. Bill Kostlevy, and David Bundy. To Bill, in particular, I owe great thanks.

Charles and Janet Morris sourced great food, conversation, and a wonderful waitress. I'm looking forward to more of each.

Rev. Jennifer Woodruff provided manuscripts, as did the British Library and the University of North Carolina.

To Stephen Strang and the team at Charisma—Barbara Dycus, Ann Mulchan, Woodley Auguste, Maureen Haner—thank you so much.

Thanks, are also due to Estrelda and the team at Seymour Press, who have given this book a new lease of life.

Last of all, though, my thanks go out to Emma, Evie, Barney, Bessie, and Libby. With you all of this makes sense.

Contents

Preface i
1 William Seymour Gains His Vision 1
2 The State of Louisiana Is Formed and Raised 7
3 Seymour's Life Begins 13
4 William Seymour Learns His Lessons 25
5 Poverty Strikes and Prophecy Inspires 35
6 Opposition and Opportunity Are Found 43
7 William Seymour Finds Unexpected Inspiration 49
8 Agnes Ozman Is Introduced 57
9 Charles Parham Becomes Better Known 65
10 Charles Parham Remains Cloaked 77
11 William Seymour Meets Alma White 85
12 William Seymour Delivers His Message to His Hosts 93
13 William Seymour Receives His First Job Appraisal 101
14 Passions Are Unleashed 105
15 William Seymour Presses Forward 111
16 The Church Delivers a Message 119
17 April 1906 Brings Change 127
18 We Meet Florence Crawford 133
19 Lives Are Transformed 141
20 William Seymour Connects With His Widest Audience 149
21 Charles Parham Delivers His Briefest Sermon 157
22 The Future Is Glimpsed 165
23 Charles Parham's Story Is Told 171
24 William Seymour's Faith Rises Even Higher 179
25 William Seymour Is Deceived 187
26 The Doors Are Closed 195
27 William Seymour Is Forced to the Edge 201
28 William Durham Wrestles for Control 207
29 The Splits Start to Split 213
30 William Seymour Considers the Future 219
31 The Story Ends and Repeats 225

Preface

Somewhere around my office is a scrap of paper. On it are ten or eleven names, most of them misspelled. Halfway down the list is scratched: "William Seymore (sic)—Azusa (sic) Street—Pentecostalism, etc." It was in 2001 that I wrote it, dictated by Chris, a good man with a good brain and a good heart. I'd asked Chris for a list of people that he thought would make a good subject for a biography, and he had come up with the goods. I'd heard of some, were confused by others, and intrigued by most.

Within twenty minutes of researching the life of William Seymour, I was hooked. Not only had I worked out how to spell his name, but I had in front of me a handful of headlines that astounded me. Son of ex-slaves…blind in one eye…mentored, and then knocked down by a racist…verandas collapsing under the weight of people eager to get close to him as he prayed…thousands getting saved at the humble meeting hall in downtown Los Angeles.

Yet as the research went deeper it became clear that this was a story I needed to learn from, not just write about. William Seymour's life started one hundred and two years before my own, but there is way more than a century's distance between us. Seymour grew up with slavery breathing down his neck and the struggles of race, religion, and civil rights defining his times. I did not. But there is something about the life and times of this man that I found irresistible, something that still feels applicable to life for me right now. Thousands of miles away in the safety of suburban England, William Seymour's story feels closer, bigger, and more important than any I've come across in a long time.

That was sixteen years ago. A lot has changed since then—for all of us.

Back then it never really occurred to me to wonder whether I, a white guy from England, had the right to tell the story of an African

American from Louisiana. If I'd really thought about that question, maybe I would have never moved forward with the book. If I was writing it today, I'd probably use different language in places—favoring the term African American over black, for example. Perhaps I'd focus more on race and dig around a little to see more clearly how events at Azusa Street directly affect the church today. But what I absolutely know for sure is that I would still have been fascinated by William Seymour, because that's exactly how I felt when I first heard of him two decades ago. And it's exactly the same way I feel today.

William Seymour matters not because of his status as Father of the Modern Pentecostal Movement. After all, few have heard of him and there are plenty who would argue that the title ought to be shared with Charles Parham—an antihero if ever there was one. It lies in the glue that holds the story together. It lies in his small steps.

William Seymour could have chosen to walk such a different path. Bitterness and resentment could so easily have defined him. Like King Lear, it appeared that Seymour was "a man more sinned against than sinning," but his end was no tragedy. In the obscurity and betrayal, we can find a man whose life lights the way. His sacrifice and obedience, his constant decision to pursue God and offer grace and peace to all around him inspire me.

There are many good reasons to celebrate his life right now. One hundred years from the beginning of the revival on Azusa Street, it is good to remember our roots. Looking back on the part he played in the dawn of Pentecostalism, it is right that we learn about our shared past. Facing the uncomfortable truths about the betrayal and racism within the faith is a bold yet essential step for us right now. We must look at today's church, admit faults, and work to heal divisions.

But more than all these good reasons for learning about the life of William Seymour, there is one that rises above the rest. His life touches the four hundred million Pentecostals around the world today, not because he preached well or promoted with skill. He simply followed Christ, taking those small steps of humility, obedience, and sacrifice.

Let's not wrestle the glory for ourselves, but, instead, let us put the gospel into practice, right here, right now, by choosing to love God and others with all that we have within us. As the man himself said: "Don't go out of here talking about tongues; talk about Jesus…" He's the real hero of this story.

CRAIG ORLASE
OXFORDSHIRE, ENGLAND
MARCH 2021

Chapter 1
William Seymour Gains His Vision

"I can no longer see."

Cincinnati, Ohio, 1902. A sick man coughs in a small room in a boarding house at 23 Longworth. The room, like the neighborhood, is unremarkable. They call it *Little Africa* or *Bucktown,* and its streets are full of identical scenes of the slow suffocation of hope. These are the places where children of ex-slaves live out their search for something better. This is how they hunt for a future that surpasses the past, for a present that delivers on the promises of old. This is the Great Migration in all its grit and glory. For the man sweating and coughing and battling a fever, his exodus might end right here.

Though the story of every migrant is unique, they are wearily lacking in variety. Here in this boarding house room the props and player could be any of hundreds in the area, any of thousands in the city, or millions currently spread across America's northern cities. These are the scenes of aspiration's collision with reality, and they contain little in the way of variety. The furniture is sparse: a bed, a washstand. In the corner, the carpetbag erupts clothes. A table beneath a Bible. A curtain hiding from the failing light beyond. No electricity of course, but intermittent, struggling, ailing power of a different source comes from the bed. Our man, coughing, fevered, aching, consciousness teasing him, taking him back to the graveyards and death-hushed bedsides of youth. How many others have slept in this bed? How many have failed to wake up?

Too many times he has sat, knelt, wept in the corners of rooms like this while others have lost life at times just like these. Brothers, sisters, a father. His brothers, his sisters, his father. All have failed to make it up from here, failed to string life's story out for a further few weeks or moments. Yet this story does not end here, not at this bedside in this city. The man will rise, weaker, scarred, yet with a strength and resolve he only previously suspected could have been his. Envisioned and inspired, walking wounded, an army of one, William Seymour's search for direction and purpose will end. His journey towards destiny will begin.

Twenty-one days was all it took. Twenty-one days ago, William Seymour was walking, talking proud. Waiting on tables in some faceless restaurant, living the free life, making the future his own in the North. Twenty-one days ago, he had nothing. Now, his body covered in sores, his left eye refusing to offer anything but the vaguest impressions of a fogged perspective, his body weak and burning, he is finally fit for the challenge ahead.

Welcome to the paradox of William Joseph Seymour. The man who had to lose sight to gain vision, the son of the ex-slave who was mentored by a racist, the soft-spoken black man who left whites aghast as races intermingled and the power of the spirit fell. Last and greatest of all the ironies about this unassuming pastor is this: His legacy touches millions of Christians today, yet his name remains all but unknown.

*

In 1902, Seymour was caught up in an outbreak of a mild form of smallpox that infected 130,000 people across a country that resisted European trends for vaccination. Ten percent of those affected were found in nearby Cleveland, where the standard 20 to 30 percent fatality rate was upheld as 224 lives were claimed.[1] Yet regardless of location, the effects of smallpox were the same. Starting with a ten- to fourteen-day incubation period, no signs would emerge. At the end of this "pre-eruptive stage" came three days of flu-like effects: headache, backache, nausea, fever, chills, convulsions, delusions, and a scarlet rash that might appear on the face or body. Strangely, playfully, the fever would then depart for a day or two, tempting the victims to believe that they had made it through some lesser infection.

Enter the "eruptive stage." The infection worsened, a rash would erupt, spread over the body, while focusing attention on the face and limbs. Soon there would be pimples, blisters, and, finally, pustules that would dry into crusts or scabs. Skin would phase from pink to red, as if it had been burned or scalded, feeling hot to the touch. At times it would peel off, flaccid sheets giving way to the touch. The internal attack was even worse: lungs, heart, liver, intestines, and other organs would all turn into battle lines. Eyes were a particularly favorite target, and ulcers on the surface left about 1 percent of smallpox survivors blind in one or both eyes. Those who survived were left wearing the same medals of deep scars upon their face.

Those who died did so within a couple of days or, at best, a couple of weeks of the start of the infection's full attack. Hemorrhaging into the skin, throat, lungs, intestines, or uterus could all claim the victim's life, as could any number of secondary infections. As for treatment, then, as now, there was little to do but to let it run its course. While early civilizations offered sacrifices in the hope of appeasing a vengeful deity, other cultures chose to bleed, overheat, or overwhelm their sick to a speedier death.

Smallpox's apocalyptic power has long inspired a mix of fear and awe. Names have been given to reflect the approach of each society: the English knew it as "the great pox" while in some parts of West Africa it was known simply as *naba*, "the chief of all diseases."[2] Like many that hold onto power, smallpox was never a respecter of class, creating an impressive alumni of victims and narrow escapers. George Washington survived, as did Queen Elizabeth I of England, while two Japanese emperors, kings of Burma and Siam, and perhaps the Roman emperor Marcus Aurelius succumbed to its ultimate death sentence. In the eighty years leading up to 1775, it boosted its credentials among the social elite by notching up some impressive results: an English queen, an Austrian emperor, a king of Spain, a tsar of Russia, a queen of Sweden, and a king of France. Abraham Lincoln found himself on the wrong end of a mild case upon his return from delivering the

Gettysburg Address in 1863. His son, Tad, may have passed it on—the young man sharing his father's resistant genes—unlike the family valet, William H. Johnson, who died.[3]

But there is something curious about smallpox that goes beyond its roll call of the rich and famous. Its power took on an almost mythical reputation. On first arriving in the Caribbean islands, courtesy of the slave trade, whole tribes were instantly obliterated. Half the native population of Puerto Rico was eradicated by smallpox within a few months in 1519.[4] Later that year, as explorers Hernán Cortés and Panfilo de Narváez introduced themselves to the Aztec civilization of Mexico, the infection made an even greater impact. Having gained immunity through previous infections, many of the Spanish seemed to be above and beyond the devastating power of the disease, which slaughtered the local population. The result? According to some estimates, as many as fifteen million out of a total population of less than thirty million were dead within only a few months of the conquistadors' first steps from the boats.

*

For William Seymour, smallpox meant something profound too. After three weeks of fevers, boils, and an expectation of death's imminent arrival, Seymour emerged. His body's physical changes told the story of the significant shifts and changes that had been played out within. Deeply scarred across his face and partially blind in a left eye that was covered in an opaque film, things would no longer look the same for the thirty-two-year-old man from Centerville, Louisiana.[5]

His sickbed had been his crucible, his testing ground for a soul that had previously been ambivalent about the future. While his body had taken the fresh attacks from the near-fatal infection, his mind had opened up old files. Childhood visions returned, aging passions resurfaced, and constant themes demanded that he finally do business and resolve the issue that burned whiter than the sores across his limbs.

The key question was simple: Was William Seymour going to show up for a life spent serving God, or was he going to choose to serve tables and himself? Was he going to choose to turn his back on the abuses handed out in the past, or would he face the future with vulnerability and determination? Was he going to open his eyes to see how a vision of races meeting together for a new Pentecost might occur, or would he turn away from such ridiculous, unheard of, and unpopular prospects?

Later, older, but still reflecting on past experiences, Seymour would tell a friend a story from his childhood. As a young boy, returning home one night he took a shortcut through the cemetery. The Louisiana sky had little to offer in the way of lunar illumination that night, but as it is with shortcuts and young boys and cemeteries and nighttime, there was little need for extra light. Or at least that was the case, until suddenly he froze. There, ahead, vaguely distinguishable, was a sight that poured fear into his every muscle.

As he remained still, the figure approached, its graceful movements doing little to counter the horror of its appearance. It was a headless man wandering among the family gravestones, but searching for what? Victims? Small boys with foolish intentions and legs that still refused to move no matter how hard he urged them to do so? The approach continued until, almost upon him, the figure appeared to rise up from within itself. Twisting, escalating, half- light shaking shadows and scattering impressions, Seymour was finally confronted with the truth. This was no headless hunter on the prowl for souls, but a horse, now interrupted from its grazing by a heavily breathing boy, now running to the distant darkness.[6]

There were other stories he would hint at in later times. Yet these did not stem from graveyard encounters, instead these visions were given to a child who hungered after illusive interpretation. They were images of angels and demons, of the good and the bad, each competing, battling, fighting. For what? That was the question that had pursued him throughout his youth. The visions, the dreams, the sights that were so hard to explain—and even harder to believe— became secrets that he held close to his heart. They had acted as spurs throughout his younger days. They had been his oxygen and his morning sun, all the fuel that he needed to ensure that his childhood days were filled with thought and study and prayer and pursuit of answers from God himself.

While other boys dreamt of glory, Seymour's mind showed images of the heavens opening up, of heavenly battles, and the ultimate victory of Christ's return. Perhaps the apocalypse was too much for such a young mind, perhaps as childhood gave way to adolescence…as the realities of grief overcame the peculiarities of fantasy, Seymour simply stopped believing.

Whatever the cause of the break, Seymour's bout of smallpox put an end to all. Recovering on his bed *he knew*, as he had suspected long before, that he had a purpose, a divine calling. Gone were the days of denial and self-fulfillment. Now was the time for action. Now was the time for change.

Chapter 2
The State of Louisiana Is Formed and Raised

French Kings and Fresh Slaves

The story of William Joseph Seymour does not start in Indianapolis. It does not begin with travel, with childhood, or even with birth. To understand the man is to understand his history, the not-quite ancient and the not-quite modern. Born at the seam of two contrasting cultures, with two hundred and fifty years of slavery ending with his father's generation, Seymour and his peers faced an uncertain future. They lived beneath the shadows of legacies of the past—a past wholly infected with oppression and abuse. But the road ahead was lit by a new sun of hope and aspiration.

Life was good in Louisiana—for a time. The state was rich in all things, from climate to natural beauty, resources to history. As it tucked into the second half of an already-intense nineteenth century, it was emerging as one of the more intriguing southern states, with a history spiced by international influence and interminable intrigue. In a little over three hundred years, it had lived under a total of ten different flags, from Spanish to French to British and beyond. Napoleon held it for a while before selling it back to the United States for $15,000,000 in 1803.[1] Named after Louis XIV of France, it even had a brief stab at life as an independent republic. After just six weeks its leaders thought better of the idea and jacked it all in, choosing to join the Confederacy instead.

All this passing of the state parcel points to one thing: value. As an asset, Louisiana was always one to hang on to. Take a look around today, and you can still see why: New Orleans guards the mouth of the Mississippi River, the route down which plenty of trade flowed from the Midwest to its cash-rich market. And what a market there was, too: the state boasted some seriously wealthy individuals, families whose empires were almost biblical in their dimensions. Even now the fertile land tells the story of a rich climate, sub- tropical, it is warm throughout the year. Winter months take it down between 40 and 50 degrees, while the summer kicks off with 100- degree heat washed down by mid-afternoon showers. In turn, indigo, sugar, and cotton have all settled into the soil, with oil now starting to rise to the surface. All in all, Louisiana offers those who control the land the chance to mark up the profits as they sell to a global market.

Enter Centerville sometime before 1860, and you would have been surrounded by a scene of natural bounty. This is bayou country with slow-moving rivers that redefine themselves every once in a while. Centerville Parish—no counties here, remember, Louisiana's Catholic background dictated a different set of rules—is on the Bayou Teche, a sometime stream, sometime river that clocks up one hundred twenty-five miles as it traces its way down through the state. Hand in hand with the bayou are the celebrated live oaks, some with a reach of up to one hundred fifty feet. These are trees with personality. The bows reach low like elephant trunks and re-root themselves in the soil, and the Spanish moss drapes their limbs like discarded scarves telling of indiscretions from the night before. Further out are cypress-gum forests, bottomland hardwoods, and a storybook full of wildlife—Louisiana black bears, alligators, wading birds, ducks, and bald eagles.

Elegant and picturesque, this was no sweltering backwater suffering under a swampy haze. The bayou shifts and sidesteps its way through a landscape marked by beauty. It may have lacked the mountains of the west, but it was not short of fuel for the artist. Perhaps caused by cynicism, perhaps by an honest desire for change, but the passing of the Civil War brought with it a shift in artistic fashions. Instead of portraits of the great and the good, higher art shifted its affections to landscapes.[2] Bayous and trappers' cabins took center stage as artists returned to nature for inspiration.

By 1866 the Civil War was over. Soon it was clear that everything had changed in its wake, that years of tradition were dry- wiped from the whiteboard, leaving plenty of people dazed and confused about where to go next. But Louisiana was always going to rise again, trusting in her own ingenuity and ability to reinvent. 1869 turned up the discovery of sulfur, while a few years later the presence of oil pretty much set things up for the next century. Add in the rise in forestry, and you had the solid assurance that the state was not going to lose too much sleep over a little thing like money. As far as Louisiana was concerned, the future always looks good.

"We don't bust ourselves trying to earn a dollar," informs one current resident of St Mary Parish. "And if we'd won, things would look a whole lot different round here today."[3]

Of that, there can be no doubt. Louisiana's DNA still carries a healthy self-regard, one of those blueprints for a positive self-image that allows for the quiet assumption that life here is as good as it gets. In many ways Louisianans are right too, but the quality has demanded some strict payment terms over the years. The luxury has come at a price, and it does not take a genius to guess who picked up the tab.

Let's start with the past. Before the Civil War, it wasn't just all this natural beauty that got people feeling fine, it was the lifestyle that was good around here. And there really was an awful lot of lifestyle to be had. On one condition—that you happened to be white. For those born on the light side of the color line life became a pleasant amble along a path marked with privilege and plenty.

As with most things, power and money enjoyed a close relationship in Louisiana, and when combined with the land it became a winning cocktail. Those whites that were part of the landowning classes were able to sign up for a lifestyle that delivered on every possible desire. For the fortunate ones, the wealth could be found in one key area: plantations. Revolving around a cash crop (usually cotton, sugar, rice, or tobacco) grown on a large scale for maximum profit, these ventures were colossal wealth creators. Like the state's namesake, plantation owners became rulers of their own kingdoms. According to one observer back in 1830, the wealth creamed off the land was such that plantations needed spare no expense. Joseph Holt

Ingraham, a Northern trader traveling throughout Louisiana in the 1830s, describes one Mississippi River plantation as looking like an entire village:

> On my left, a few hundred yards from the house, and adjoining the pasture stood the stables and other plantation appurtenances, constituting a village in themselves—for planters always have a separate building for everything. To the right stood the humble yet picturesque village or quarter of the slaves, embowered in trees, beyond which, farther toward the interior of the plantation, arose the lofty walls and turreted chimneys of the sugar-house, which, combined with the bell-tower, presented the appearance of a country village with its church-tower and the walls of some public edifice, lifting themselves above the trees.[4]

Such wealth spread throughout the state as it thrived on rules and hidden assumptions. The revival of Greek architectural sympathies throughout the middle of the nineteenth century had laid down the law for architectural desirability. Pillars and columns were in and should be erected wherever possible. Skin tone was preferred white; the sun was avoided by young ladies; and freckles were considered a blemish on an otherwise beautiful pallor.

For young men, aspirations were tied with the preservation of all that was considered good. With a cultural history suffused with European ideals, the sense of tradition was a powerful force. While residents of New York fought tooth and nail along the streets of Five Points, the white gentleman of Louisiana stepped into the game with the odds already stacked in his favor. Education was a right; land ownership an option. And perhaps most significantly, he found at his disposal a workforce that made good his dreams and secured his future. Or so he thought.

Of all the states Louisiana boasted the biggest slave population. Here is another fact: Depending on your source, it's said that between half and three-quarters of the country's millionaires lived here, even through the war. Of course, the two were linked, as slavery had been as vital an ingredient in the state's wealth as the climate, the soil, and the desire to rake in the profits.

Before the war, slave ownership ran at about 40 percent for white families. A total of 47 percent of the state's total population were slaves, with some of them being owned by private individuals, some by the state. The average plantation had between ten and twenty-five slaves, although the state's largest plantation was close by at Houma. There they had one thousand slaves.[5]

Slaves were assets, tools to be taken as an indicator of wealth or potential. If a plantation was auctioned, you'd see its slaves listed right there among the agricultural machinery, the livestock, and the buildings. Life, it seemed, could be bought at a price.

On paper the Civil War changed this aspect of Louisiana life forever, but who are we kidding? Regardless of whether you saw it as a harsh imposition of alien ideals or a decisive amputation of outmoded values, the battles for hearts and minds were never going to be over with the end of the Civil War. According to white historian Alcee Fortier, writing at the end of the century, at the end of the war the outlook on slavery in the state was relaxed and self-congratulatory. The white masters did their bit, and their consciences were clean:

> [Slaves] were, as a rule, well treated by their masters, and, in spite of their slavery, they were contented and happy. In addition, the Negroes, as all ignorant people, are very superstitious.[6]

When Fortier turned his attention to the legislation passed in 1870, which demanded the integration of public schools, his opinions are just as revealing:

> Colored children, instigated to apply for admission to white schools, were firmly refused.... In several instances, where the colored pupils

had been admitted, upon a concerted movement, large companies of parents visited the school and required the obnoxious classes to withdraw.[7]

But if Fortier aimed to convince us that life for the black slaves under their white masters was as good as it could get, he was clearly wrong. While life was good for the whites, those who were black found that life in the fading light of the nineteenth century was a blur of half-formed hopes and looming demons. Back then, slavery cast a shadow overall, a shadow that would stretch beyond emancipation, beyond Reconstruction, beyond the last generation of those in chains and those with keys. Slavery's legacy was an infection that went beyond business, beyond education, beyond the church. But like all diseases, the cure took time to be perfected. Such was the harsh reality of life for those enslaved that even the passing of a century and a half cannot undo its damage.

Chapter 3
Seymour's Life Begins

In no Way Remarkable

The story of life for slaves was told in a thousand whispers. The minute details added tones and themes that the big picture found hard to include. Like the names, for example. It was common for owners to give their slaves classical names.[1] Either these were clumsy attempts at undermining the individuality of the slave, of mocking their lowly state with such esteemed names, or it was an illustration of the low regard with which the slaves' identities were held. Whatever the motives, as the white masters surrounded themselves with their Plato, Caesar, or Julius clones, they created in their minds an association with the splendor of ancient Rome.

Make no mistake, slaves were expensive. In 1853 one-man "in no way remarkable" went for $2,300.[2] When someone paid that type of money, they looked after their investment. Some owners were clearly better than others, yet there was a difference between ensuring that a slave was in a fit state to work and providing them with basic human rights. Married couples were rarely kept together, although under Louisiana law a child under ten years of age was required to be sold or imported with his or her mother.[3] Slaves were forbidden from being taught how to read or write. Curfews were imposed at nightfall, and written permission was needed if a slave was to leave his or her master's land.

The truth about slavery is shocking. The law upheld a barbaric regime that allowed a black person to be killed if that person hit a white person hard enough to bruise the skin. Permission to fire upon a fleeing slave was granted if the slave did not stop when ordered. The Louisiana Supreme Court suggested aiming to avoid inflicting a fatal wound, but if the slave died no charges were to be made.

Punishments were severe. As one observer notes, they were also creative. Sergeant Charles O. Dewey described a device he found around the neck of a fleeing slave who fled from the territories held by Confederate troops into the safety of the Unionists' camp:

> The form of the instrument prevented him from lying down and taking his rest at night. Because of its weight and close fit, it was very burdensome during the day. It consisted of a heavy iron ring that fit closely around the neck. Three prongs extended from the neck ring, each two feet in length. A ring was formed on the end of each prong. The design of the instrument allowed a chain to be attached to each ring, thus securing the victim beyond all possible hope of escape.[4]

*

Change was certainly happening, but the pace was slow. While slaves had been imported from Africa for over two hundred and fifty years, the abolitionists' noise had been gathering for decades. In 1777, Vermont changed its constitution to ban slavery. Over the next twenty-five years, other northern states joined in. In 1808 Congress banned the import of slaves.

But down in the South, the story was not so simple or smooth. It wasn't until 1831 that things started to catch up with the cousins in the north. That year, Nat Turner, a Virginia slave who had been taught to read by his master's son, and who believed he was chosen, as Moses had been chosen, to lead his people to freedom, instigated a slave revolt in Southampton County, Virginia. As a result, fifty-five white people and as many as two hundred slaves were killed.[5] In the fallout the state narrowly rejected a bill to emancipate their slaves, and, as a reaction, the owners dealt with their fears for their own safety by tightening the reins that bound their own slaves. Throughout the South expressions of anti-slavery sentiment were suppressed through state and private censorship.

As for how we made it on from there, much of it was down to one man—John Brown. John Brown was a militant abolitionist, a "conductor" on the Underground Railroad, and the organizer of a self-protection league for free blacks and fugitive slaves.[6] In 1856, responding to an attack by a bunch of proslavery thugs in Lawrence, Kansas, a free town, Brown and his followers attacked one of their settlements, killing five white men. Push turned to shove, and within a year two hundred Kansas residents had been killed and up to $2 million worth of damage had been handed out to the property.[7] A couple of years later in 1859, Brown was back, but this time failing in an attempt to capture the federal arsenal at Harper's Ferry, Virginia. His plan was to use the weapons to kick start a slave rebellion, yet he wound up hanged alongside many of his followers. Of course, everyone needs a hero, and in the eyes of some abolitionists, Brown became a martyr to the anti-slavery cause.[8]

But there was one other hero who wound up a martyr. Abraham Lincoln became the Republican Senator for Illinois in 1858, and just two years later he was president. But the reaction was not uniformly joyous. Playing the anti-slavery ticket meant that Lincoln presided over a divided country. Soon seven states of the deep South, including Louisiana, left the Union to form the Confederate States of America.

Within four months the Civil War began, and four more states joined the Southern reaction to the Unionists. Over the next four years, there were 10,455 military engagements. The war claimed 1,094,453 lives.[9] The financial cost was equally great: just two years into the war and the government estimated that each day was already costing $2.5 million. The final figure would reach $6,190,000,000, but that figure would pale next to the amount paid out in benefits to surviving soldiers in the coming decades.[10]

This brings us to Centerville in 1870. An end to slavery, an end to war, but bloodshed and oppression were still part of life. The physical devastation of the war, almost all of it borne by the South, had been enormous. The countryside had been ransacked, houses burned or plundered, homes, crops, and farm animals destroyed. In places, the infrastructure looked like a ruin. Neglect and despair were all around.

For Southern Louisiana the impact of the war was tangible. Before it, all kicked off the total sugar crop was one hundred thousand tons. A decade later, and it had fallen to forty-five thousand tons.[11] Thanks to the abolition of slavery, plantation owners were left without the means to work such vast quantities of land. Again, it had taken just one decade to halve the average size from 536 to 247 acres. Seven years later, only twenty-five of the ninety landowners in 1860 who kept more than fifty slaves were still in possession of their farms.[12]

But for all the change handed out to the white man, the ex-slaves had it worse. Left without the basic provisions of their former masters, many found themselves utterly alone and without help. The economy had been shot, and there was not too much goodwill and charity flying around. Despite millions of rations being handed out to former slaves through the Freedman's Bureau, as many as one hundred thousand former slaves died from starvation or disease in 1865.[13]

Some were able to find work. St Mary's Parish paid $20 per month for work as field laborers, but for many who stayed around, the archaic laws still favored white supremacy over black.[14] Those who found themselves arrested for vagrancy were fined. Without the money to pay, they were forced to work for the government or were hired out as cheap labor. For those on the wrong end of it, the difference between this and slavery seemed pretty thin.

There was a sense of faded glory about Seymour's birthplace. Of course, life for the elite had been fine, but in the run-up to our hero's birth, Centerville and the surrounding parish of St Mary had something of a reputation as being a sickly place. In 1869 the Franklin Planters' Banner ran an advertisement trying to draw people into the region. The key selling points were simple and transparent: "There are a great many more young ladies than young men."[15] Even better, these white young ladies are pretty resistant to death too: "There has not been a single death among the young ladies of this parish from diseases of the climate, in four years…" [16] Those young white men were supposed to be flocking here when they read it.

In 1869 a true renaissance man by the name of Colonel Samuel H. Lockett came through the area researching *Louisiana as It Is: A Geographical and Topographical Description of the State*.[17] Part author, part artist, part engineer, part Confederate soldier, Lockett described the impact of recent years on the landscape:

> As an agricultural district, it is difficult to conceive of its superior. And yet, a want of labor caused much of even this fine country to be lying untilled and idle…Much of this excellent country is lying waste, the fields grew up in cocklebur and other weeds, roads reduced to narrow trails, plantation houses, and fences in a depleted condition. A general air of desertion and desolation pervades the scene.[18]

While he called Centerville a "neat little village," you can read between the lines and figure out the cause and effect of this ghost-like decay. Without the workers, the landowners found themselves facing some hefty changes in lifestyle. In the absence of slavery, many found room for resentment and hate.

The real enemy for these once-wealthy lords was, of course, the force that took away their power—the Unionists and their federal troops. Even with the post-war peace reaching its fifth birthday, it appeared that Louisiana was going through somewhat of a difficult phase.

The person with duty of care for this volatile state was General Shepley—the man that Lincoln charged with the task of re-establishing civil government in the state during 1863. It seemed like the general knew the land as well as the people. While his troops supervised the reconstruction of the infrastructure, they also witnessed the resistance to change. According to Shepley, this was "the obstinate proslavery parish of St Mary."[19] In a few years Shepley took charge of a whole new detachment of soldiers in nearby Franklin, simply as a reaction to the increase of hostilities against former slaves by their former rulers.

The truth about life for the freedmen was known by all. As the free-thinking national newspaper *Harper's Weekly* put it: "The war left the late slaves free among a population that had always despised them as a servile race, and that now hated them as men who had loved and trusted the Government."[20] The reasons were complex, yet it is clear that Louisiana had become a testing ground for the government's reconstruction policies.

That hatred had a face. In fact, it had many faces, most of them looking a lot like the Ku Klux Klan. Founded just four years previously in Tennessee, the Klan created so much havoc in such a short space of time that its infamy was widespread. Yet when it came to Louisiana, the Klan's influence was less direct. Instead, it was up to groups like Seymour's Knights to drag this state further down into the swamps of racial hatred. Formed to support the presidential aspirations of Horatio Seymour, it protested innocence, yet the people all knew who was to blame when the State Governor asked for military support in 1868:

> Men are shot down in the streets and at their homes, and no efforts are made to bring the criminals to justice. One of the Judges refuses to go into a certain parish without soldiers to protect him, and the Sheriff of the same parish has resigned, owning his inability to arrest offenders. In another parish men, women, and children are murdered by bands of assassins who remain unmolested. In another, the peace is preserved only by armed bodies of volunteer citizens.[21]

As many as one hundred and fifty people were murdered in the state during that summer, and, despite the fact that the group was only a few months old, their secret was already out:

> A secret organization, hostile to the colored population, has been

formed with the intention of coercing the colored vote; that it was its known intention to assassinate, under certain circumstances, the Lieutenant-Governor and the Speaker of the House… it unquestionably meditates a bloody revolution.[22]

It would all get worse too. The battles would start up again, the lynchings would intensify, and the resistance would only grow stronger. In the middle of it all were the freedmen. But not all battles are fought about the past. For some the passing of the war brought new opportunities and hope—opportunities and hope that acted as fresh salt in the wounds of proslavery throwbacks. Like Senator Hiram Revels, one of seven black Senators to be taking a seat around the time of Seymour's birth. In a twist of fate, Senator Revels occupied the seat formerly warmed by Jefferson Davis, former president of the Confederate States of America. His obvious displeasure was the purest of all fuels for the press.[23]

It may have been less than a decade since the war started, but the pace of change was breathtaking. For so long the color line had dressed the races in their pre-determined uniforms that to see black faces crowning soldiers' jackets or senators' gowns appeared to some as an unthinkable horror. It was in January 1863 that President Lincoln clarified plans to enlist black men as soldiers, creating the first all-black regiments. Opposition was clear from the start. Many white soldiers refused to fight alongside black ones, and at first few were paid. Towards the end of the war, as two hundred thousand black men had enlisted to fight or support those on the front line, Congress bowed to pressure and equalized the pay of black and white servicemen.[24]

One of the two hundred thousand men was Simon Seymour. Born around 1841, it seems like Simon was the kind of man who wanted to focus on the future more than the past. Ask about the identity of his former white slave owner, and you'd hear little in the way of a response. What Simon would tell you about was the war. He was one of the first black soldiers to fight under the Union flag, enlisting a few months after Lincoln's Emancipation Proclamation.[25] His unit started out life as the 25th Regiment Infantry, but soon changed to reflect the sense of identity to which soldiers like himself clung. In April 1864 the unit changed to 93rd Regiment Infantry, United States Colored Troops, and as before the troops were based in southern Louisiana. The unit was only engaged in one skirmish and we don't know what part Simon played, but as the war drew to a close and the unit disbanded, he spent four months in the hospital, suffering from fevers, rheumatism, and bronchitis. Later in life he continued to suffer from chronic diarrhea and hemorrhoids, which seems likely to have been picked up while on excursion throughout the swamps of Louisiana and, later, with the 82nd Regiment Infantry throughout Apalachicola in Florida. Simon's unit disbanded in September 1866, and he moved to Bayou Sale, close to where he had served with the 93rd. History is a little short on reasons why, but it is possible to join the dots a little—it was at the meeting point of Bayou Sale and Teche that, in January 1867 Simon met Phillis Salabar. Six months later she became his wife.[26]

Like everyone of her color, Phillis's history was marked by slavery. Perhaps her former owners were kinder than husband's, but Phillis had more to say about her past. She was born on the plantation owned by Adilard Carlin on November 23, 1844. Close by was Centerville, and Carlin's presence was easily felt. In 1860 his land was valued at $150,000, and his property topped $160,000. Phillis was one of one hundred and twelve slaves before the war. After the fighting and the Emancipation Proclamation, many of them stayed on as farm laborers, and it was to the plantation that Phillis and Simon returned on the day of their wedding on July 27, 1867.[27]

On that day the wedding party made its way to Franklin, the legal center of St Mary Parish, five miles from Centerville. Carlin was typically generous, allowing the guests the use of the horse and trap to make the journey. The ceremony was conducted at the First Methodist Church on Main Street, by Reverend R. K. Diossy.[28] A controversial figure, Diossy bought plots of land throughout the parish, building churches wherever possible. As a white preacher, he felt strongly that the Methodist Church needed to do something about the exit of black people from the pews.[29]

His work was at great personal expense. He performed dozens of marriage ceremonies for freedmen and took unlimited abuse from angry whites. There were parts of the parish where he felt unsafe to travel, the hatred stirred up in part by the *Planters' Banner* article that hung around for years. Under the title "Disturbance in Franklin" Diossy and his fellow ministers were accused of whipping "up the worst spirit among the Negroes. What little talent they have is in the service of Satan."[30]

Well, on the wedding day there didn't seem to be much evidence of him being in Satan's service. With Phillis's father as official witness, alongside Jefferson Ellis and Charles Brown, there were plenty of people there to see the couple united. Simon had borrowed the $100 bond required by the parish for the marriage license, but once it was all legal the party returned to Carlin where the boss had put on, as Morris Bowens described it, "dinner and supper…to celebrate the said marriage."[31]

*

In 1870 Simon and Phillis were back in Franklin on official business, this time attending the Catholic Church of the Assumption for a baptism. With them were Charles Morette and Azelie Peter, the godparents. There too, were the children: two-year-old Rosalie, and six-month-old William Joseph Seymour, the man of the moment.[32] Again the family returned home to the Carlin plantation, but by then it was not wise to parade your joy too freely if you were black.

The experiment known as *Reconstruction* throughout Louisiana was heading for meltdown. It was common knowledge that for every reported lynching, beating, or raping, one hundred more would be suffered in silence.

The state election was just around the corner, too. More than any other current event, this promised to turn up the heat on the tension between the opposing political forces. The result was be disputed both by regular Republicans and a coalition of Liberal Republicans and Democrats. Each side tried to tough it out by putting their own governors in power and drawing up their own legislation, but the federal judge's ruling that the regular Republicans should be declared the victors did nothing to ease the tension.[33] War hero and second-term president, Ulysses S. Grant, sent in the troops to ensure compliance, but he received none. A shadow government was formed, paramilitary units attacked blacks and Republicans, while the law stood by, impotent and unable to rein in the terror.

Thankfully Simon, Phillis, and their children were not near Colfax, Louisiana, on April 13, 1873, but they, like everyone else, would have heard of the events. William may have been told the news of the fighting, which left two white men and seventy black men dead—half of whom were slaughtered after their surrender. He may also have heard, in the years that followed, of the infamous pursuit of justice for the victims, and how all of the one hundred white men who were arrested for the murders walked free from court.[34]

There were other events that became part of the backdrop to Louisiana life. In Grant Parish, for example, on Easter Sunday 1873, somewhere between one hundred and fifty and two hundred black men were murdered, shot down—as a witness would later testify—"like dogs."[35] Many were shot in the back of the head, and all had multiple bullet wounds. Their bodies were burnt beyond recognition.

A week after Seymour's third birthday, *Harper's Weekly* published an illustration of black men hiding in the swamps of Louisiana to avoid violence. Some of his father's fellow soldiers were among them. The Seymours and friends would have felt the fear as the reconstruction entered its bleakest phase.

Years later, William Seymour refused to hide from the troubles that surrounded him, pleading with his congregation to put aside the racial hatred and segregation of the past. William Seymour's passion and purpose changed the face of America.

Chapter 4
William Seymour Learns His Lessons

The Invisible Institution

According to the legend of Lake Chitimacha, the area around Centerville once played host to a romantic tragedy that rivals even that played out by the original star-crossed lovers.[1] Two tribes—the Chitimacha and the Attakapas—shared the region in relative peace, their lands meeting along the edge of the tranquil Lake Chitimacha. It was here that Gentle Fawn, the beautiful innocent maiden at the heart of the tale, met Massangoit, a noble brave ranked high in the neighboring Attakapas tribe. Beneath the draping oaks, the two soon fell in love, and as the autumn moon looked on, they whispered their affections to one another.

Yet neither peace nor love was to last. Without her knowledge, Gentle Fawn's father had betrothed his only daughter to the chief of a different tribe, a man whose impatience was legendary. Soon he arrived to claim his bride. Gentle Fawn was paraded before this man and informed of her father's contract. Standing at the side of the lake where so many kind words had already been spoken, Gentle Fawn's silence betrayed her true feelings. *Where*, echoed her heart's cries, *was the brave Massangoit?*

Suddenly an arrow fell at her feet. It could have come from only one bow—her true love's. She knew its meaning: She must have faith, hold on, and remain strong. Hastened by his suspicions, her father informed her that the following sunrise would signal her departure from Chitimacha with her betrothed. Gentle Fawn chose to trust her noble Massangoit.

The following morning as the sun's rays began to warm the great live oaks, Gentle Fawn was brought out to say farewell to her father. Time was almost gone, and the sound of an approaching horse heralded the arrival of what Gentle Fawn was convinced was the escape she had longed for throughout the night.

But it was not Massangoit who descended from the horse; it was a messenger. In one hand he held a pipe of peace; in the other, a tomahawk.

"Massangoit bids me tell you," announced the young man, "that if you give him the Fawn for a bride, he will smoke with you. Refuse, and he will bury the tomahawk in your heart."

The father paused. He approached the youth. As the messenger shrunk back under the chief's gaze, the elder reached out and took the pipe.

"Go," he said, "and prepare for war. But before you leave see how the Chitimacha avenges his people."

Turning to his daughter, he raised his bow and fired an arrow directly into her heart. Plucking it from her lifeless body, the chief placed it in the now empty hand of the messenger.

"There," he said. "Tell your master to meet the Chitimachas here before the next morning sun rises above the horizon."

By the time that sun was in the sky, the battle had been fought. The Attakapas had lost; Massangoit's tomahawk was buried deep within his own chest, and none of his tribe remained alive. The Chitimacha gained in power, yet their pre-eminence was to be short-lived. Soon another tribe would come from far away, and the Chitimacha would exist only through Indian legend.[2]

*

Whether you believe the story or not, Gentle Fawn's fate and her father's fury have a shared DNA with the post-Civil War era in Louisiana. Anger, a strong sense of injustice, and a castrated desire for retribution—these were the hallmarks that branded the ex-slave owners in the decade following Lee's surrender at Appomattox.

Depending on your politics—both then and now—the state of Louisiana was either the prime villain or an innocent victim. There are those who, even today, hold onto a sense of injustice, a grudge (albeit a little watered down) against those who imposed rules and change with such overbearing force. As one part-time duck hunter/land owner/boxing promoter recounted, "Things would be a whole lot different round here if the South had won."

"Oh, yes?"

"Well, for one, we wouldn't be busting ourselves trying to make a dollar."[3]

*

If I ever get through this war,
And Lincoln's chains don't bind me,
I'll make my way to Tennessee,
To the girl I left behind me.[4]

So, went one of many songs that were popular among soldiers at the end of the Civil War. It was this air of defeat that took longer to clear than the cannon smoke that clung to the battlefields of Mansfield and Port Hudson. Yet the depth of pain went beyond missing one's girl or worrying about getting caught. The long walk home from battle, for those fortunate enough to be making the trip, brought home to many just how much destruction had been handed out to the South. As one soldier commented: "Never was there greater nakedness and destitution in a civilized community."[5]

While the end of the Civil War prompted the closing of one painful chapter, it also signified the start of yet another. Reconstruction may have sounded like a unified drive forward, but for members of the South who had lost so much through the war, the process was as painful as it was protracted. Of all the Southern states, Louisiana's occupation by their former enemies lasted the longest. Indeed, it was a full decade before the troops withdrew and the state was allowed to walk free of the guiding hand of discipline held over it by the North.

Reconstruction was difficult. White folk resented the occupation of their homes, the destruction of their infrastructure, and the eradication of their ability to harness the labors of a previously pliable army of slaves. In Franklin, at least, it didn't take a genius to determine the mood of the people. All one had to do was open the newspaper.

Of the handful of newspapers in the area at the time, *Planter's Banner* had the edge, the advantage of the rest of the competition. The local rag's particular joker in the pack came in the form of one Daniel Dennet—editor, informal leader, and possessor of a withering tongue that loved to unleash venom on any who displeased.[6] Writing of the minority local group of political opponents, he commented:

> There was an unusually large meeting of the friends of General Pierce in the parish of St Mary, under an umbrella, at the corner of Odd Fellows Hall, on Wednesday last.[7]

Yet Dennet's actions did not stop at high-caliber playground insults. His fingerprints are to be found all over the local equivalent to Seymour's Knights and the infamous Ku Klux Klan, known as the *Knights of the White Camellia,* formed in Franklin on May 22 1867.[8] Named after the snow-white bloom of a local flower, it symbolized the purity of the white race, which they considered at the heart of their ambitions. The group made certain demands on new members. Initiation required that they swear to help fellow White Camellians to:

> …defend the superiority of the white race on this continent, and at all times observe a marked difference between the whites and the Negro of African race; that he would do all in his power to prevent the political affairs of this country, in whole or in part, from passing into the hands of the Negro or other inferior race.[9]

The White Camellians even had a secret signal: left index finger drawn over left eye, plus a secret knock and a whole bunch of passwords. Despite all the marks of childish role-play, the assumed innocence should not be misleading. As a keen supporter, Daniel Dennet was in a position to comment on the group's eventual size, which he put at twenty thousand members, many of whom were living 120 miles away in New Orleans.[10]

Dennet, and members of the Knights of the White Camellia, tried their best to justify their racist actions. "In no part of the world," wrote the editor in *Planer's Banner*, "is the colored race treated better than in Louisiana. We want peace in this state, and we wish to give no encouragement to disturbers of the peace and mischief makers of the carpetbag persuasion."[11]

Carpetbaggers—that breed of freedman on the road to better prospects, with their worldly possessions crammed into one voluminous, durable bag—were symptoms of the climate in the South just after the Civil War. As visible signs of the rapid change in society's structure, the carpetbaggers contributed to a shift in the democratic process. This was evidenced in the 1863 election in St. Mary Parish for judge and sheriff. With the sudden opening up of the vote to the black population, former slaves of Franklin, Centerville, and beyond outnumbered the former white ruling class by three to one. The winners, Colonel H. H. Pope and Judge Chase, both black, held their posts for five years.

Pope and Chase formed a close bond, and, understandably, kept in close contact. So, it was not surprising for them to be found in animated conversation on the gallery of O'Neil's Hotel on Main Street one night. On April 17th, 1868, five masked men exited a nearby bar and rushed to O'Neill's where they shot and stabbed both men in full view of Pope's wife.

Dennet's response to their murder was revealing. Writing in the paper, he declares:

> Since the shocking events of the night of the 17th, all parts of our parish have been diligently patrolled by armed police every night. We have reports that the colored people are settling down quietly....Most of the Negroes now show a disposition to vote the Democratic ticket and live on friendly terms with the white people of the parish.

White Camellia denied any involvement. Dennet denied any knowledge. The war was far from over.[12]

*

Life for Seymour in Centerville was set against a backdrop of tension, hatred, and hardship amid the prospect of potential improvement. Having fought against the Confederate troops, Simon Seymour did what perhaps was sensible and pursued a quiet life, purchasing a four-acre slice of land in 1883. Together in their new home in Verdunville, a settlement east of Centerville, bordering the Bayou Teche, the family now consisted of Simon and Phillis, plus thirteen-year-old William, eleven-year-old Simon Junior, seven- year-old Amos, and three-year-old Julia.[13] Caleb, an infant, had not yet reached his first birthday, and never would. Like seven other Seymour's children, his early death must have added an agonizing punctuation to the regularity of sorrow experienced throughout William Seymour's early years. Little is known of his first decade, but the presence of grief and suffering outweigh any petty facts that could possibly be uncovered.

What we do know is that Simon and Phillis were able to send William to school at the age of ten. At this time, like his adult father, William was illiterate. Yet the rumors about his early experiences of God imply that he was remarkable for other reasons. In years to come, William Seymour would hint at the "visions" he received while still a child.[14] We cannot be sure whether they were received in the Baptist church of Little Jerusalem, located a mile or so further south from Centerville in Ricohoc, or in Verdunville's Church of the Immaculate Conception. Perhaps they came to the young man under the wide skies carpeted with towering sugar cane, on the banks of the sluggish Bayou Teche or draped over the bows of one of the ancient live oaks. Wherever, whenever, and however Seymour received his divine inspiration, his pursuit of divine revelation would at least have offered a distraction from the tensions and agonies that formed the backdrop to his childhood.

*

Health in the parish was not good. With a family death toll approaching double figures, the Seymours may have been particularly cruelly affected, but others had an all-too-familiar relationship with death. Disease struck at various times, such as when the floods of 1865 and 1867 were followed by outbreaks of yellow fever. Another flood in 1874, as well as tropical storms in 1878 and 1879, reintroduced the region to the fatal disease, with the death toll climbing highest among the poor. By the time another yellow fever outbreak hit in 1897, the public reaction was set to a default of panic. Treatment was primitive: a hot mustard foot bath to act as a purgative, plenty of hot tea, and no solid food.[15]

While death was common, the church appears to have struggled to offer much in the way of guidance and consolation. Instead of practical help, social niceties and smug self-satisfaction were high on the clergy hit list as religious groups preferred to focus on the perceived social rather than the actual physical ills of the day. The Temperance movement was one of the more recognizable religious groups spawned during this period, and included smaller sects like The Sons of Temperance, begun in Franklin in 1849, and the Young Brothers, who splintered from the Sons of Temperance with a goal of ridding the land of the "demon rum." Other splinter groups included the Good

Samaritans and the Daughters of Samaria, fine names that may have led to assumptions about their desire to alleviate suffering, to reach out across the racial divide, and to offer radical care and practical love to their neighbors. Unfortunately, in reality they set their sights a little lower, desiring only to: "To promote literature among the young people of this place, to afford rational public entertainment to the ladies and gentlemen of this community."[16]

Despite the presence of eight churches in Franklin by 1860— four Roman Catholic, two Methodist, one Baptist and one Episcopal, and a large Baptist revival earlier in 1854— religion seemed to have made little impact on things.[17] "The grogshops," complained one religious minister looking back, "were more crowded on Sundays than the houses of worship, and the ministers were starving while the saloon keepers grew fat and wealthy."[18]

And so, we arrive at the heart of the matter—the fact that religion had little or nothing to say about the injustice of the day. While every edition of *Planters' Banner* carried a front-page sermon from a prominent vicar, their words rarely connected with the concerns that mattered. The lead article on Saturday, March 24, 1900, is typical, kicking off with a potentially exciting title that wonders "what religion does for the prolongation of human life," and suggests that "care of the health [is] a positive Christian duty." Good points, perhaps, but the meat that follows the entrée adopts a narrow obsession with platitudes and legalistic mumblings: "Adam lived 930 years" it says, with the implication that we could all do likewise if only we read our Bibles more often.[19] Neither the paper nor the preacher are around today to expand on such a radical theory.

*

What William Seymour tapped into was something far more profound, something far more potent, yet far less obvious. While the local white church appeared to duck the issues of the day, and polite society obsessed about absorbing the latest fashions from England, Seymour was plugged into a different network altogether. Like millions of others with a past connecting them to the yoke of slavery, Seymour found freedom in the very religion that his family's former masters had contorted to suit their oppressive ends. While others like those in the White Camellia took on the mantle of revenge and hatred epitomized by Gentle Fawn's father, Seymour chose a different path—a profound faith in a God whose power transcended segregation and oppression. Out of the pain of grief at the loss of so many siblings came profound revelation that would shape his theology for years to come. For William Seymour, the message of the cross underlined the fact that Jesus came into the world not to confirm the mighty in their seats but to exalt the humble and meek. Like his peers, he was discovering that "God never made us to be slaves for white people."[20] Even at a young age, the seeds were sown.

Chapter 5
Poverty Strikes and Prophecy Inspires

"I'll lie in de grave and stretch out my arms."

Death and grief were not finished with William Seymour. Though the potential of youth had been robbed from the Seymour family with agonizing regularity throughout his early years, William was about to experience a whole new type of suffering. In November 1891, his father died. It had been a slow, lonely descent for Simon Seymour, with little help offered, save from his immediate family.

The state for whom he had risked his life refused to make good on the promises made while recruiting black soldiers to fight alongside white soldiers in the Civil War. In June of 1891, Simon was described as "weak, feeble, and hardly conscious" by the New Orleans doctor who refused to sign off on a full pension for Simon, in spite of a mixed-bag of symptoms including rheumatism, diarrhea, and an affliction of the eyes. According to the physician's verdict, Simon was suffering with the pain and indignity of severe piles—for which he was awarded a limited pension, yet he was otherwise "healthy."[1]

Simon carried on being "healthy" for 153 more days, by which time his ailments overwhelmed him. It is thought that he may have picked up a parasite while on duty with the army in the marshes of Florida, and he had spent time in the hospital before being discharged. On his last night on earth, slipping out of consciousness, Phillis called for the doctor. He never came. The priest arrived too late to administer last rites, and Simon was buried the next day in an unmarked grave in Centerville's New Providence Baptist Church cemetery. Two weeks later a final blow hit the remaining head of the family—her application for a widow's pension was denied.[2]

Phillis and her three teenage children—William, Simon Jr., and Amos—were left with nothing. In her pension application she made it clear that she had "no means of income whatsoever," and that the four acres of land on which they lived produced too little to sustain the four of them. With a full register of possessions amounting to little more than "one old bedstead, one old chair and one old mattress," the Seymours were left with salable assets—excluding their stubborn land—of just fifty-five cents.[3]

Determined to pursue justice, Phillis fought for the pension she deserved. It was eventually granted in June 1894, when she was awarded $8 per month plus $2 for each of the children.[4] It kept them alive, barely. And not for long either. One year later she sold half her farm for a mere $30.[5]

Yet things were not supposed to have turned out this way. According to the Technicolor dream of Reconstruction, the transition from slavery to freedom was supposed to be bold and absolute. For twelve years the process of rebuilding the nation made radical changes: over one thousand schools were built, the fourteenth and fifteenth amendments were added to the Constitution (declaring equality among races and opening up voting rights), teacher-training institutions were created, and several black colleges were founded.[6]

Despite some of the gains made during Reconstruction, it soon faded as a viable plan for uniting the nation. Federal troops were withdrawn from the South in 1877, and white voting power predominated once more. White Southern Democrats soon took control from black and white Republican office holders. By the end of 1877, all of the gains of Reconstruction had disappeared, and blacks were again relegated to second-class citizenship. It would not be until the Civil Rights movement in the 1960s that this would change.

Opposition took many faces. The sense of indignation, anger, and blatant hatred for those who had imposed their ethics upon the south was tangible. While the military battles against had already been fought and lost, new fields of combat were opening up to those fueled by resentment. The Jim Crow laws imposed racial segregation in ways that lasted up until the latter half of the twentieth century. The gains of Reconstruction were eroded by a twin attack of apathy and legal maneuverings. Whites in the north and south grew less supportive of civil rights, allowing those hung over with previous agendas to draw the color line once again.

In an act of defiance that would echo in the future with Rosa Park, Homer Plessy challenged Louisiana's law of 1890 requiring blacks to travel in separate rail compartments. Plessy, seven-eighths Caucasian, boarded a train on June 7, 1892, and sat in a whites-only car. His refusal to move prompted an arrest, and in a trial in a local court, the judge ruled against him. Appeals took the case all the way to the Supreme Court in 1896, yet while the surroundings differed, the verdict remained the same. In fact, it paved the way for further segregation. The decision made people conclude that separate but equal travel arrangements did not violate Plessy's rights, nor did they stamp him with a badge of inferiority.[7] The result was a cascade of apartheid previews as blacks were refused access to schools, restaurants, hospitals, and public places. In 1905, Georgia passed a law requiring separate public parks. In 1909, Mobile, Alabama, created a 10 P.M. curfew for blacks, and in 1915, blacks and whites in South Carolina were restricted from working together in the same rooms of textile factories.[8]

"Separate but equal" sent a message to those feeling resentful. In just one generation, with the national declaration of emancipation, a mass of privilege had been removed from the whites. As a result, a desire for retribution began to move down the power chain toward those without the means to respond.

One particularly hateful form of retribution that raised its ugly head during this period was lynching. Lynching was nothing new, for Colonel Charles Lynch, a revolutionary war soldier turned Judge, ordered the perpetrators of a Tory plot to sabotage lead ore from the mines on his property to be court-martialed and then tied to the black walnut tree on his property and given 39 lashings, possibly the first lynching on American soil.[9]

Lynching carried on long after its eponymous antihero died. Like the Jim Crow laws, they would bridge the centuries, only dying out in 1968, but not before their death toll stretched into the thousands. From 1882 to 1968 a colossal 4,743 people died of lynching, with 3,446 of those victims being black. The role of shame places Mississippi at the head with a total of 539 black victims and 42 white. Louisiana rated fourth in the charts with 356 black and 56 white people murdered in this way over the years.[10]

The truth about lynching is that it was often unrecorded and covered a variety of *techniques*. When the victim was black, it would often be a more savage, sadistic, and even public affair. By the time that Simon Seymour died, lynchers increasingly relied upon burning, torture, and dismemberment in order to prolong suffering. These abuses had a further payoff too—they helped to create and maintain a carnival atmosphere among both the killers and onlookers. White families brought small children to watch, newspapers sometimes carried advance notices, railroad agents sold excursion tickets to announced lynching sites, and mobs cut off black victims' fingers, toes, ears, or genitalia as souvenirs. Nor was it necessarily the handiwork of a local rabble; not infrequently, the mob was encouraged or led by people prominent in the area's political and business circles.

According to historian Robert L. Zangrando "lynching had become a ritual of interracial social control and recreation rather than simply a punishment for crime."[11] Surrounding the people reconstructing their lives amid the debris of Reconstruction were a host of messages intent on perpetuating prejudice. It was nearly impossible to find a newspaper report where the victim was referred to other than "Negro," or where it is not implied that they were guilty therefore deserving of public torture and murder. One hundred and thirty miles from Centerville, Hammond, Louisiana, in 1911 was the stage for the lynching of a black man accused of robbery. The New Orleans *Picayune* described him as a "big, burly negro" and a "black wretch". Seventy miles closer to home in St. Mary's Parish, four black men would be lynched in Lafayette in March 1911, two months after

Oval Poulard was lynched for murder in nearby Opelousa, and eight months before another man would be lynched back in Lafayette.[12]

The state appeared powerless to intervene. In fact, in many cases those dressed in the robes of political offices were the very ones encouraging such violent hatred. To see just how far from grace the new century fell, read the words of Mississippi Senator James K. Vardaman written in 1910:

> The door of hope might have remained closed as far as the progress the Negro was to make for himself was concerned. He has never created for himself any civilization. He has never risen above the government of club. He has never written a language. His achievements in architecture are limited to the thatched roof hut or hole in the ground. No monuments have been built by him to body forth and perpetuate in the memory posterity the virtues of his ancestors. For countless ages he has looked upon the rolling sea and never dreamed of a sail. In truth, he has never progressed, save and except when under the influence and absolute control of a superior race.[13]

*

So, what were the results of all this betrayal, hatred, and watered-down promise? What came out of this torment? Was it hatred, anger, and a determination to rail against a system that took and took then failed to give an ounce of grace when death approached? In part, this was true. There were those who fought fire with fire. Yet the ultimate success of the Civil Rights movement had its roots in a far more nutritious soil. In an ironic twist of fate, Seymour, like so many other African Americans, discovered that the faith of his oppressors offered the power not just to endure, but to gloriously succeed.

One of the first to write about this was Colonel Thomas Wentworth Higginson of the First South Carolina Volunteer Infantry,

Colored U.S. A white writer, liberal, abolitionist, and former soldier, he had served alongside black troops in the Civil War. There he witnessed black troops expressing their faith by singing spirituals and songs handed across the scarred generations. Writing in the *Atlantic Monthly* in June 1867, he unpacked his experiences while wandering through the soldier camps after dark. Two songs stood out in particular, and he related them to his audience with care:

> Hold your light, Brudder Robert,
> Hold your light,
> Hold your light on Canaan's shore.
> "What make ole Satan for follow me so?
> Satan ain't got notin' for do wid me.
> Hold your light,
> Hold your light,
> Hold your light on Canaan's shore.[14]

"This," wrote Higginson, "would be sung for half an hour at a time, perhaps, each person present being named in turn. It seemed the simplest primitive type of 'spiritual.'" [15]

He was right. At the heart of the faith was a profound belief in the sustaining power of the Christian message. Theirs was a suffering that they saw reflected across the pages, a pain that echoed throughout the stories from both Testaments. Theirs was an attitude that would overcome even the greatest darkness.

> I know moon-rise, I know star-rise,
> Lay dis body down.
> I walk in de moonlight, I walk in de starlight,
> To lay dis body down.
> I 'll walk in de graveyard, I 'll walk through de graveyard,
> To lay dis body down.
> I 'll lie in de grave and stretch out my arms;

Lay dis body down.
I go to de judgment in de evenin' of de day,
When I lay dis body down;
And my soul and your soul will meet in de day
When I lay dis body down.[16]

Higginson was impressed: "'I'll lie in de grave and stretch out my arms.' Never, it seems to me, since man first lived and suffered, was his infinite longing for peace uttered more plaintively than in that line."[17]

William Seymour's spiritual education started with similar lessons in the value of peace, unity, and an embracing of suffering. The opportunities for practice were ever-present as he made his way out into a world far different from the promises handed out earlier in his life. Was he bitter at the failings, or did he choose to put his head down and pursue whatever freedom he could find? It seems that the latter appealed. Bitterness never managed to find a handhold on Seymour's heart. Instead, he turned away from his earlier passions for scriptural revelation and headed for something altogether more certain and less controversial.

Chapter 6
Opposition and Opportunity Are Found

Ice Cream and Elevators

What happened next is unclear. All we know for sure is that Seymour's life did not find a different setting until he was halfway through his twenties. His teenage years, it is safe to assume, continued to be played out under the sweat and passions of the Louisianan skies. The seemingly endless ranks of sugar cane held down the flattened earth like so many tent pegs and gave the skies a sense of power and purpose. But the cane fields inevitably ended at a line of trees or a slow-moving bayou. Round here, everyone knew the boundaries—even the vegetation.

So, William Seymour did what so many others would eventually do to the South—he turned his back on it and headed North. In time the trickle of men on the move like Seymour, who were in search of better things, would become an exodus. Like all things popular, it would grow its own industry, and eventually every conceivable method of attracting Southern workers would be employed by those eager for cheap, willing labor. Yet once again— and not for the last time—black men would be recruited with the offer of inducements and treats. Travel costs were sometimes paid for, and street corners became the marketplace where labor agents would tout for business.[1]

Of course, this time around the offers didn't come with chains or bullets. The hope of a better life was fueled with genuine reports of success and freedom found in the arms of a welcoming North. Migration fever, so it seemed, was a benign condition, perhaps even one that purged the system of old germs and wounds. Freed from slavery, many looked for a new Canaan, where promises landed the right way up.

They found their Moses in one Benjamin "Pap" Singleton. Born a slave in 1809, he escaped in 1846—a couple of decades ahead of emancipation. Regardless of the changes yet to come, Tennessee was not a good place for an ex-slave on the run in the mid-nineteenth century, and Singleton headed for the progressive safety of Detroit.[2] It was a return to his own personal Egypt that prompted a change in Singleton. Reconstruction's dream soon ended, the Jim Crow laws quickly re-established the color line, and the Ku Klux Klan emerged. It was time for a second exit from the state of oppression. But this time Singleton's movements would be accompanied by a mass of followers.

Kansas had been home to John Brown's rebel uprising, and understandably represented the promise of a brighter future for men like Singleton. So, with nearly three hundred ex-slaves in tow, Singleton escorted his first wave of the exodus to Cherokee county, coming to rest in his colony near Dunlop, Kansas in June of 1879. Over the years, tens of thousands followed to Kansas and other Northern states, with Singleton overseeing the organized colonization of entire black communities.[3]

Singleton's death in 1892 brought an end to his role as "Father of the Negro Exodus," and the final decade of the nineteenth century saw William Seymour prepare for the next phase of his own development into a phenomenal leader. Of course, back then, there were few indications of the man's destiny. His early years are shrouded, and perhaps rightly so. We do not know precisely why he left Centerville, what education he had received there, or how he chose his next destination. He may have first headed to Memphis by boat, and then on to St Louis.[4] Or he may have taken the train directly to Indiana in 1895. Either way, there is something appropriate about the mystery of Seymour's past, providing a contrast against which the later changes can be clearly set.

Indianapolis was an obvious choice for a young black man eager to escape the South, even if Seymour was a little ahead of the game. It was not until the first two decades of the twentieth century that things really exploded, with the number of African Americans in Indianapolis growing from 15,931 in 1900 to 34,678 in 1920.[5] The Great Migration was about to kick off for real, but in the meantime, plenty of others would be leaving behind a troubled past for the chance of a better future, leaving the wintry south and heading for a northern summer of cooler heads and warmer hearts.

The state of Indiana had made a deliberate decision to open up its doors. In 1866 the state supreme court voided the article of the 1851 state constitution that had prohibited African Americans from settling in Indiana, and the number of black residents increased by nearly 500 percent between 1860 and 1870. By 1900, nearly sixteen thousand blacks lived in Indianapolis, comprising almost 10 percent of the city's population.[6] This far outweighed the racial mix of much larger cities like New York and Chicago where the proportion was closer to one in fifty.

With churches, businesses, and social organizations, Indianapolis offered its new arrivals a ready-made black culture. Seymour's arrival coincided with the birth of the *Indianapolis Recorder*, one of the city's first newspapers targeting the black community. Often including directories of African American businesses, the paper was something of a Bible for fresh arrivals like Seymour. With details of restaurants, hotels, and grocery stores, as well as barbers, physicians, dentists, lawyers, dealers in coal, ice, oil, and junk—even a clairvoyant, Indianapolis appealed to the masses as a city of fresh opportunity previously unheard of.[7]

It was to one of these restaurants that Seymour headed on arrival: the Bates Hotel. There he found work as a waiter before moving on to the Grand Hotel Café. Don't be fooled by the servile role—waiting on tables in such a venue was a valued profession, one that came with the dignity of union membership. Seymour joined the Association of Head and Side Waiters, a union of black workers that offered protection in an insecure job market.[8] The Association was one of the few all-black unions to exist in the city, including the Hod Carriers' Union and the Shovelers' Union. Such groups protected their own and were prepared for action if necessary. According to one report "the hod-carriers' industry was almost wholly in the hands of Negroes who had a strong union, with a large strike fund put aside."[9]

There is another reason for Seymour's choice of career to spark interest. Turn back to Acts 6 and we see the twelve apostles selecting seven strong believers to carry out the vital task of meeting the needs of the local community of Greek Jews. Among them was Stephen, whose martyrdom follows in the next chapter. These seven offered practical help to those in need, and were known by the Greek word *diakonos*, often translated as *servant* or more specifically *waiter*. Like modern-day deacons, William Seymour's time spent waiting on table, serving others in such a literal capacity was an essential first step in his spiritual growth.

Though some found protection and security in their work, others emerged with a different experience of life in the North. While nowhere near as harsh as the South, underlying attitudes created a paradoxical situation across the city. Thousands had come to find freedom, and the place throbbed with the prosperity generated from a thriving black subculture and equal voting rights for all. Yet, often, the promises went undelivered. Black voters found, perhaps unsurprisingly, that white politicians flirted with their concerns to gain their support during elections, only to ignore them afterward. One need to look no further than the falling arc of the Republican party's morality in the years following the Civil War for an example of this. Back then, most black voters in Indianapolis supported the Republican party, the party of Lincoln. Yet a cancer was growing within, and by the 1920s the Ku Klux Klan dominated the Republican organization in Indiana.[10]

Such developments took time of course, but their fermentation was easily witnessed in the hardening of attitudes. While some white-owned businesses did search for black customers in the pages of the *Recorder*, other white storekeepers, restaurant and theater owners redrew the color line. By simply refusing to serve African Americans, or by dissuading their presence with inflated prices, the undertow threatened to destabilize the law. Indiana's civil rights ruling of 1885 stated that places of public accommodation had to serve all people "regardless of color or race," but African Americans who tried to challenge discriminatory practices in court found themselves the victim of petty literalism acting as a thin veil to racist attitudes. In 1900 a black hairdresser sued an Indianapolis hotel when she was denied permission to use the elevator to reach the room of her customer. The Marion County Superior Court accepted the argument that because the hairdresser was not a guest herself, she had no right to use the hotel's elevator. In a similar decision in 1920, the Appellate Court ruled that an ice cream parlor was not technically an "eating place" and so was not covered by the civil rights law.[11]

Indianapolis, so it seemed, was a paradox. It was the starting place for Seymour's attempts to move on from the past, yet a city whose potential for unity was dogged by retrograde attitudes and cheapened promises. Like Reconstruction itself, Indianapolis was a small step taken by a big boot, a slow shuffle forward from one with far greater athletic potential.

If this left Seymour disillusioned, there is little evidence. In fact, it seems clear that such semi-progress only served to spur the young man on. He may have chosen to join the biggest urban black community of the day, living in the heart of downtown (first at 127 1/2 Indiana Ave then 309 Bird Street), yet Seymour was not closing himself off. The work as a waiter brought him into contact with a racial mix beyond his own, and his choice of church spoke volumes. Instead of joining one of the many all-black churches that were part of the wallpaper of downtown Indianapolis, Seymour chose a spiritual home that promoted a message of integration and unity. Well, nearly. The truth is that the Simpson Chapel Methodist Episcopal Church was comprised of an all-black congregation, yet it was part of the interracial Methodist church.[12]

The Methodist church—having split over the slavery issue in

1844—had actively tried to reach out to slaves as the Civil War approached. They provided churches and schools—establishing two schools in Franklin and Baton Rouge during Seymour's childhood. The Northern Methodists remained resolute not to split down racial lines, and despite numerous offshoots formed in the mists of time, in the Simpson Chapel, Seymour had chosen a spiritual home that was known for its unique stance on a key issue.[13]

However, as is becoming clear with Seymour's story, statements about the generally progressive nature of the Methodist church at the time must be served with warnings and clauses. To say that Seymour found a home in Methodism is true, but unfortunately, that particular home life was about to change. Despite the bold glories of the 1844 split, the color line was becoming increasingly clear within the church.

Chapter 7
William Seymour Finds Unexpected Inspiration

"Is the Negro a Beast?"

And so, Seymour's spiritual journey continued to be a tour of the varied landscape of the nineteenth century American church. Brought up a Baptist, but with Catholic influence, he would have held tight to certain key doctrines, primarily believing that above all things faith was the key. Things would have gotten muddied as the two traditions fought over the issue of the sacraments—with the Catholic school of thought emphasizing the importance of the sacraments and the Baptist church playing them down. Therefore, Methodism would have been a fresh start, not only because of its apparently progressive Northern stance, but also because of the movement's role as a historical stepping stone to a vibrant, wholly new phenomenon: the Holiness movement. This cross-denominational drive did exactly what its name proclaimed— encouraged members to pursue personal integrity, to let their lifestyle match the rhetoric.

Even this slice of the Seymour story comes complete with its side order of irony. The holiness movement took ground, energy, and people away from the Methodist church. In comparison, both the Northern and Southern arms appeared conservative and repressive. Yet urging the masses to pursue holiness was precisely what Methodist founder, John Wesley, had done himself. His experiences had led him to believe that the evolution of a Christian was marked by two phases: the first *work of grace*, being conversion, and the second, getting the tag "Christian perfection" or sanctification. The latter, he argued, could be attained instantly as a *second work of grace*, usually followed by a good deal of hard work as the believer put in the effort to live a less sinful life. These phases or "works of grace" were to become increasingly important to the development of contemporary theology at the time, and for the Holiness movement, they represented the drive for more of God's power, a longing for a repeat of the events of Pentecost as described in Acts chapter 2[1]. Seymour would have felt the pull, the thrill of the chase as the promises and power of old were believed to be close at hand.

*

And so, in 1900, Seymour moved on from Indianapolis.[2] Popular belief has it that he may have moved to Chicago, where, like many other ex-Methodists, he would have found himself within the gravitational pull of integrationist preachers like James Alexander Dowie. With over ten thousand members attending meetings across the city, the pastor insisted on integrated seating in his Christian Catholic Church.[2] At least one man serving on his board of twelve apostles would be black, and, according to Dowie, it was high time for "this horrible, so-called 'race prejudice' to be wiped out." Why? As the man saw it, "The whiter you are the less strong you are."[3]

What is clear is that before long Seymour had moved again. This time he chose Cincinnati, Ohio, retracing the one hundred and eighty miles back south to Indianapolis and then on a further one hundred miles to what would prove to be a life-changing destination. Here Seymour would lose his sight but gain his vision.

Again, he found work as a waiter, lodging first at 23 Longworth and then at 437 Carlisle Avenue.[4] Again Seymour was surrounded by a social climate that brought out both the best and the worst in people. The church he eventually chose to join was pastored by the Reverend Daniel S, Warner. Along with the rest of his Evening Light Saints, Warner was, depending on your point of view (or affection for the Methodist cause), either a bold pioneer shaking off the dust or a dangerous radical who threatened to neuter the Methodist church entirely. Either way, the preacher and his flock were influential. Their territory spread beyond the city and throughout Ohio, Indiana, and Michigan, placing Seymour at the heart of the action.

From his vantage point, Seymour would have been aware of the interplay between politics and faith represented by Warner and his followers, as well as the spiritual dimension to the work. According to Warner, the longed-for Pentecost experience was not far off. Nor, it seemed, was the apocalypse that heralded the return of Christ. The Spirit (called *the evening light* by Warner) was about to be poured out on the saints in a prelude to history's end. Warner's pre- millennialist views attracted more than a little interest. The Saints made noise, attracted notice, and circulated thirty-five thousand copies of their newspaper *The Gospel Trumpet*.[5] Circulation at this level gave the group a voice, one which they were not afraid to use given the right circumstances.

If ever there was an opportune time for the Saints to speak out, it was in response to a racially charged piece of venomous spiritual hijacking titled, *The Negro A Beast*. The work of Charles Carroll, throughout its 165 pages it pours out racist bile fueled by an abuse of Scripture. Take a look at Carroll's text, and it is clear that back in that day racism took many guises—from violent lynchings to pseudo-intellectual musings.

At times Warner's agenda was so obvious and his arguments so weak as to be almost amusing. Take these partisan musings on the intellectual capacities of the modern man:

> The average weight of the European brain, males and females, is 1340 grammes; that of the Negro is 1178; of the Hottentot, 974; and of the Australian, 907. The significance of these comparisons appears when we learn that Broca, the most eminent of French anthropologists, states that when the European brain falls below 978 grammes (mean of males and females), the result is idiocy. In this opinion Thurman coincides. The color of the Negro brain is darker than that of the White, and its density and texture are inferior. The convolutions are fewer and more simple, and, Agassiz

and others long ago pointed out, approximate those of the quadrumama.⁶

Fearing that he may not have made a strong enough case thus far, Carroll refines his argument further:

> Had these estimates extended to every class of people in the United States the average of whites would doubtless have been raised to 1,500 grammes.⁷

While often ridiculous, the text is more frequently disturbing. Published by the American Book and Bible House, St Louis in 1900, the work reflected a disturbing trend within the church, as the publisher makes clear in the foreword:

> In placing this book entitled *The Negro a Beast* or *In the Image of God* upon the American market, we do so knowing that there will be many learned men who will take issue with us, but while we are fully convinced of this, we are also convinced that when this book is read and its contents duly weighed and considered in an intelligent and prayerful manner, that it will be to the minds of the American people like unto the voice of God from the clouds appealing unto Paul on his way to Damascus.⁸

The use of illustrations throughout clarifies and condenses the thrust. One pen-and-ink sketch depicts Adam and Eve in the garden of Eden. The white couple stand apart from a crying black baby, the first woman protected by the strong arms of the first man. "Is the negro an offspring of Adam and Eve?" the text asks. "Can the rose produce a thistle?"

Later the illustrations tap into more contemporary fears as a dazed-looking white bride stands alongside a mischievous looking black man in front of a white preacher. "Can you find a white preacher who would unite in holy wedlock a burly negro to a white lady?" we are asked. "Ah! parents, you would rather see your daughter burned and her ashes scattered to the winds of heaven."[9]

This was a time of betrayal. The book became a bestseller, and much of the church was complicit in the crime. However, in 1901 the Evening Light Saints used their publishing house to promote William G Schell's response to Carroll's vitriol. *Is The Negro a Beast?* was a reply that promoted equality. Sadly, it was the last major effort of any Christian group to do so.[10]

As well as opposing the segregationist rantings of Carroll, the Saints were marked by their desire to dig in a little deeper and soak up a little more fully the stuff of the Holy Spirit. Like John Wesley before them, they saw Pentecost as a relevant lesson for the times rather than an historical curio destined never to leave the display case of religious phenomena. As much as the Saints valued racial inclusion, an abandonment to overwhelming spiritual power was similarly upheld as a goal worth pursuing. For a son of ex-slaves such as Seymour—one whose very skin tone was argued by some fellow believers as being evidence for inferiority and a status equivalent to a farm animal—the prospect of a powerful spiritual encounter was highly attractive. As a sign of inclusion and success in a struggle against overwhelming social oppression, there could be little better than a personal Pentecost.

Seymour, it seems, was a soul in conflict. On the one hand his spiritual upbringing offered him the fruits of a life less ordinary, the promise of the ultimate satisfaction of a life spent serving God. Yet wherever he turned he could see betrayal and hypocrisy, living examples of bigoted attitudes dressed up in religion's robes. Or perhaps the conflict took on a different nature; perhaps it was played out between twin passions of his ambitions. It may have been wealth or status that he craved while the lure of the church promised a higher (and lowlier) reward. Whatever the cause of this inner turmoil, Seymour's three weeks spent pole axed by smallpox put it all to rest. He emerged envisioned, inspired, and determined to put the past into place. He was finally ready to accept the destiny the had always suspected was on offer.

Cincinnati was the ideal place to make the decision to push ahead with life as a preacher. The Evening Light Saints were at the cutting edge of things, pushing the boundaries and encouraging members to find a radical, dynamic aspect to their faith. Personal Pentecost was all part of the plan.

Yet while Seymour would have to wait five years before fully receiving what he would later consider to be the sign of such a blessing— speaking in tongues, or *glossolalia*—his time with the Evening Light Saints was not without reward. It would later be claimed about him that he believed, at the time, that he had been sanctified during one evening meeting. According to the story he returned to the altar a second time, refusing to leave until he felt sure that he had received his second blessing.

Perhaps what we can be more sure of, however, is the lesson learned by a process of osmosis from the leaders of the movement. Theirs was a stricter, perhaps more integrity-laden, faith. Members were to drink no tea or coffee; they were not permitted to wear lace or ruffles if they were women, or ties if they were men. Neither gender was allowed the extravagances of gold, nor were they allowed to indulge in the enjoyment of professional entertainments.[11]

The preachers epitomized the concept of a strong work ethic. Warner, for example, would preach daily for weeks on end, sometimes up to four times a day.[12] These were radical, dangerous men caught up in a battle not only for souls but for the future shape of the church itself. Men like Martin Wells Knapp, Cincinnati-based Methodist evangelist, who opened up doors and altar to blacks as well as whites. His nightly meetings held in the revivalist chapel were an open invitation to all who cared to attend. Of course, controversy was not far behind, and the pressure on Knapp the maverick was too great. In 1901 he resigned from the Methodist Episcopal Church.[13]

However, this old-style Methodism, this fervent, inclusive, and radical approach to faith found a fan in the newly inspired and freshly determined William Seymour. The waiter became the part-time student while in Cincinnati, attending Knapp's God's Bible School and gaining a deeper understanding of holiness theology.[14] Knapp's strong pre-millennialist views, which predicted the imminent arrival of Christ, were controversial. Yet they were also familiar to Seymour, tying up in part with the images and visions that punctuated his youth.

A retrospective view from today's vantage point shows that change and conflict were a constant in all aspects of life. Church, constitution, and culture were all in a state of flux, like cotton caught on the wind, preparing to settle yet still twitching in all directions until the very last moment of flight. Of course, Seymour's life bore the hallmarks of the same genetic code—the frequent movement around the country betrayed the heart of a man on a quest. Partly in a bid to escape a past, partly in search of a better future, Seymour's movements were brought to an end in the midst of Cincinnati's 1902 smallpox epidemic. It was then that he made his choice, it was after his illness that he took his first steps. As the smallpox gathered force within his body, its cells replicating, attacking, and overpowering, the host approached his own moment of surrender. Before long, William Seymour had been delivered yet another lesson in the omnipotent power of the paradox: By facing the prospect of an unremarkable death, he discovered the power and purpose for a remarkable life.

Chapter 8
Agnes Ozman Is Introduced

"Glory Hallelujah!"

Topeka, Kansas, January 1st, 1901. If you're that way inclined, it was the first day of a new year, the ideal time for fresh starts and new resolve. For the thirty-five individuals meeting underneath the Disneyland-like turrets and fantasia ceilings of the building known by the curious locals as *Stone's Folly*, the menu offered far more than off-the-peg good intentions for the coming year. The collected faithful, under the gaze of their master, were hungry for nothing less than manna from heaven, spiritual gifts from the Creator Himself.

Left alone by their leader for the previous three days, these pupils had prayed, studied, discussed, and moved ever closer to what always seemed like the inevitable conclusion. For seventy-two hours they had pondered just one question: What does the Bible say is an accurate indicator of a person being baptized with the Holy Spirit? The answer? A unanimous vote for *glossolalia*, "speaking with other tongues."

Their conclusions went against the grain of popular thought. Tongues at that time were viewed with suspicion by the mainstream church. Of course, if you deal in centuries rather than decades, it is possible to find plenty of other believers in the importance of God's ability to replicate the phenomenon described in Mark 16, Acts 2, 10, 19, and 1 Corinthians 12, 13, and 14.

Like the early believers in Corinth, Jerusalem, Caesarea, and Ephesus, there had been others who had been on the receiving end of the experience. The list reads like a roll call of the mysterious and the bizarre, with many of them being branded heretics in their day as the watching world observed them chase down tongues and many other ecstatic experiences:

Donatus lead the Donatists in receiving the gift in the latter part of the third century. The Beghards were a splinter from the Franciscan movement in the thirteenth century. They joined a little later with the Calixtines at a camp meeting near Prague and became known as the Taborites. Lead by a man named Ziska they too pursued the gift of tongues. There were the Vaudois, the Zwickau Prophets, the Davidists and the awkward sounding Convulsionaries, although it is stretching credibility to believe that the English Muggletonians of the seventeenth century were anything other than a joke name. However, they were real enough for William Penn to go on record with a damning critique of their affection for apocalyptic teachings and manifestations in his book, *The New Witnesses Proven Old Heretics*.[1]

In the century just ended, *glossolalia* had made a limited impact despite a significant development across the Atlantic. Edward Irving started out his preaching career as the archetypal celebrity. His sermons were reproduced in the London papers, and demand for pew space was so high that admission to services at which he preached was by ticket only. During the services the police dispatched a special unit to regulate traffic around the church before and after the Sunday services. Later in life, Irving was to be found at the center of an outbreak of full-scale *glossolalia*. However, some say that it was not until he was on his deathbed that he received the gift himself, exhaling a perfect Hebrew rendition of the 23rd Psalm.[2]

Forty years later, another preacher, Dwight L. Moody, would experience the fire of the Holy Spirit. Yet despite the influence, the passion, and the controversy, the new Pentecost had failed to dig in and settle into an established pattern. At least that was the case back in the days of the nineteenth century. For the select few meetings in the mansion as the old sun rose on the new year, the potential represented by possible receipt of the gift of tongues was significant. During preceding years, the spiritual bar had been raised by the increasing influence of the holiness movement. With all this extra devotion flying around, students and participants alike assumed that it would all lead to something significant, that something big was about to happen. The imminent change, many agreed, was about as big as things could get: global revival. Many were convinced that it was close. Add to that all the optimism and reflection that comes with the dawning of a new century, and it was logical for many to conclude that God would soon be sending a sign that His people were on the right track. Previous practitioners of tongues believed that *glossolalia* was the key to the receipt of other gifts. Others believed that it had a practical value all of its own. For the people gathered in Topeka to pray, two facts appeared clear: History was about to draw to a close with Christ's imminent return; and a major outpouring was precisely what was needed to sort out the faithful with a little last-minute maturing in advance of the imminent harvest.

Back in that Topeka room, the students enrolled in Charles Parham's Bethel Bible School prayed in earnest. It was past midnight when one, a young lady named Agnes Ozman broke the pattern.[3] She asked the man in charge to lay his hands on her head and pray for her to receive the Holy Spirit and the gift of tongues. That man—Charles Parham—remained a mysterious figure. Rumors of childhood ailments and dramatic healing accentuated the mystique. His elfin figure and dramatic public speaking persona added to it, leaving his followers inspired by his leadership. To cut a short story not much shorter, she received what she asked for. Reports have it that her mid-western tongue gave way to a cascade of Chinese. It wasn't a momentary event, either. For three days Ozman was unable to communicate in any other language, either verbally or by writing. Whenever she attempted to write, her hand would produce nothing other than Chinese characters.[4]

Both the news and the tongues spread. Before long, all of Ozman's fellow students (each one American) began speaking in tongues. Between them they covered twenty-one known languages, all verified by native speakers who turned up to one of the many meetings at which Parham and his students spoke over the coming weeks.[5]

The press caught on and returned a generally positive verdict upon the strange proceedings. The *Cincinnati Enquirer* suggested that little in recent years had "mystified the people" as much, while the *Kansas City World* spluttered that "these people have a faith almost incomprehensible at this day."[6]

To Charles Parham, this was exciting yet perfectly normal. Ever the practical man, he saw this as the perfect ramp up to the higher levels of world mission. With such linguistic blessings on hand, he felt assured that there would no longer be any need for missionaries to study the language of their destination country. All they needed was a decent soaking in the power of the Holy Spirit, and the language barriers would vanish like dawn mist.[7]

According to Parham, this was the way that things would be from now on. Speaking in tongues would be as useful an everyday tool as the telephone. This stance toward the gift marked him apart from others, a state of being with which Parham was already well acquainted. In time he would find himself even more so, yet in 1901 his peculiarities were limited to his tastes in architecture and friends. His choice to rent the mock-European castle, Stone's Folly, as a base for his Bethel Bible School was unorthodox. Thought by locals to be haunted, Stone's Folly had lain empty since its creator (tycoon Erastus R. Stone) had fled to California to escape financial ruin in the 1890s.[8] It was one of those grand buildings that dominated the landscape the way its owner's ego dominated a crowded room. It was perfect for Parham, the man who had previously been inspired on more levels than one by Frank Sandford's church at Shiloh, Maine. Shiloh's community of believers were surrounded by architecture that made grand statements and invited enquiry.[9]

Shiloh had impressed upon Parham more than a taste for architectural oddities. It was there that he heard *glossolalia* for the first time, and there that he saw the links between the gift of tongues and the possibilities for evangelism to far-flung countries. It was at Shiloh that he met Sandford, an ex-professional baseball player and holiness preacher who signed up for the "restorationism"—although certainly not integration—of Chicago's John Alexander Dowie. Dowie was convinced that it was only a matter of time before the powers given to the disciples would be restored to the church as an overture to the second coming.

Sandford was impressed by Dowie's energy, commenting in his diary that: "Dr. Dowie of Chicago prays with or for as many as 70,000 sick people a year, and thousands of the most astounding and remarkable miracles have taken place."[10]

Clearly a magnetic and dynamic personality, Sandford had more than a few cracks in his armor. First, he was influenced by the writings of Charles Totten, a biblical scholar and professor at Yale who fervently taught the racist doctrine of British Israelitism.[11] According to Totten, the modern-day Anglo-Saxons were, in reality, the "ten lost tribes of Israel" who were subsequently scattered when the Kingdom of Israel was conquered by the Assyrians. (See 1 Kings 17.) This teaching was a thin veil for racist rhetoric and was strongly at odds with the Wesleyan holiness tradition, which had played such a key part in the fight against slavery.

Sandford was convinced that the end of the world was near, and that he had a role to play. In fact, his role had a name: *Elijah*. Sandford believed that he was to operate in the same power and spirit as the Old Testament prophet. Unfortunately, his impression was flawed, as there is no record of Elijah encountering such opposition as a ten-year prison term for manslaughter, Sandford's most infamous public appearance.[12]

Conditions at Sandford's church at Shiloh were poor. One member who broke away from the church, later revealed:

> I have endured the tortures of hell since I joined....They have taken all my money, deprived me of my family, ruined my health and were starving me to death.[13]

Sandford's charges eventually included the manslaughter of a boy whom he had refused permission to take medicine while suffering from diphtheria. Rumors suggested that the faithful were permitted only one meal a day, usually mush and milk, and that sickness was ravaging the disciples. A state investigation uncovered what were identified as cases of cruelty to children, and it was declared that Sandford was, "ruling his people with fear, they following his merest suggestions implicitly." Sandford was called "insane."[14]

Eventually Sandford was indicted and convicted on six counts of causing deaths among his people. He was sentenced to ten years in prison and, in 1918, seven years later, was paroled on good behavior.[15]

So, this was the man that Parham liked, the leader on whom he based part of his theology. Tongues clearly fitted with Sandford's view of a restoration of gifts in the closing bars of the earth's pre-apocalyptic state, and Parham made all the right noises. Writing again in his journal, Sandford recalled a meeting a few months prior to Agnes Ozman's experience on New Year's Day:

> At Kansas City…The services Saturday and Sunday were richly blessed, and Brother Parham, a religious leader who had come from Topeka to attend the services, insisted that we accompany him home. The bond of union Sunday afternoon which had united the three leaders of three great movements, one in the extreme west, another in the extreme east and the third in the center of our vast country, must have brought rejoicing among the angels…here was my Brother Parham from Topeka, leader of a work similar to our own, divine healing, church, Bible School, and publisher of a paper…[16]

*

Meanwhile, back in Cincinnati William Seymour was about to undergo his own informal discipleship at the feet of a radical practitioner. Having escaped the death-hold of smallpox and having made a decision to pursue a life in line with what he was convinced was a divine calling, Seymour applied himself to the life of the Evening Light Saints. It was there that he was ordained, although the title implies a rather grander process than the reality. Ordination within the movement involved kneeling at the altar and praying in earnest for divine guidance. The ordained lived out their life of dedication by preaching God's Word.[17] As simple as that, and Seymour was on track, pursuing the path he had spent so long avoiding.

His first stop was Jackson, Mississippi, where he encountered Charles Jones.[18] Raised a Baptist, Jones was one half of the Mason/Jones partnership, a duo that, impacted by holiness teaching they had heard, introduced the concept of sanctification to their fellow Baptist churchgoers. They were promptly introduced to life as ex-Baptist ministers, yet things worked out well. They formed the Church of God in Christ, which became the first southern holiness denomination to be legally chartered, enjoying a status and influence that grew phenomenally over the coming years.

Yet for William Seymour, Charles Jones' influence was rather more practical: It honed and deepened his conviction that life in the early twentieth century was indeed life at the edge of history. The latter rains were coming, and the ending was about to begin.

Chapter 9
Charles Parham Becomes Better Known

A Sincere and Extremely Optimistic Fanatic

Remember that bit about Agnes Ozman speaking in tongues as the fresh light of a new century threatened to break through the windows as New Year's Eve merged into New Year's Day? Well, there's a problem with it, a slight tremor of instability around the foundations of its truth. Then there's the matter of the students deciding independently of their master that tongues was the sign of second blessing. Similarly, they're struggling to hold their own under scrutiny. You see, these versions of events both come from one source, but there are others that contradict and counter these neater retellings of the story. The unreliable, highly polished version belongs to Charles Parham. The truth belonged to Agnes Ozman.

Charles Parham was no stranger to critical opinion, and certainly did not seem to complain when it came his way. Whether you mark him down as countercultural maverick or self-seeking antagonist, his bold moves make for good reading even now. Take his first book, self-published in 1902 with the catchy title *Kol Kare Bomidbar: A Voice Crying In The Wilderness*. Comparing oneself to John the Baptist while still in your twenties takes a certain amount of self-assurance. Yet Parham's confidence was always high, and while Seymour struggled alone with the pox and the calling, the Kansas man was telling anyone who would listen that he was walking on this earth with a serious task at hand. Parham, like the original outcast on the fringes of society, believed fervently that there was a new baptism, a fresh blessing about to be delivered to any who chose to approach. He was right, too, yet perhaps a little too right for comfort, though his own plot did not follow John's all the way to include dancing girls, infatuated rulers, and severed heads. In years to come he would reflect on what had passed. "Should we expect something else?" are words that could so easily be transplanted into his aging lips.

Whatever the ending, it fails to alter the fact that two of the most important accounts of what went on at Stone's Folly fail to match up. The official version of events comes from numerous newspaper reports based on interviews with Parham as well as through his wife's 1930 biography.[1] Other reports were based on interviews with the man himself and quoted in two theses written by Charles Shumway, the student interested in sharpening his analytical carving knives on the whole tongues phenomenon. So, while we know Charles Parham's version—the three-day pupil-only Bible study, the revelation to one and all of tongues as the sign of God's blessing, followed by the New Year's receipt of that gift—but we need go no further than Agnes Ozman for a different version of events.

Like Parham she too grew up surrounded by the empty wilderness of the American frontier. In her case, it was Nebraska, as opposed to her mentor's two-step childhood based first in Iowa and then in the emergent wheat wealth of Kansas. Similarly, Ozman suffered ill health as a child, although unlike Parham's prolonged list of ailments, her afflictions numbered just two: "la grippe and pneumonia."[2]

Like Sandford and possibly Seymour she too had spent time hearing the message from Dowie's lips in Chicago. Then, aged thirty, single and in Kansas, Ozman got the chance to pursue her street-preaching passions by signing up for the Bethel Bible School. According to her accounts, *glossolalia* kicked off at 11 P.M. on January 1st, rather than the wee small hours of the night before.[3] Perhaps not the most outrageous of errors, but there's a little more soil that shifts with not-so-careful digging. It appears that this whole baptism in the Holy Spirit—whenever it was—was not Agnes Ozman's first experience of tongues. Writing twenty years after the event, she reflected that:

> One night three of us girls were praying together, and I spoke three words in another tongue. This was a hallowed experience and was held in my heart as sacred.[4]

Not only was this experience held as sacred, it was held pretty secret too: she credits the event as taking place some three weeks before New Year's Eve. There's more too, coming in the form of significant doubt about the extent to which the students chimed together their response about the value of tongues as a sign of blessing. Again, Agnes has the adjacent opinion worth listening to:

> Before receiving the comforter I did not know that I would speak in tongues when I received the Holy Ghost for I did not know it was Bible [sic]. But after I received the Holy Spirit speaking in tongues it was revealed to me that I had the promise of the father as it is written and Jesus said…I did not know then that anyone else would speak in tongues.[5]

She was then "greatly surprised to find so much written on the subject" when she conducted a Bible study on the phenomenon.[6] So much for the unified conclusions at the end of a three-day Bible study on the New Testament. Yet beyond being able to highlight inconsistencies, this field of study exposes a more valid point. Parham, it appears, had already made up his mind that the gift of tongues was the way forward—his experiences at Shiloh had led him to that particular conclusion. So why would he decide to play down his role in leading his students toward the events in January of 1901? Could he have been perturbed by the possible introduction of such a controversial doctrine, or were his later reports simply trimmed back in the name of self-effacing humility? Neither explanation appears particularly likely.

Perhaps the truth lies in the area of Parham's health. He was constantly dogged by medical problems, advised even to give up preaching while at college for fear of the stress it induced and the potential damage to his already weak heart. Once, while praying for healing in someone else he stopped. What was he doing? Shouldn't the physician heal himself? Transferring the focus of his prayers onto his own ailments, he quickly experienced what he later claimed to be total healing. His faith was high, and the results were tangible. It was soon even clearer: He had been praying for divine healing while hoping for help from the medical profession. This equated a conflict of faith in his mind, and from then on, he was clear about the way forward. With a God on board who held the power of the sun and stars in His hand, a God who healed His created beings, what need was there of man-made solutions and insurance? From then on divine healings were part of his evangelistic message while medical intervention was wiped clean of the agenda.[7] Even on his deathbed he refused medical attention for a fatal heart condition. Dismissive of human wisdom, dependent on interpretation of the divine will, Parham's mixture of arrogance and faith fueled his every decision.

In the wake of the January 1901 events at Stone's Folly—events that would later become known as the *Topeka Outpouring*, the *Topeka Revival* and the *Birth of Pentecostalism*—controversy received a power surge. Informed regularly of events, newspapers shocked and bemused their readers with accounts of what was going on, and a minority of students became disgruntled. One, Samuel J. Riggins, left on January 5th and headed for the press:

"I believe the whole of them are crazy," reported page 2 of the *Topeka Daily Capital*, quoting the escapee.[8] Few others left, and the crew remained solid in their purpose. With a man like Parham in the lead, following was simply a case of trying to keep up. His penchant for planning was matched only by his flair for picking a fight and seizing an opportunity to drive his message home.

Within days of the outpouring Parham was inspiring his students about a forthcoming mission to Kansas City. His intentions were clear: he would preach at meetings held over several weeks, the power would fall, healing would be received, and the city would surely be transformed. Thousands would crowd forward, and the blessing would make its logical progression to the next level of intensity. Unfortunately, while he talked positively about the event to his team, his refusal to have his team members vaccinated against smallpox per the authorities' requests did not go down well. The unpopular move was accompanied by some unimpressive newspaper appraisals. Dubbed "a sincere and extremely optimistic fanatic" by one reporter, the flock were treated slightly less kindly. They were "about as tacky looking an outfit as one would see in a trip around the world." Despite the public relations work on the Bethel believers' behalf, the crowds stayed away, and where Parham had promised thousands, the reality was a far more spacious crowd of one hundred or so.[9]

For six weeks Parham and his students applied themselves to the task, eventually admitting defeat (well, almost). Their return to Topeka was billed to reporters as a need to "to clear up a problem at the school."[10] Not much time needed to pass before the plans and the passion were back on full display, as Parham was soon touting his intentions to commence fundraising for a significant building program at Topeka, erecting an auditorium capable of seating the masses soon to be brought in by a fresh mission drive. Yet holiness churches were largely indifferent to the tongues and healing message, despite Parham's claims of having five hundred followers in Topeka and thousands around the country and beyond.

Within days of announcing the plans, silence fell. His year-old son Charles Parham, Jr. died suddenly on March 16th.[11] Some followers believed in the potential for resurrection of the child, but it looks as if the grieving father just didn't have that particular fight within him.

Shortly after, as Agnes Ozman later put it, life at Stone's Folly continued in the way to which they had all become accustomed: "a voice which was followed was not the Lord's."[12] Missions failed to live up to Parham's hype and the big crowds that were promised never showed up. Disillusionment set in, and even the bricks and mortar seemed to be against them. Stone's Folly gave up the power of the mascot, finally getting sold in July 1901. The new owner favored spirit of a different kind, and Parham was sickened by the knowledge that his beloved Bible school was now owned by a common bootlegger. Many local residents shared Parham's dislike of the new owner, and so when early one morning in December 1901 Stone's Folly burned down "under somewhat mysterious circumstances"[13] many claimed it as a victory for Godly standards.

Is it possible to get the measure of a man like Charles Parham? With all his ego and pain and passion and plain anointing, things get more than a little confusing. History has painted many portraits of him over time, each one catching a different side of his character according to the light. The truth is…well who knows what the truth is? There is more of Parham's story to play out yet, including what you must now know is the inevitable interweaving with Seymour's own adventure. With the two men's histories so varied in tone and texture, all that can be said for sure is that it is bound to have to take a fairly remarkable set of events to join them together. On the one side will be the calculating white preacher, while on the other will be the softly spoken, self-effacing black wanderer. Smallpox started the inevitable collision of the planets, with Seymour's escape from the disease prompting him to begin to move in some of the same spheres as Parham. Yet it would be some time before the two men stood face to face, no matter how briefly.

*

To talk of the years linking 1902 to 1905 as a collision of planets is slightly misleading. Far better to consider the progress over the thirty-six months as a series of climate shifts, some sudden and shocking, others more gradual and guarded. Things started as 1901 ended. The promise represented by the opening days of the year had failed to deliver, and 1902 began with no building for the Bible school, fewer followers than predicted, and virtually none of the public enthusiasm Parham had previously enjoyed. These were days on which Parham would later reflect as those when "my wife, her sister, and myself seemed to stand alone."[14] A new Bible school that opened in Kansas City did not live to see its fifth month, and later in the year the Parham family moved forty miles west to Lawrence, Kansas. There they met with little more than total apathy as a series of evangelistic meetings failed to find a spark, let alone fan a flame.

Call it a hunch or a direct word from God, Parham then embarked on a trip one hundred and fifty miles south to El Dorado Springs. The spa town had something of a reputation for attracting the sick, so Parham's message of divine healing at least had a few natural routes in with the punters. A few came, a few were healed, making the trip a good deal more better failure but a long way short of the kind of success that Parham liked to promise. Until August 17, 1903.

That was the day when Mary Arthur—a long-term sufferer of what seemed like most conditions medical science had identified—arrived at the Parham house to hear the sermon and receive the prayers. In short, she was miraculously, instantly, and completely healed. Such was her joy that on return to her morally dubious mining town of Galena, Missouri, her enthusiasm for Parham's prayers was so vocal that an invite to the preacher himself was the obvious next step.[15]

And so continued Parham's gradual inch southward, towards the heat, towards the furnace. Galena, close to the border with Arkansas, was to be a significant, if not total confirmation of all that Parham had long suspected. For a man whose dreams dwarfed the clouds, such a statement is quite something.

At Galena everything went Parham's way. Within six months the booty of souls passed the eight hundred mark, and more than a thousand individuals had stories of healing handed out from on high at any one of the numerous meetings. The year closed with a prayer meeting at which twenty-five hundred turned up, with as many as four hundred still there at dawn.[16] Twenty-four months had passed since the thirty-four students had received their baptism in the Holy Spirit back in Topeka. Now there were several hundred receiving theirs for the first time on one night alone.

Parham had broken through the doubt. Missions followed missions, revival tours peppered the calendar, and 1904 was the stuff of which Parham's dreams were made. A three-week mission to Baxter Springs, Kansas, (population one thousand) yielded two hundred and fifty new converts. What could be better?

But the better story did not follow on. Instead, Parham was dragged back down toward the mire of controversy and confusion. The primer that broke the code of 1904's success was death—nine-year-old Nettie Smith from Baxter Springs died in October.[17] Her illness was brief, yet long enough for her father to refuse medical treatment on the grounds that it conflicted with his Parham-shaped beliefs. The community felt the death was wholly unnecessary, and Parham took both the blame and the opportunity for moving on. However, it was not until the following April that he was able to put the episode behind him. For six months Parham and his movement were neutered, chained up again in their original state, unable to escape the failings of dreams that had failed to find sustained flight.

Whether it was destiny's gravity or God's pull, Parham's journey continued south. Again, at the invitation of a previous attendee of a meeting, this time to Orchard, Texas, he received the tonic he needed. Having relapsed into previous states of ill health during the Nettie Smith affair, it took just three days within the new environs of Orchard for Parham to declare that "a great revival broke out and I was strengthened for the campaign."[18] What followed were meetings, sermons, prayers, and conversions. The number of sinners shrank as the saints rose in the town, and soon the old ambition was back, this time with the metropolis of Houston in his sights. They were to lay siege to it, pour out their arsenal and, for once, sustain little in the way of collateral damage.

The campaign that lasted throughout July and August brought many strands together. Mrs. J. M. Dulaney was one. Married to a prominent local attorney, she had spent three years partially paralyzed after a streetcar accident. A lawsuit assured that the case was known to all, popular enough for a newspaper report in May 1905 to include a quote from the lady herself, stating that she believed she was to be healed and that a vision had made it clear that a man as yet unknown to her would be instrumental in the act. When she saw Parham preaching from the pavement in July, she recognized him from her vision. Her full healing was only a matter of days away, delivered in one of Parham's evening meetings. From that point on, the buzz was out.[19]

Other strands joined together, including one involving Mrs. Lucy Farrow. Born a slave in Virginia in 1851, she was the niece of abolitionist Frederick Douglas. Farrow moved to Texas in 1900 and eventually assumed leadership of a small black holiness church in Houston, finding secular work where she could support herself. A widow and mother of seven, she mourned at the graveside of five of her children. Such sorrows were not uncommon, yet perhaps it was the pain that bound her closer to her faith. When she attended one of Parham's meetings in her home city and witnessed the healings and experienced the Holy Spirit baptism through *glossolalia* for herself, something must have clicked. Soon she would leave the city with Parham and his family, heading a thousand miles north to Kansas. There, throughout September and October she would teach his children and learn from the master.

It is hard to say what it was about Parham's teaching that attracted Farrow. He was certainly entertaining in delivery, the sort of preacher in front of whom "people sat spellbound, one moment weeping, the next rocking with laughter, as the words flowed from his lips like water gushing from a fountain."[20] These were the reflections of Howard Goss, a man who felt that "through it all he was sending home with clean, incisive, powerful strokes, the unadulterated word of God."[21] With hundreds of members signed up to the swelling ranks of Houston evangelists loyal to Parham's message, it's hard to deny Goss's assessment.

Yet Farrow must surely have been uncomfortable at times during his more left-field moments. Parham was fond of raising the subject of Zionism, backing up previously publicized opinions that the Jewish race would soon return home in a prelude to the coming apocalypse. Parham put his own twist on these familiar theories, adding a secret confession to the mix. He would confide in his congregations that he had discovered a secret tip about the location of the Ark of the Covenant. Like a turn-of-the-century Indiana Jones, he told of his plans to travel to Palestine, track down the Ark, and do his bit for the formation of the State of Israel. One more thing: Such sermons were often delivered in costume—an authentic Palestinian robe bought as part of a set from a Bible lecturer. Add to that the idea he borrowed from Sandford about having colorful flags and banners proclaiming words like "unity" and "victory," and it becomes clear that even if Parham's credentials as the father of Pentecostalism may be under question, he certainly set the trend for an arresting pulpit style.

It gets better, too. The gem in the crown of bizarre theories came in the form of Parham's musings about Genesis, the first couple, and the location of Eden. Paradise, he said while sounding remarkably like a modern-day Antiguan marketing consultant, was to be found somewhere in the Caribbean. When Adam and Eve left, it was hidden from their view and, probably then became the lost city of Atlantis.[22]

His "Disneyfication" of the Old Testament carried a darker side. Moving on through Genesis, he would narrate the Fall of man through the lens of racial interplay, taking a literal stance on God's reaction to Cain's choice of marriage partner. The Houston *Daily Post* picked up the story on August 13, 1905, printing his sermon titled "Creation and Formation":

> Thus began the woeful intermarriage of races for which cause the flood was sent in punishment and has ever been followed by plagues

and incurable diseases upon the third and fourth generations, the offspring of such marriages. Were time to last and intermarriage continue between the whites, the blacks and the reds of America, consumption and other diseases would soon wipe the mixed bloods off the face of the earth.[23]

Still, there was enough about Parham that inspired Farrow to uproot her life and commit to a two-month period with him. The only problem was the care of her congregation in her absence. What she needed was a safe pair of hands, yet belonging to a man whose passions for mission, blessing, and holiness matched her own. For a task like that the choice was obvious.

Chapter 10
Charles Parham Remains Cloaked

Beneath the Surface

While Lucy Farrow passed the handful of weeks as governess to his children and pupil to Parham himself, the small Holiness church was placed in the care of one of the group's members: William Joseph Seymour.[1] For little more than eight weeks, the Louisianan took charge of the meetings, preached, and cared for Farrow's flock of believers. This was William Seymour's first time in such a role, but it was not to be his last. Similarly, while this was also the first time that Seymour's life moved close to Charles Parham's, there was more to come.

The plot around this time is simplicity itself. Farrow left with Parham's party, while Seymour remained in Houston, elevated to the position of church leader. Within six months Parham and Farrow would return, the latter inspired at having experienced her own Pentecostal blessing, and the former determined to equip believers with the theological and practical tools necessary to help spread what he felt convinced was to be an imminent revival. Meanwhile Seymour had, by all accounts, done a good job with his caretaker role.

On her return, Farrow's infectious enthusiasm rubbed off on him, and he signed up for Parham's newly established Bible school. Yet within a matter of weeks, he was off, boarding a train that would take him to the west coast to that city of angels, demons, and plenty more in between.

Yet while the period from September 1905 to February 1906 may be relatively easy to follow, the significance of what happened in that time is colossal. In a bizarre parallel preview of events that would take place twelve months later, these first encounters between Parham and Seymour throw up what is perhaps the defining issue of this whole story—Parham's racism.

Or lack of it. The truth is that his attitudes still promote controversy and frustrate those looking for a definitive take on things. Even today people cannot agree on whether Charles Parham deserves the title *Father of Modern Pentecostalism*. No two histories of the Pentecostal movement contain the same depiction of the mustachioed maverick's part in the tale. With a century's gap between us, his actions appear as alien as the culture in which he operated. True, Parham's behavior in later life made it slightly easier to criticize, yet should a fall from grace negate what went before?

But we're rushing too far ahead of ourselves. There's something about the story that makes this impatience almost impossible to avoid. Like a class full of over-amped children on return from summer vacation, there are too many things to be said in too little time. So, for now a little discipline is in order, holding us back to the sequence of events as they occurred.

Parham's decision to return to Kansas in the summer of 1905 left many in Houston feeling increasingly abandoned. To overcome the problems thrown up by his absence, Parham did the next best thing: he sent them handkerchiefs.[2] Not just any old hankies, you understand, but ones over which he had prayed. It is a measure of the man that he would imitate the apostle Paul so blatantly, whose own touch was enough to elevate such items to the status of vehicles for healing. Parham's ego, it seems was in rude health, and it was at about this time that he chose for himself a new title. Instead of leader, pastor, or founder, Parham decided that he was to be known as *Projector of the Apostolic Faith Movement*.[3]

Yet as well as what the whole hanky incident suggests, it also illuminates the attitude that his followers had toward him. He must, after all, have inspired plenty of devotion and trust if such tokens were to be taken seriously, and there is no evidence to suggest that the reaction was anything other than devotion.

Parham, along with his family and the children's temporary governess, made their way back to Houston in October. On his return,

Parham made a choice that would alter the course of church history from then on. With several hundred new Christians around as evidence of the fruit of recent evangelistic missions in Houston and the surrounding areas, it made sense to assume that the longed- for revival was just around the corner.

He was right, within a year the whole world would be talking about the events of the American Pentecost. Unfortunately for Parham the corner around which such good things were to be found happened to be a thousand miles away in Los Angeles. Still, ignorant of the future yet sure of his intentions, Parham came to the obvious conclusion that if events were to proceed as planned, it would be absolutely vital that enough workers would be on hand to help out. What was needed was a means of preparing those who were willing to become the next wave of missionaries and evangelists. What he came up with was the formation of a ten-week Bible school.

Starting in December 1905, the Houston affair had much in common with its predecessor in Topeka. For those who signed up for study—as well as those in charge—this was a chance to live life by nothing more than faith. The venue for the school was a large, rented house on the corner of Rusk and Brazos streets, and to his credit Parham made no charge to those attending, even though finances were inevitably tight. The budgets were shoestring, and the message coursing through the veins was clear: If you believed, then you would receive. Correction—the main message promoted was that the second blessing known as *sanctification* cleansed and purified the believer, while it was the third blessing, *the baptism in power of Holy Spirit*, that brought power for service.

Power was necessary too, as the Bible school rolled out a demanding and ambitious program. Howard Goss was one such attendee, and his reflections on his time at the school serve to illuminate our understanding of life within it:

We were given a thorough workout and a rigid training in prayer, fastings, consecration, Bible study and evangelistic work. Our week day schedule consisted of Bible Study in the morning, shop and jail meetings at noon, house to house visitations in the afternoon, and a six o'clock street meeting followed by an evangelistic service at 7.30 or 8 o'clock.[4]

Clearly this was hard work, yet the sense of purpose and energy is tangible. Perhaps it was this that attracted Seymour, a man who, since his own Damascus road experience back in Cincinnati, had spent the intervening three years searching for opportunities to preach, to serve, and to see his faith shift up a gear. We do know that Farrow returned from her Kansas trip inspired, envisioned, and impassioned. There she had learned directly from Parham about the need for the third blessing, the power of the Holy Spirit, and the evidence of tongues as proof of receipt. She got it too; the knowledge, the blessing, tongues and all. We have to assume that she took back the reins from Seymour in October, leaving him possibly hungry for more.

The eight weeks or so had certainly made an impression, not least on one female friend of Farrow's, a Los Angeles resident named Neeley Terry, out in Texas visiting relatives. Her time in Houston included attendance at Farrow's Holiness church, where she met Seymour. She left with an impression of him that would again change the course of the church from that point on.[5]

Prior to leaving the west coast, Terry found herself confronted by controversy. Her passion for Holiness teaching—encouraged by Seymour but with roots that predated her trip eastwards—came with a price. Such theology did not sit well with her home church, and the Baptist congregation ensured that she, as well as a handful of other holiness fans, were freshly ejected. Houston not only cemented her beliefs but also provided her with a suggestion to take back to the small group of wandering ex-Baptist believers struggling to find a way forward in Los Angeles. Later Seymour would describe what happened in typical God-focused style:

> It was the divine call that brought me from Houston to Los Angeles....The Lord put it on the heart of one of the saints in Los Angeles to write to me that she felt the Lord wanted me to come there, and I felt that was the leading of the Lord.... The Lord provided the means and I came to take charge of a mission on Santa Fe street.[6]

Little time passed between Seymour's meeting Terry and joining her church in the February of 1906. Written in bold across those months was one name: Charles Parham. The period that closed 1905 and opened 1906 would be the time when Seymour and Parham were at their closest. They spent more time together then than at any other point, and their friendship would never again have such currency.

Friendship was a reality for the white master and black pupil, despite the fact that when it came to matters of theology, they "they sometimes disagreed rather vociferously."[7] Parham did not agree with Seymour's take on the nature of the second blessing, who believed that it was itself the point at which a person was entirely cleansed. There were other points of disagreement, too. Parham took a more liberal line on the possibility of remarriage for those who were divorced, while Seymour's line was far harder and more conservative. They also failed to step in time on the subject of other sexual liberties, but more importantly, the key difference between them was one of attitude to race.[8]

Parham allowed Seymour to join his Bible school. According to the Jim Crow laws that dominated racial interaction, blacks were not allowed to worship or study alongside whites. Yet it is clear that Parham wanted to find a way around this, that he was keen for Seymour to learn, that he saw a place for Seymour (and his fellow blacks) in the coming revival. So, Seymour sat outside the classroom and listened to the master through the door that was left ajar.[9] A defining image, perhaps? Certainly, it's one with multiple interpretations, and one that places front and center the key question of the hour: Was Parham a racist?

Clearly there are two extremes of response. To respond with an affirmative, one needs only to picture October 1906, when Parham stood in front of a crowd of assorted races, pouring out venom and bile that centered on the crossing of the color line.[10] You could flick back to his theories of biblical division as the roots in the soil of racial prejudice, to his interpretation of Cain's sin being the root of his beliefs about racial intermarriage. And if you wanted to be really unkind, you could drop hints about the shameful end he would encounter. But there's plenty of time for all that later on.

However, if you wanted to be kind to Parham, you would mention cultural indoctrination and point to the fact that he took a bold step in allowing Seymour to even study at the Houston Bible school. You would make it clear that he spent time drawing all races into the kingdom, that those considered "inferior" were not to be precluded from the End-times rescue mission. You would get the highlighter pen out for the parts where some describe his attitude toward African Americans as "paternalistic." You would find comfort in the part of James Goff's biography where he argues that in the context of the day his approach could hardly be argued as "racist."[11]

Yet, what would one have had to do in order to be branded a racist one hundred years back? Clearly the white hoods and impromptu gallows were the extreme, but segregation and oppression made it the case that surely racism was the norm, the default by which many in the South played. If this was not the case, then what was it that the Civil Rights movement was fighting against? When it comes to the question of Parham's racism, the trouble is that guys like him were supposed to play by a different set of rules. Wesley, Wilberforce, Lincoln, Dowie, and a whole army of others had added Christianity to contemporary life and concluded that such attitudes were wrong. Surely it is naïve to suggest that Parham did not know better. For one who emphasized the importance of Pentecost, he sure missed a whole load from Acts that describes the interracial elements of the early church. Simply put, his attitudes were not good enough for a man of his faith.

It is better to stick to the facts. There had been no black people at Bethel college, but three had converted during the previous campaign in Texas.[12] Seymour was not alone as Messrs. Hall, Viney and Robinson also served alongside on the Houston mission fields. It is clear too that Parham was liberal compared to fellow member of the Apostolic Faith, W. F. Carothers. Here was a man who abhorred any form of social interaction between races. and, while he did permit the idea of both races receiving the Pentecostal blessing, he was convinced that it could only be handed out with due respect paid to current social trends and expectations. In the hands of Carothers, the church, so it would seem, was to be defined by the world.

The topic was as essential then as it is now, and Carothers took it upon himself to give advice to the new workers traveling down from the North to harvest souls. He was clear as to how these liberals should behave:

> Take the word of a native southerner, who, through the sanctifying grace of Jesus Christ is incapable of prejudice, loving the colored man's soul equally as much as the white man's, and let the race question alone until you have been South long enough to know by experience what it seems impossible for our northern brethren to learn through other sources.[13]

So, Parham was moderate. Over the years his tannin and toxins would strengthen, his flavor develops, as his racial "tolerance" declined. While his later critique of the Azusa meetings would mark a key shift in his approach, there is other evidence to suggest that even though he could claim to be a moderate voice on the issue while in Houston, his failures outweighed his successes. The truth is that while he had not prevented Lucy Farrow from attaining her blessing, he made it almost impossible for Seymour and others to secure theirs. Only whites were allowed to approach the altar during the evening meetings.[14] Seeing as how it was at the altar that everything kicked off, this made things difficult not only for Seymour, Hall, Viney, and Robinson, but for those who had been encouraged along to the meeting by street preaching earlier in the day. Parham stood alongside Seymour and others when they approached the black districts, but as soon as they were back on his home turf, segregation was back in play, and Parham disappeared off to the front.

Parham was clearly prejudiced. Perhaps he was also in some way intimidated by Seymour. We know that power was a key jewel for the white preacher, yet all of this is little more than guesswork and gossip. What counts in the story of the birth of Pentecostalism is just the same as that which counted in the months and years that followed the very first Pentecost. Put simply, it is the good that was done that needs to be in bold rather than the bad. Sadly, in this, Parham missed many opportunities to get his name remembered for the right reasons. His wife would later write briefly about the reasons why she and her husband shared such a passive acceptance of social inequality[15]. In searching for the future highs of revival, Charles Parham missed the battle against injustice that was all around him. Had he played things differently, who knows where the church would be today.

Chapter 11
William Seymour Meets Alma White

"I am only a man myself."

Welcome to the story, Alma White—unusually tall, unfeasibly loud, and, according to common opinion, unremarkably "homely." But oddly remarkable too, as Alma White was capable of creating a stir wherever she went. She could inspire hope as well as fear and found herself fueled by desires and passions that set her up for decades of conflict—conflict that would continue beyond her death, subjecting today's opinion of her to debate and diverse opinion.

Born into poverty in rural Kentucky in 1862, Alma Bridwell's transformation began at the age of twenty-five when she married Kent White, a Methodist preacher. Their work together passed through phases with the regularity of the passing seasons, all the time shifting them away from the establishment's center, toward the fringes of power. It was while leading a succession of small, backwater congregations throughout Colorado that Alma White began to find herself moving closer to that power, which would multiply her influence dramatically. Starting by leading hymns and prayers as well as delivering the occasional sermon, her first lesson was fundamental to her understanding of communication with others. Through preaching she discovered a vital lesson. When she wanted to, she could move a congregation to the extreme reaches of the emotions. Joy or tears, the choice was hers.[1]

White is a contradiction tied up in controversy. At the heart of the problem is a question of reading—how do you interpret an extraordinary life lived in extraordinary times? While only sixty years have passed since her death, those six decades have blueprinted enough cultural change to make superficial judgments of White something volatile, something that must be handled with care. For those who fight in her corner, White was a true feminist icon, a woman who fought the oppressive male powers that infected and inhibited the Methodist Episcopal Church. The journey started, they say, when she was refused permission to preach at the camp meetings of the Colorado Holiness Association. She responded by claiming that she was "ready to lay my life down in sacrifice on the altar of the Methodist Church" that "made no provision for me to preach the Gospel."[2]

For a woman to take on such a potent masculine force as the church politic was a mark of significant bravery, and it is true that in many ways White fits the profile of a truly influential woman. Along with others, White's work shifted the foundations of the Methodist Church, driving it forward where other denominations lagged at the back. Their fight for women's rights raised the standard for changes that would roll out across the century. During her eighty-four years, Alma notched up plenty more achievements. She became one of the first female bishops of any Christian church. She made twenty-nine transatlantic trips, each one dedicated to delivering her gospel message to the lost souls of Great Britain.[3] She argued passionately for the scriptural and historical case that supported vegetarianism. She founded the Pillar of Fire sect at the turn of the century and saw it grow in influence and size until, in 1936, its membership topped four thousand, and its property portfolio exceeded $4,000,000.[4]

But there's another way to read White's life. Her appetite for controversy did not exist out of a desire to get people wound up for the sake of it. Her rages were not some type of teenage emotional hangover. Instead, there are plenty around who argue that there's a reason for White's relative obscurity today. History, as we know, favors the brave, but White's appetite for risk was of a type that many would rather forget. In 1925, she published "The Ku Klux Klan in Prophecy," a venomous number detailing biblical justification for the existence of such an organization dedicated to inciting anti-Semitism and further racism.[5]

Her sermons also underlined the points at the heart of the book, and, by now living in New Jersey, her Zarephath Pillar of Fire Church near Bound Brook provided the state's Klan group with ardent and determined supporters. Under the guise of preserving "traditional American values," with a particular focus for a hatred of Catholicism, White's life's work is, for many, soiled by her politics.[6]

Whatever view you choose to take of Alma White, it is difficult not to be struck by the brutal force of her passions. Misguided, and simply wrong as some of them were, White was a character—100 percent proof. Put it this way, if all this ever made it to film, they'd be queuing up to take on the cameo role of the feisty feminist. Imagine the scene when Kent declares his passion for the Pentecostal movement. Alma's reaction is cinema magic—in the one hand she holds her marriage of twenty-two years, in the other is a zealous belief that speaking in tongues is nothing less than satanic. The result? Exit Kent, stage left. Despite his best attempts at reconciliation, his wife's will was as solid as the mountain ranges through which they had previously picked their way together. To her Pentecostalism was evil. End of discussion.

*

But why raise Alma White now? Why detour just when Seymour's progress hits a faster pace? The anxious truth is that it was into this woman's domain that Seymour stumbled, weary from travel, in need of refreshment, shelter, and nurture on the way to a bolder future. Denver, Colorado, may have been a convenient midway point for a break while traveling to Los Angeles, but for our eponymous hero, it was a step back to all he hoped to have left behind.

It was in January 1906 that Seymour left Houston to take up Neely Terry's offer of work on the west coast. As a passenger on the railroad in 1906, Seymour anticipated a ninety-six-hour trek from Houston to Los Angeles. The 1,371 mile journey was one that many of the ten thousand black people leaving the state of Texas during the year would have taken. Under the Jim Crow laws, each member of the exodus would have been barred from taking up a place in either of the first two classes of carriage. That meant no sleeper, no space, and a minimal chance of relaxation. It meant signing up for the risk of having to move out of even the third-class carriage if too many whites wanted to travel by train at that point. Should that be the case, then black passengers were expected to travel in the aisles, between carriages or in with the freight. Breaking up the journey would have been an obvious, certainly necessary choice to take when back in Houston. As a traveling clergyman, Seymour was afforded certain privileges—although none by the rail operators at the time. Instead, Seymour was able to plug into a network of nineteen houses country-wide that offered free accommodation to the traveling man of the cloth. It just so happened that Colorado's venue was owned by Alma White, and while Seymour was welcome as a clergyman, his roots as a black man risen from poverty did not escape White's attention.

In her book "Demons and Tongues," she reflects on her guest's visit to her Pillar of Fire holiness center.[7] She wasn't exactly impressed by his appearance. She criticized him for not wearing a collar and complained that his odor was less than pleasant. She suggested that when he prayed, she was reminded of "serpents" and "slimy creatures." A curious comment, perhaps, one muddied by an overactive imagination or heightened sensitivity to urban odors, having been privileged by the rarefied mountain airs. No chance for such an excuse, as this is simply the warm-up. Once in full flow, Alma White laid into Seymour with an imaginative ferocity that would surely prompt calls today for fast-acting medication. According to her Seymour was "devil possessed," and his later work in Los Angeles was "the most hellish outburst of demoniacal power that has ever been known under the name of religion…the climax of demon worship." News of races mixing was more fuel to the fire, with her pen spitting out accusations of Seymour leading people into "Satan's slime pits, sealing their doom for damnation."[8] Forget the venom for a brief while… you have to admit that she does a nice line in metaphors and alliteration.

Sadly, we will never know what happened during Seymour's stay with Alma White. We do know that this was the only time they met and can be reasonably sure that White's impressions were passed through the filters of her own personal prejudice, rather than through grievous fault on Seymour's part.

White's criticism of Seymour's dress illustrates how segregated and insular many within the wider church had become. Like gangs from rival schools, groups adapted uniforms to create identity. The only difference being that instead of issues of fashion, these were issues of faith. White's men all wore ties. Seymour's spiritual upbringing had taught him the importance of not wearing a tie. Ironically, far from being disheveled through choice or neglect, Seymour was later criticized for being too well dressed.

Of course, there's more to all this than fashion. White's antipathy toward Pentecostals led to the demise of her marriage. But while it is kind of tempting to picture her as being a little devoid of feeling— some type of spiritual automaton plowing the fields for harvest regardless of the wildlife disturbed along the way—the facts suggest otherwise. She had been quiet on the subject of Seymour since their meeting in 1906, and it was not until four years had passed that she decided to commit her thoughts to paper. The spleen vented had a clear focus, and it appears that it was his Pentecostal credentials that she despised above all the rest of Seymour's so- called faults.

1910 was a busy year for Alma White. Apart from publishing *Demons and Tongues,* she also suffered what must have felt like a colossal betrayal as Kent declared his passions for speaking in tongues. Put it in context, and White's vitriol starts to make sense, particularly when you add into the mix the fact that she reserved a particular distaste for Christians based in Los Angeles. There's no record of phobias related to sun, sand, or future sensitivities toward a thriving film industry, so we have to conclude that White's antipathy was personal.

And it was. Prior to Seymour's 1906 visit, she had led a well-healed campaign to convert the good people of Los Angeles. The right churches sent the right pastors along, but the success was limited. In fact, the mission was essentially a failure, earning for itself a particular White-esque diatribe. Labeling the Angeleno Christians *deplorable* and *backslidden*, she saw her own mission as the city's last chance of salvation. According to her they failed, and Seymour's interracial Pentecostalism was therefore a fair judgment on the lot of them. Within a year of Seymour's visit to White's holiness center in Colorado, her own Pillar of Fire congregation on 8th and Maple atrophied and died, unable to pay the rent. In a pleasant twist of fate, the building remained in use as a place of religious worship, soaking up the overflow from those unable to cram into another local congregation, the one on Azusa Street.

*

So, there was Seymour, back on the train for the second half of his journey to the city that promised him so much. His exit from Houston had been hasty, and the words of his mentors there may well have rung in his ears. They expected him back within a month. Hardly the type of endorsement to set you up with a tub-full of self-confidence, yet Seymour's story was beginning to settle around certain essential themes, determination finding itself at the top of the list.

But if the assumptions flying around as he left were less than inspiring, those that greeted his arrival in Los Angeles were from the other end of the spectrum. The entire congregation from 9th and Santa Fe turned out in welcome, with one member later commenting that the arrival of their new pastor was as significant as that of the apostle Peter at the house of Cornelius in Acts 10. They may not have thrown themselves at Seymour's feet, but after Colorado, there's every chance that he was chewing over Peter's words: "I am only a man myself."

And so, in February 1906, William Seymour arrived in the city that would cement both sides to the story of his place in history—as a remarkable man whose gracious determination would underpin a movement of which millions would benefit in the coming years, but also as one too often pushed aside, neglected, and abused. The following twelve months would change the course of history, but Seymour's story still had decades left to run.

Chapter 12
William Seymour Delivers His Message to His Hosts

"This may be our answer to our hunger for God."

Within hours of stepping off the train, Seymour was at the front of the congregation, stuck in to precisely what he had been invited to Los Angeles for.[1] As the forty-eight-hours' worth of odors and cramps unbuckled themselves from their host, Seymour's message to his new flock was untied. Parham, and virtually all earthly authority was now far away, and Seymour took full advantage of the freedom available to him. With Neely Terry the only link between past and present, the pupil finally became the teacher.

And what a lesson he delivered. There was no chance of Seymour holding back or allowing for a gentle warm-up phase with his new congregation. Or, at least, if Seymour was in the market for warming the crew up gently, this was to be done in the matter of minutes rather than weeks, more flash-fry than slow roast. He waded in with the assurance of one who knows his time has come, laying out his stall for all to see.

He tackled the importance of conversion and holy living. Nothing too controversial about that, and for the cynics among the crowd at 9th and Bonnie Brae, his opening words provided very little to complain about. Yet the safety catch was soon discarded, with Seymour launching into a passionate diatribe on what were widely considered to be the defining issues dividing the church of the day. Seymour claimed that divine healing was the birthright of every Christian. He preached the imminent return of Jesus. He declared that unless a person spoke "in tongues," they had not been baptized by the Holy Spirit. To many today these three issues may be confusing, unremarkable or more than a little passé, yet in that time, in that place, William Seymour had lit the fuse wire on a very large bomb indeed.[2]

*

That time and that place made for a unique duo. Los Angeles at the turn of the twentieth century was, well, changing. From the car window as he traveled the short distance from the train station to the church meeting, Seymour would have absorbed a new landscape, one whose story was barely settled into its second century. It was just over one hundred and thirty years since the first group of missionaries, sailors, and other men laid claim to the land, declaring that San Gabriel was the name of choice for the location.

Of course, it did not stay that way. From the start, the place had something special about it, something that meant the name would need to be changed. Those first settlers met the Indians who weren't too pleased to be joined out here, and violence seemed imminent. The settlers were understandably nervous, but it was one of the priests who had the idea of bringing out his painting of Mary. That was it. They were hooked just as soon as they saw her, the spell cast by the mother of God. No wonder Alma White hated the place.

The sights from the window would have been a little different than those surrounding Seymour's youth. Clusters of Chinese merchants, traders staring back at him, a black policeman talking to some white youths. The mix of races was nothing unusual, but the roles were. Seymour had seen blacks in power before, men like Mason and Jones and their Church of God in Christ. He knew the Senate had representation, but was this different? Was there any significance in the fact that this policeman was out in the open for the masses to see, not shut away in a museum for the elite?

From the start the city had always thrived on racial integration. The first colonizers were a tapestry of Spanish, Black, and Indian, and including their families in total there were twenty-six black faces among the original founders.[3] Yet the city was not free from racial tension. Just three months before Seymour's arrival, Los Angeles had been awakened by an incident that brought underground tensions up into full, unavoidable public view. Having arrested a white man for brawling, Special Officer Arrington found himself on the wrong end of a swiftly forming mob, a mob who objected to the black officer's employment as much as his conduct. Within minutes, as many as one hundred angry protestors had gathered, threatening to kill him or any other black policeman who chose to visit. Arrington kept them at bay for twenty minutes before help arrived and dispersed the crowd. He got his man, too, and became something of a hero among the local black population.[4]

For their own reasons, the congregation that had invited Seymour wanted their own Special Officer Arrington. They wanted a leader, someone to rally behind, yet they were also in need of a defender, someone to hold off the mob that threatened to engulf their own progress. They also wanted a patroller, someone to challenge them and force them to move on from a place of potential apathy. And yes, there was the question of race, too. For the city's second- ever black congregation, race was, and still would be, an issue they could not escape from.

If Seymour thought that he had escaped the petty politics of patriarchs and powerhouses like Parham and Carothers when he left Houston, he was mistaken. On the West coast the church scene was highly politicized, and debates raged across the denominations. At the heart of the problem was the name—or rather, there was a problem with the name itself. It simply didn't fit. Far from being a city made up of angels, Los Angeles was tickling up a reputation for itself as one controlled more by demons. At the turn of the century the city's population was doubling with every decade that passed, and, like the earlier gold rush, the influx of people was a chaotic, unplanned, and unstable affair. With a little under a quarter of a million residents, Los Angeles had doubled its population in the six years since the 1900 census was taken.[5]

The Church was responding with a desperate cry for something to change, yet there seemed to be little agreement on exactly what that change should look like. The Methodists—perhaps still in recovery from their previous year's visit by Alma White and her subsequent "appraisal" of their moral status—were planning their own ten days of Pentecost in the form of a convention, due to start the following month.[6] The Baptists had thrown out the brightest light—Englishman Joseph Smale—for allowing the preaching at the First Baptist to run with the slogan "Pentecost has not yet come, but it is coming."[7] Too much focus on revival, they said. These conservative forces were everywhere, and the battles were raking up the casualties. It seemed like the choice was simple—stay and submit or break away and start over with your own set of values and ambitions.

Which is precisely what happened to the group headed up by Julia Hutchins, which had previously belonged to the Second Baptist church. Neeley Terry and others joined in the call for revival, but the rest of their church somehow lost their voices. While it had been considered progressive when it was founded in 1885, the second black congregation in the city had become too caught up with profile to take a risk of calling for what amounted to a serious dose of the Holy Spirit.[8] One controversial issue was at the heart of the matter: Were the problems of the day to be solved by God or man, by grace or effort, by a serious dose of the Holy Spirit or some profound preaching that brought the city to its knees? The sense of mistrust about those who advocated a wholesale abandon toward the Holy Spirit was intense. According to the conservative mind-set, those on the other side of the divide were opening a particularly ungodly set of fireworks. As the reactions to what happened around Azusa Street throughout 1906 would show, these emotions were rawer and deeper than many would have expected.

For Julia Hutchins and her clan—among them Neely Terry, Edward and Mattie Lee, Ruth and Richard Asberry—the Second Baptist church was on the wrong end of the divide. So, they left. Or rather they were pushed. A wandering band of estranged believers was a common enough occurrence at the time, and for a while they joined the congregation led by William Manley, meeting under the name of the Household of Faith in a tent near 1st and Bonnie Brae Street. This time the larger group separated on color lines, with Julia's all-black group eventually moving on to their own tent near 7th and Broadway.[9]

Tents and winter don't make for the best of church services, and eventually in 1905 they moved their meetings into the home of Ruth and Richard Asberry at 214 Bonnie Brae Street. An office building janitor, Richard epitomized the rising ranks of middle-class black men whose deep south past had given way to west coast progress. Born in Louisiana in 1865, Richard's change in fortunes enabled the group to meet on Monday nights, staging a gospel concert at the front of the house. Neighbors stopped to find out more, and among them was Jennie Evans Moore, a cook in a wealthy white household across the road.[10]

By February 1905 the group had outgrown its domestic setting and leased a building at 9th and Santa Fe for their meetings. The change in venue prompted a change in approach, and while Hutchins remained leader, other members of the congregation shared preaching duties. It was not a success. With too many people pouring out too many different ideas, bad doctrines were delivered. Inevitably people struggled for power over others, and Hutchins was wise enough to know when and how to end the chaos. They needed a strong leader, a "holiness man" to take them where they wanted to go. Neely Terry— a cousin of the Asberry's—knew just the man for the job, a "very godly man" at that. Hutchins was sold, and William was invited.[11]

*

The congregation had expected many things. They assumed that their new teacher had already received his own personal baptism in the Holy Spirit. They were wrong. Yet William's first sermon made it perfectly clear that he did not intend to hide this from them. He, like many other Christian leaders before him, was on a journey. The destination may have been clear, but it was a journey, nevertheless. Among those who heard his first innings from the pulpit was W.H.

McGowan, a white farm worker who had made a similar journey from Texas. His Methodist background was strong, and his appraisal of his new teacher's words was equally intense. He immediately relayed the contents of the sermon to his pastor, William Pendleton. On the strength of McGowan's recommendations, Pendleton claimed: "This may be our answer to our hunger for God."[12] McGowan also ensured that President J. M. Roberts of the Southern California Holiness Association received an invite to hear this remarkable man, blind in one eye but with a vision that they had craved for years.

But there were other reactions. Hutchins rejected the strong emphasis that her guest was placing on the importance of the gift of tongues. According to her, such an approach undermined the experience that many valued so strongly. In other words, all the train fare appeared to have bought them was a double dose of condemnation. In many ways she was right. Seymour was preaching that unless his fellow believers spoke in tongues, they had not fully soaked up the full dose on offer from the heavenlies. It was not a double-sided coin, however, as tongues did not necessarily imply a full blessing. In short, William saw it as an essential rite of passage, a badge that indicated inclusion, a mark of proof that a person should strive for.

For the following three nights William retained his focus, preaching the doctrine of Spirit baptism that Parham had so vehemently supported himself. Yet, was this a case of the pupil blindly imitating the master? Was William stuck in a groove he had no knowledge how to get out of? Perhaps not. Perhaps William's single focus was an indication of how much he had changed rather than how little he remembered. While it may have taken four days to cross the Rockies, it seems that ninety-six hours in Los Angeles was all it took for an even more monumental journey to take place. He had left Houston with Parham's prediction of failure weighing him down. As soon as the train stopped, it appears that he was utterly determined to fight assumption's tide and prove the critics wrong. Did Seymour adopt this approach out of a desire to be deliberately controversial? It appears unlikely and wholly out of character for a man whose critics have hurled accusations of nearly everything at him, everything, that is, except obstinacy. William stuck to his message because it had been the fuel that had driven him for years. This was the core belief that he had clung to, the light that revealed the path from the time when he, previously blinded by apathy and foolishness, received his vision and became determined to follow his true calling.

Hutchins disagreed with the importance Seymour placed on Holy Spirit baptism, yet that may have been of little consequence. When President Roberts appeared with fellow leading lights from the Holiness movement to hear William's fourth sermon in as many days, the Roberts' presence, along with his entourage, would clearly have shown William that he was making an impact. Of course, the message remained the same, but the reaction from Roberts and the others was less than positive. Roberts publicly disagreed with William, rolling out the party line that claimed that baptism had already taken care of the whole Holy Spirit thing.[13] Tongues were an unnecessary optional extra. At the end of the meeting he gave Seymour some advice—ditch the controversial message and play things a whole lot safer.

With four years as an evangelist, preacher, and pastor behind him, Seymour was used to preaching, yet this was something different. The passion and conviction suggest a man inspired, a man with a message to deliver no matter what opposition may present itself. This was no Jonah, begrudgingly delivering his master's commands as briefly as possible before turning tail and leaving on the first camel out of town. Seymour's first four days show that he had already thrown off expectation's baggage. If he had wanted to make a name for himself, to carve a William Seymour-shaped hole at the heart of the city's spiritual power base, then he was going about it the wrong way. Suddenly Seymour was at the heart of the action, and the chance to become another Parham was at hand. His choice? Declare a radical intention to chase after God with all his strength, taking whoever would come along with him. From Wednesday until Saturday Seymour laid out his agenda, repeatedly, shaking things up a little for those inside 9th and Bonnie Brae. On Sunday things would be different. The storm would break out.

Chapter 13
William Seymour Receives His First Job Appraisal

Locked Out

William Seymour's journey had located him in Los Angeles, handed him the role of pastor, and placed him at the center of controversy. In as much time as it had taken him to travel to the coast from Houston, Seymour's world had been truly shaken. Turned upside down? Perhaps not. Since his decision in 1902 to redirect his life's energies, he had been treading an inevitable path to conflict and challenge. Not that he was looking for trouble for trouble's sake. Instead, Seymour simply held tight to his convictions. All that had changed since Cincinnati was the introduction of Parham's contemporary message, which went against the tide of many in the church.

The church in question—the hall on the corner of 9th and Santa Fe—had quickly become Seymour's home. He ate, slept and spent most of his time there. If we can guess anything of his behavior from later events, there is one thing we can be sure of—that Seymour would have used the time wisely, filling his days with prayer for a visitation of the Holy Spirit upon the people who gathered together in that little hall.

With the words of Roberts loud in his ear—words delivered either as half-veiled threats or stiffly wrapped encouragement— Seymour prepared to deliver his fifth sermon on his first Californian Sunday morning. We know little of the actual message he preached, although it is clear that his very first sermon to the holiness group had ripped into the second chapter of Acts, exploring, expounding, and generally dreaming up the glories represented by the retelling of the very first Pentecost outpouring of the power of the Holy Spirit.[1] This would be a familiar theme that fueled his sermons, one to which he returned frequently, as he would do in January of the following year:

> Many people say today that tongues are the least gift of any that the Lord can give, and they do not need it, and ask what good is it to us? But by careful study of the word, we see in the 14th chapter of Corinthians, Paul telling the church to "follow after charity and desire spiritual gifts." Charity means divine love, without which we will never be able to enter heaven. Gifts all will fail, but divine love will last through all eternity…But he says in the next verse, "For he that speaketh in an unknown tongue, speaketh not unto men, but unto God."[2]

Whatever the actual words spoken back on that first Sunday sermon, Seymour was clearly, as one eyewitness later described him, "a man alive and on fire" with news of spiritual revivals in Kansas City and Houston.[3]

When the congregation disappeared after the service, Seymour was invited back to the home of Edward Lee and his wife. The couple were previous members of the local Peniel Mission, a group thoroughly uninterested in the extremes of Pentecost.[4] What drove Lee to invite Seymour back was simply a desire to act "solely out of Christian courtesy."[5] Together they trekked to his home on South Union Avenue, a street marked by houses that fell far short of the double-parlored solidity of the Asberry residence on Bonnie Brae Street. South Union Avenue catered for a different market: one with less money and fewer prospects of changing their circumstances. There was little space, in fact no space at all, between the houses. The borders between street and house were barely defined.

Power. Grace. Mercy. Baptism. Reconciliation. Revival. Sanctification. Healing. Wholeness. The area of discussion may have been any one of many, but as the two men walked back to the mission in the early evening, there could only have been one topic worth discussing. As they turned the corner of 9th onto Santa Fe, they saw a crowd gathered for the scheduled evening meeting. Yet they were troubled by the fact that their entry was barred. Closer inspection revealed the truth—the wooden doors had been padlocked shut.[6] Seymour was officially out of favor.

He was also out of a job. And his home. And just about every form of security he had with him in this still strange and unfamiliar city. Again, it was Edward Lee who came to the rescue. His hospitality lasted longer than one lunch as he invited Seymour back to his home.

What Seymour did next was simple. He prayed and fasted. For days he kept it up, refusing food but not, eventually, company. While Lee's wife in particular had been unsure about their guest, the couple gradually warmed to the idea of Seymour's presence. They began to pray with him. Whether the simple act was offered out of curiosity about what might follow, frustration over this earnestly praying man, or something in between is unclear, yet their decision to get on their knees alongside the man who spoke so passionately about his beliefs was one of the defining steps forward in the Azusa Street story. Together they completed a selection of ingredients where the sum was far greater than the parts—three people of the *wrong* color, living in the *wrong* neighborhood, praying for the *wrong* things. It could only go in one direction from that point on.

Soon, as the hours in prayer turned into days, there were others who wanted to join in with Seymour's vigils. Seymour was starting a movement or tickling up a revival. He was merely doing what he knew to be right, pressing on with integrity to reach his own next destination. Whether or not there had been others to join him Seymour's integrity and determination pushed him on in the only direction he was happy traveling. As he pressed ahead, asking God for his own third blessing, looking for the divine power that he knew was vital if the promised future were to be seen, Seymour's reputation shifted from freshman maverick to man of prayer.

Of those people who expressed an interest and crossed the line that had previously divided Seymour from the flock he had come to care for, perhaps the most significant were Ruth and Richard Asberrys. As friends of Julia Hutchins, their decision to establish contact with Seymour could have been taken as a display of disloyalty, yet their resolve matched their sense of intrigue. When eventually the numbers of those joining in prayer threatened to overwhelm the cramped Lee residence, it was the Asberrys who delivered the solution in the form of an open invitation for Seymour and the others to meet together to pray in the parlor of their home on 214 North Bonnie Brae Street.[7] Again, another step was taken toward Seymour's role in the formation of a new future for the church, yet one that at the time was a simple matter of unglamorous obedience. Just like before when smallpox was at large in his veins, Seymour took small steps that carried big significance. Like his decision to get serious about his faith and secure ordination by the Evening Light Saints, Seymour's acceptance of the Asberry's invitation may have felt like a humble, symbolic gesture, but its significance cannot be overstated. This is what made the difference with William Seymour, just as it does with all the heroes of the faith. These were the small steps of obedience taken that led to a remarkable destiny. As Seymour found out, God's power and our submission enjoy a close relationship and a glorious range of conclusions.

Chapter 14
Passions Are Unleashed

The Fire Within

In between the days when padlocks were applied and then removed, Seymour's reputation spread. Those who were drawn out of positive regard for him found their expectations met, fulfilled, and exceeded. Yet there were plenty of others skulking around the city intent on seeing the outsider brought down low. If this troubled Seymour, he had clearly nurtured an innate talent for maintaining a premium quality poker face, as there are no accounts to contradict the image of him doing anything other than prayerfully, peacefully, waiting to see what God might do next.

It was left to Julia Hutchins to act as God's courier. She got word to her short-lived employee that he was to attend a meeting where he could defend his views against an inquiring panel of the city's holiness leaders.[1] What may have started out as an inquiry, trial, or social lynching would turn out to be something rather different altogether.

From the early days to the fading years, Seymour's time in Los Angeles was marked by the attempts of others to use him as target practice. Whether it was his theology, his social and political agenda, or simply his race, Seymour was doubtless an appealing prey for those hungry to test their power. Despite their attempts, few would succeed.

One such attempt was carried out by holiness pastor Rev. Glen A Cook. Reflecting on his encounter with Seymour sometime later, his words describe not only the appeal of the attack, but display with absolute clarity precisely why so many failed to quash the man's belief in the baptism of the Holy Spirit:

> I was not alone in this effort, as many more preachers and gospel workers began to gather and contend with brother Seymour. But the contention was all on our part. I have never met a man who had

such control over his spirit. The scripture that reads, "Great peace have they that love thy law, and nothing shall offend them," was literally fulfilled in this man. No amount of confession and accusation seemed to disturb him. He would sit behind that packing case and smile at us until we were all condemned by our own activities.

Although almost all of the holiness people who attended continued to reject the preaching, all had a secret reverence and admiration for this man who really lived what he had been preaching for years, a sanctified life. It was the wonderful character of this man whom God had chosen that attracted people to keep coming to this humble meeting.[2]

Self-control, peace, integrity. These three qualities formed the bedrock of Seymour's character and proved more than a match for the assorted parade of leaders and detractors that lined up for a meeting with him in February 1906. Hutchins was there, as too was Roberts, the President of the Southern California Holiness Association, called in yet again for oversight. What it came down to was a simple matter of theology. The holiness people naturally refused to believe that a third blessing should be required, while Seymour echoed Parham's words by claiming that without godly power in evidence, there was little or no indication that an individual had drunk as deep as they could from God's well.

For a man arguing for the importance of baptism in the power of the Holy Spirit, Seymour's lack of personal experience did relatively little to undermine his position. Instead, it appears that his determined approach left the audience more intrigued than they were outraged. Seymour played it to his advantage, sticking to a simple, biblical argument. It was, he said, a misreading of the scripture to suggest that this third blessing, this release of power, was superfluous. Such a view ignored Acts chapter two, and that simply would not do.

He was right, too. Yet if Hutchins' liberal use of the padlock had surprised him before, Roberts' reaction would have truly left him confused. While the meeting concluded that Seymour's theology was wrong, Roberts approached him at the end and suggested that as soon as Seymour received his own personal Pentecost, he ought to make sure that he was the first to know.[3] Even though Hutchins still refused to allow Seymour to assume the role of pastor, the unemployed, homeless preacher was clearly in no way finished.

Of course, it is beautiful irony that Julia Hutchins was not far from feeling the positive pull of Seymour's passions. Within a matter of months, she would be fully signed up to the theology, speaking in tongues and ready to turn her life upside down at the first hint of the Holy Spirit at work in her life. The October 1906 of the *Apostolic Faith* newspaper—Seymour's mouthpiece to the world—takes up the story in full:

> On the sixth of last month, while out in my back yard one afternoon, I heard a voice speaking to me these words: "On the 15th day of September, take your husband and baby and start out for Africa." And I looked around and about me to see if there was not someone speaking to me, but I did not see anyone, and I soon recognized that it was the voice of God. I looked up into the heavens and said: "Lord, I will obey." Since then, I have had many tests and temptations from the devil. He has at times told me that I would not even live to see the 15th of September, but I never once doubted God. I knew that He was able to bring everything to pass that He told me to do.
>
> After hearing the voice telling me to leave Los Angeles on the 15th, I went to one of my neighbors and testified to her that the Lord had told me to leave for Africa on the 15th of September. She looked at me with a smile. I asked her what she was smiling about She said: "Because you have not got streetcar fare to go to Azusa Street Mission tonight, and you're talking about going to Africa." But I

told her I was trusting in a God that could bring all things to pass that He wanted us to do. He has really supplied all my needs in every way, for the work where He has called me."4

She went, too. So did her husband, who, by the way, happened to be an atheist when his wife heard the call to Africa. Nine days later he was at the head of the queue to take the gospel message back to the motherland.

Throughout February and March, the prayer meetings continued as the Asberry home on Bonnie Brae. Today the road occupies a lower-middle ranking in the city's hierarchy. Not as bad as others, yet too crowded and creaking to be polished up too much that would turn a handsome enough profit. Its days may well be numbered, but a century ago the house and its surroundings symbolized the potential success available to members of the black community. 214's entry steps brought visitors up to a narrow veranda, from which they moved into the solid and spacious downstairs parlors. With a piano on hand and small kitchen out the back, the house kept it simple, yet easily met the needs of those gathering to pray.

So, in a way Seymour was liberated by Hutchins' antipathy. While he was in a financially precarious position, he rose to the challenge of being in spiritual limbo with precisely the right attitude. Prayer and persistence became his guiding stars, and there is little to suggest that he even had any concrete ambitions for the immediate future. None, at least, other than the hope that he would soon reach his treasured prize of a powerful spiritual encounter. It was as if the script was truly blank, as if whatever happened next was simply a matter of following God, rather than fitting into another person's lecture hall.

While February saw Seymour sustained by a diet of prayer and fasting, it also introduced a key player in what was soon to be known as the Azusa Street story. Into focus came a white gentleman, a patchy beard clinging to a thin crag of a face. Frank Bartleman's own journey had been marked by sacrifice and sorrow, as the opening words of his version of the Azusa Street story make perfectly clear:

> I arrived in Los Angeles, California, with my wife and two young daughters, on December 22, 1904. Little Esther, our oldest child, three years old, was seized with convulsions and passed away to be with Jesus on January 7, at 4 A.M. Little "Queen Esther" seemed to have been born "for such a time as this" (Esther 4:14).
>
> Beside that little coffin, with heart bleeding, I pledged my life anew for God's service. In the presence of death, how real eternal issues become. I promised the rest of my life should be spent wholly for Him.[5]

Within a week, he began preaching at the Peniel Mission in Pasadena. Within a year he was out, forced by politics and pressure from rival groups such as Burning Bush and Pillar of Fire. It was particularly galling for a man whose determination, carved by tears of grief, was to see all denominations responding to the spirit of God.

Having spent time in Chicago, where the influence of Dowie would have again been unavoidable, it is not surprising that Bartleman was shocked by the lack of justice being offered to Seymour's fellow black citizens. In time, this thoughtful, open-minded man would become the chief chronicler of the Azusa events. But in these early days of Bonnie Brae meetings, Bartleman's white face offered perhaps a more symbolic value. Unlike many gatherings before, Seymour's informal group was already challenging social prejudice.

*

Fast forward to the parlor at 214 on the evening of Thursday, March 8, and Edward Lee—janitor at a local bank and loyal believer hungry for more of whatever was being offered—rose to his feet. He had a message to deliver to the assembled crowd.

He had been at work, but not working. Hiding in the basement for hours on end he had prayed long and hard for the Holy Spirit experience about which Seymour had excited so many of them. Eventually he had experienced something of a breakthrough, a vision that seemed as real as the chairs on which his fellow believers sat as they listened to his story. What he had seen, or rather *who* he had seen, were the apostles Peter and John. They looked at him, lifted their hands, began to shake under the power of something mightier than usual, and spoke in tongues. The vision ended, and Lee was left shaken yet convinced that he had experienced a front- row demonstration of precisely what it was that they were all in pursuit of.[6]

The retelling done; Lee's vision had raised the bar. Excited, expectant, the future was clearly at hand. Seymour laid hands on his friend, who instantly keeled over. Lee was falling, his legs giving way inch by inch as his joints doubled under themselves, tendons and muscles fleeing for some other body. Before anything else could happen—Pentecost or otherwise—Lee's wife, the Mary who played more of a Martha role, intervened. There was no way she was allowing her husband to remain in such a state on the floor.[7] The meeting may have been over, but it was clear to all that something profound had just begun.

Seymour knew this, as well as his limitations. With the potential outpouring of heavenly power so tangibly close, he recognized the need for assistance. Easter was approaching, the climate was warming up, and reinforcements were sent for from Houston. Sister Farrow and Brother Warren would come and were given the train fare.[8] The time was right for independence, for instinct and action. The time was right for harvest.

Chapter 15
William Seymour Presses Forward

"Will you stay and pray?"

The urgency was unmistakable. With Easter just days away, and the encouragement of Lee's vision still fresh, the collected believers pushed ahead with increasing determination. According to one researcher who interviewed many of those involved at the time:

> ...their whole souls, minds, bodies and all, seemed to center on the desire to obtain the baptism of the Spirit and the sign of the tongues and to determine to remain in prayer until it came. Men left their daily work and spent the time in prayer.[1]

The researcher in question happened to be Charles Shumway, putting together an undergraduate thesis while studying at the University of Southern California. But he was no casual observer, nor was he a limp-minded acolyte desperate to get close to the action. Charles Shumway came from a different mold, an altogether far more critical one.

Meanwhile, on Friday, April 6, one week ahead of Good Friday and five weeks since he had been looked out by Julia Hutchins, Seymour had encouraged his fellow believers to kick off a week-long fast in order that they might be suitably focused on the wisps of future that appeared to be tickling their palms.

Things happened, too. On the evening of April 6, the meeting extended due to little more than enthusiasm and nothing less than a sense of the imminent release of divine power. Seymour was clear, passionate, perhaps even a little overenthusiastic in his encouragement of what was now clearly his flock. With the fast on their minds, Seymour was clear about the sacrifice needed if they were to reach their goal.

After a late night on Friday, the same recipe was on the menu for Saturday and Sunday—more prayer, more singing, more determination that people would stick out the waiting just as long as it took. Whether it was a quiet determination or dress rehearsal of the emotional intensity Seymour and others believed was around the corner, the next step forward was typically out of sync with expectation. The first three days of the fast had begun to show on Edward Lee, who was laid up at home suffering from fever and cramps.[2] After a three-year quest for the gift of tongues, to be kept home from meetings that were so clearly bolted to the tracks of destiny must have been galling.[3]

Still, Seymour visited him late in the afternoon of Monday, April 9. Lee's intention was that after a little prayer from the pastor, the illness would lift, and he would be able to attend that evening's meeting. Seymour did as he was asked, finding himself yet again at the side of a sickbed containing a patient. Yet this time around the patient would rise. Immediately after Seymour began to pray. Lee felt better.

Yet the janitor wanted more. He asked Seymour to carry on down the wish list, to pray that Lee might get his own baptism right there, right then. What else to do but obey? Seymour did what he was told.

The sound was indescribable. Lee was caught up in praises that neither could understand but which astonished both of them. The two men radiated joy, peace, and more besides.[4] Pentecost had come. Pentecost was among them.

Within the hour they were back at the Asberry home, where Seymour resisted the urge to reveal immediately all that had happened, holding back on any desire to wallpaper the mission with the experience from the minute they entered. He knew that however much he and Lee were in on it; the encounter should not become a freak show. He spent much of the first part of the service narrating the events that had just unfurled, linking them with the bedrock of Scripture that had woven its way into so many sermons since his west coast arrival[5]: "And they were filled with the Holy Ghost, and began to speak with other tongues, as the spirit gave them utterance."

There was little chance of getting much further with Acts, chapter 2. Lee stood, raised his hands, and opened his mouth. As before, he poured out a sound that was beyond comprehension but full of meaning. The entire room fell to their knees as fires of baptism ignited spontaneously among them.[6] Joy. Chaos. Beauty. Sounds. Songs. Nothing could be defined but everything could be felt.

Some were crying, some dancing. The Asberry's son may have decided to flee out of primal fear, but of the rest who stayed, all were feeling the intensity of a personal encounter with the Holy Spirit.[7] The servant girl from across the street, Jennie Evans Moore—a relative of Neely Terry and the Asberrys—approached the dark wood piano, lifted the lid, and played a simple melody, high up, rolling, harmonized with simple chords given greater depth and tone by her pure voice. She sang out in French first of all, then in other languages—Spanish, Latin, Greek, Hebrew and Hindustani.[8] Interpretations came from all over, each one reflecting the theme of God's glory and the power of His presence. Perhaps it was Neely, Richard, and Ruth Asberry who wept hardest, for they knew the truth that the rest of the congregation suspected: How could a girl without education have ever hoped to learn the piano? How could a girl with no knowledge of any language other than English utter such words?

*

Reading the thoughts of Charles Shumway on the matter of speaking in tongues is like pressing one's nose up against a curiously lit club in a foreign city. The student was a keen observer of the whole tongues scene, devoting two key phases of his academic life to its exploration. As well as his undergraduate work in 1914, Shumway sunk his postgraduate teeth in with "A Critical History of Glossolalia" while working toward his 1918 Doctorate from the University of Boston. In both cases Shumway's take on the popularity of the gift of tongues betrays his true feelings on the matter. What Parham and Seymour were involved in was modern, contemporary, and a challenge to the previously dominant views and mindsets. Shumway's awkwardness and critique of the emotional aspect of the proceeding's casts him as a rather uptight nineteenth- century throwback. He may well have had a problem with phones and motorcars, too.

The researcher was unimpressed by either Parham or Seymour, despite having met and interviewed them both. Yet what really counts are his pronouncements on the movement that was just starting to gather true momentum, even with such humble beginnings as the lifting of Lee's cramps, the raising of his arms, and the outpouring of all manner of curiosities in the double parlor on 214 Bonnie Brae, on April 9th, 1906.

Writing twelve years later, Shumway gets to the heart of the matter early on:

> The sect has been troublesome to thousands of pastors; its teachings have divided scores of churches in different parts of the world; and its rise has created fresh interest in certain passages in the New Testament.[9]

Ignoring for a moment the confusion over whether the creation of "fresh interest" in the Bible really should be part of a list of such troublesome divisions, it is soon clear that Shumway sees tongues as a solely emotional rather than spiritual response to God. He chooses to adopt pseudo intellectual language to dissect, analyze, and define the experience, talking of the "up rush" and the "releasing agents." More interestingly still, he labels all involved as mentally weak:

> The nervous instability which characterizes so many of them may be either temperamental or congenital, or it may be acquired through disease, fastings, vigils, prolonged attention to one idea, by weariness, or in other similar ways.[10]

Weakness, nervous instability, and congenital problems aside, Los Angeles in April 1906 was a fascinating place to be. More specifically, as a new sun rose on the events of the day before, 214 Bonnie Brae continued to fizz and sparkle with the events of Monday, April 9. Somewhere among the glorious chaos of the previous evening, those filled with the Holy Spirit had spilled out from the parlor onto the porch and the tree-lined street in front. There they had continued to shake, to pray, and to experience their own Pentecost. Just as happened back in time, there were observers—and they were fascinated. By Tuesday morning a crowd of onlookers had gathered around the Asberry home, wondering what on earth was going on.[11]

Yet these were no passive bystanders. Within the house, as well as outside it, things were getting increasingly dramatic. The faithful that had been there to experience the gathering momentum found themselves caught up in an experience the like of which no one had seen before. As people crowded closer to listen to and see what was going on, many found themselves drawn into a firsthand encounter with God's Spirit.

Of those who were not speaking in tongues, Seymour may have been the most surprised to find himself on the peripheries. He was not baptized in the Holy Spirit, even though plenty of others were. Yet his role at this time appeared to be equally important as he began to explain the occurrences to the waiting audience. Soon it was as if "the porch became the pulpit and the street became the pews," with Seymour drawing together the threads, making the connections, and providing the opportunities for others to join in.[12] So many decided to do so that at one point the crowds on the front porch proved too much for the timbers, and the structure began to give way. Of course, it was duly fixed, yet the experience must have caught Seymour's eye. Surely this was a case of demand for the divine outstripping the earthly supply?

Other things would have caught Seymour's attention, too. So far—or at least on the night of Monday, April 9th—the assembled faithful had all been black. With Tuesday came the increased interest from neighbors and passersby, many of whom were white. This, it seemed, was a little different from the way things had happened back in Houston. There was no altar, no separate seating, and no color line. What there was could not be so easily prescribed—men and women in trances of up to five hours each, and healings that had been ruled out of range of the possible by the medical profession.[13] One such miracle was handed out to Emma Cotton. Her facial cancer was severe, yet as she later wrote:

> The noise of the great outpouring of the Spirit drew me. I had been nothing but a walking drug store all my life, with weak lungs and cancer. As they looked at me, they said, "Child, God will heal you." In those days of that great outpouring, when they said God would heal you, you were healed. For thirty-three years, I have never gone back to the doctors, thank God, nor any of that old medicine! The Lord saved me, baptized me with the Holy Ghost, healed me, and sent me on my way rejoicing.[14]

This was it. Pentecost had come. People whispered it, believed it, saw it there in black and white. Yet Seymour remained, at best, its narrator. For three days the power increased as 214 Bonnie Brae played host to that which he had been hungering after for so long. Did he worry? Did he fear that the whole experience might never be his? Was it possible that these three days might fade from memory too?

*

Thursday, April 12, 1906. 214 Bonnie Brae. All questions were answered. It was late, and many were too tired to continue, but this was the time when Seymour knew things would change. With just two men left praying in the room, one half blind and black, the other perplexed and white, Seymour was determined to "pray through." Too much time passed, and the second man was convinced that now was not the time.

"Yes, it is," replied Seymour. "I am not going to give up."[15]

According to Douglas Nelson—a less cynical scholar interested in Seymour's experiences— what happened next was as simple as it was profound:

> He kept on, alone, and in response to his last prayer, a sphere of white hot brilliance seemed to appear, draw near, and fall upon him. Divine love melted his heart; he sank to the floor seemingly unconscious. Words of deep healing and encouragement spoke to him. As from a great distance he heard unutterable words being uttered—was it angelic adoration and praise? Slowly he realized the indescribably lovely language belonged to him. A broad smile wreathed his face. At last he arose and embraced those around him.[16]

Chapter 16
The Church Delivers a Message

Awful Destruction for the City

"The present worldwide Pentecostal manifestation did not break out in a moment, like a huge prairie fire, and set the world on fire. In fact, no work of God ever appears that way. There is a necessary time for preparation. The finished article is not realized at the beginning.... So it was with this present work in its beginning. The enemy did much counterfeiting. God kept the young child well hid for a season from the Herods, until he could gain strength and discernment to resist them."[1]

The eyes of Frank Bartleman saw many of the same things that were placed in front of William Seymour. Born within a year of each other, both men shared a childhood that was marked by farm work and Baptist teaching. Both men were drawn to Los Angeles as the new century bolted into life. Both played their part. But it was Bartleman who, for a season, played scribe to Seymour's passions, Lois Lane to the unassuming Clark Kent, articulating, appraising, and analyzing the events at the edge of the ocean.

> God found his Moses in the person of Brother Smale, to lead us to the Jordan crossing. But he chose Brother Seymour for our Joshua, to lead us over.[2]

Smale—the local holiness pastor at First New Testament Church, whose belief in the imminent arrival of a dramatic move of God in Los Angeles had been fueled by a visit to Evan Roberts in the United Kingdom. He was still awestruck by the Welsh Revival and adopted the role of drum beater—and agitator fits with the analogy. His courting of controversy was powered by a sense of purpose: that revival was imminent. As for the modern-day Joshua, it certainly did not take long for the army of the faithful to gather in force. Less than one hundred hours after the chaos of Monday night, it was clear that 214 Bonnie Brae was too small a venue for the meetings. With the speed of conviction, new premises were found almost immediately. Some of those who had soaked up the passion at 214 recalled a building they met in previously when they were members of the city's first black church, the First African Methodist Episcopal Church. It had since moved from 312 Azusa Street, and the building had failed to establish a permanent identity since they left. And so, for $8 a month it ceased its incarnation as a storage facility for construction materials and became the new home of the still unnamed congregation.[3]

Even the term *congregation* felt a little awkward, and history raises its hand in testimony to the fact that the building of a brand was never the group's main concern. To this day, the words *Azusa Street revival* will reap a far more bountiful Google harvest than *Apostolic Faith revival*, and reviewing events from a century ago it appears as if there was too much pace at large to worry about things like names, power, or reputation. What mattered was harnessing every opportunity to give time and space to God and his people.

*

The move to 312 Azusa Street was an obvious choice; it was big, cheap, and available. Added to that was the fact that Seymour would be able to live in one of the rooms upstairs, although everybody knew that it was downstairs where things would really come to life. Yet there were some subtle facts about the building that reinforced its suitability for the purpose. Its internal dirt floor seemed to flow almost out onto the unpaved street. Single, bare electric bulbs provided light, which showed fire damage and cobwebs.[4] The absence of plumbing meant that the outdoor latrine was the only facility on offer. The squat, flat-roofed building had once been a church, yet an earlier fire had stripped it of its pitched roof, its one interesting architectural feature. What was left was a wooden box that was for one person at least "the most humble place I was ever in for a meeting."[5] Back then it was in the heart of the black district, and its current proximity to Skid Row hints at an area that authorities have failed to know what to do with. It was, in short, unimpressively frayed. It was also perfect. From stables to dead-end towns, God's greatest moves appear to have always favored the humble starting place, and Azusa Street was no exception.

Upon leasing the building, Seymour and others were faced with the immediate task of cleaning it. Having been used as a storehouse for construction materials and hay, the urban barn needed work. Enter, stage left, Arthur G. Osterberg and his pushy mother. The family came from Chicago where their pastor, William H Durham, was making a name for himself. Joining the procession south to California, and arriving in Los Angeles, Arthur Osterberg eventually signed on as pastor at the Full Gospel Church at 68th and Denver. Yet when his mother got wind of something marvelous taking place on Bonnie Brae Street, the dutiful son headed off and witnessed the meetings at first hand:

> The meeting on Bonnie Brae convinced me, not so much because of the speaking in tongues or the pattern of the meeting; but I could sense these were spiritual people. There was no nonsense going on. Although I didn't quite understand the matter of speaking in tongues, I was convinced these people were sincere. That night as I drove home, I felt quite disturbed and asked myself, what are you going to do? What are you going to do about your church? It was evident that this teaching could revolutionize our whole theory.[6]

His arrival in the story was timely. As well as a pastor, Osterberg worked for a construction company, where he bumped into three men in search of overtime in the days before Easter. Out of his own pocket the part time pastor paid for them to accompany him to Azusa Street and clear 312.[7] When they arrived, they met several members of the

Bonnie Brae meetings already at work on the chaos. All female, all black, the first thing that these cleaners wanted to do was to blow away a few of the more spiritually oriented cobwebs. So, they prayed, inviting the workmen to join them. The next thing Osterberg saw was one of the workmen felled to his knees, weeping and "getting soundly converted."[8]

The workman happened to be a Roman Catholic and proved to be the first of many to make the jump from Rome. Later there was one man in particular who grabbed Osterberg's attention when he was miraculously healed of a clubfoot. When asked about his conversion, the man's reply was simple: "Conversion? I no understand. All I know…one day Jesus He jump into my heart." In Osterberg's version the story concludes with a nod at one of the bricks of Azusa's success:

> For a while we even held up the whole program until we came to see God was doing something we didn't recognize. We had made our own formula that one must do so-and-so and repent according to the letter of the formula. But that doesn't always work out to be the Lord's way.[9]

The theme of the foolish being used to shame the wise is written in bold across the Azusa Street story. Along with the obvious facts about race and social standing, even the very name by which the events would come to be known was drawn from the mouths of those whose blood had been shed by the first settlers. *Azusa* was taken from an American Indian tribe's settlement. Literally translated, it means "blessed miracle."[10]

Among the tears of converted construction workers and the delight of faithful cleaners, the building prepped for the hundred or so people they hoped would eventually come. Planks were laid across whatever would support them—nail boxes, broken chairs— making backless benches that gave a nod to the past heritage of black Christianity that liked room to move, room to pray.[11] Sawdust went on the floor, while two large wooden shoe crates stacked and covered with cotton cloth became the pulpit. This homemade object was the room's central feature, with the altar placed in front of it and the benches circling them both. Unusual? Undoubtedly. Deliberate? Of course. Seymour was building a different ark; one where traditional ideas of status were challenged. While it may seem that the arrangement drew focus toward the preacher, Seymour's own preference for spending almost the entire duration of each meeting on his knees beside the altar dispels any claims of hypocrisy.

*

News of what happened at Bonnie Brae spread quickly and simply. The meetings were made up of people who belonged to other churches, and as they took news of the events back with them, the buzz inevitably spread. Playing her part in all this was Jennie Evans Moore—the monolingual, unmusical, miraculous pianist and multilingual singer. She went back to her New Testament Church on Easter Sunday. An explanation from the front followed by a burst of *glossolalia*—itself interpreted by Ruth Asberry—stunned and excited the congregation. After the meeting, clusters of people clogged up the sidewalk, wondering about whatever might happen next.[12]

The answer was simple. The first meeting at 321 Azusa Street drew in a hundred people. The second drew in more, and the third even more. By now the word was spreading, and fascination hooked such a variety of people that within a few days the congregation has shifted from being solely black to representing something of the mix of the city. At one meeting, Seymour could be found praying with a white man, desperately tired from the prayer, his willpower starting to fade. In a symmetrical echo of Seymour's own baptism, the pastor knew what was to come next as the young man started to tire.

"It is not the time," he told Seymour who was kneeling beside him.

"Yes, it is," Seymour replied. "I am not going to give up."

Later the young man described what followed as like a sphere of fiery white-hot radiance falling upon him, melting his heart with divine love.[13]

Within a week the building was crowded with three daily meetings, often without a discernible beginning or end, merging into one another, just as the color line blurred.

While the people gathered after the testimony of Jennie Evans Moore on Tuesday night might just have been able to predict some of the scenes described above, there was one event that followed that shocked them all. Even the unexpected interpretation of Moore's strange words given by Ruth Asberry at the meeting failed to prepare the masses. Ruth's words were few: she claimed, "[t]his is that prophesied by Joel."[14] Armies, judgment, destruction… the message was not clear.

It was clear to Rabbi Gold and the reporter from the *Los Angeles Times* he brought with him to the meeting on Tuesday April 17th. The Rabbi found himself converted on the spot, while the reporter left shocked and amazed some hours later. The journalist could not decide what to be more astounded by—the sense of something powerful yet invisible rampaging throughout the room or the sight of black and white leaning on, praying for, and weeping, laughing, and rejoicing with each other. What was it? Pandemonium. He described the "old exhorter" who stood at the front urging people to "let tongues come forth." This was a scene that shocked, surprised, and intrigued. Yet one comment he recorded came back and stood out high above all his other observations. Sometime near the end of the meeting he heard a man at the side of the hall start to talk about the future. He spoke of "awful destruction" for Los Angeles unless the city turns to God.[15]

The next day's paper carried the story but opted to emphasize the "weird babel of tongues" over the prophesied doom. The feature revealed how the "sect" encouraged utterances "which no mortal could understand."[16]

An old colored exhorter, blind in one eye, is the major-duomo of the company. With his stony optic fixed upon some luckless unbeliever, the old man yells his defiance and challenges an answer....Clasped in his big fist the colored brother holds a miniature Bible from which he reads at intervals one or two words—never more. After an hour... pandemonium breaks loose, and the bounds of reason are passed by those who are "filled with the spirit," whatever that may be.

"You-oo-oo gou-loo-loo come under the bloo-oo-oo boo-loo," shouts an old colored "mammy," in a frenzy of religious zeal. Swinging her arms wildly about her she continues with the strangest harangue ever uttered...listened to with awe by the company.[17]

Despite being tagged "old," at thirty-six, William Seymour was still very much alive and well, full of energy and passion for whatever would come next. He needed it too, for at the end of the piece, almost as an afterthought, came the report of the man who "prophesied awful destruction to this city unless its citizens are brought to a belief in the tenets of the new faith." As the very words were being printed and delivered to the readers, San Francisco was shaken by an earthquake that was felt as far away as Los Angeles and Nevada. Awful destruction, you say? As many as three thousand people were dead and three-quarters of the city's population made homeless by the most powerful earthquake in living memory.[18]

Chapter 17
April 1906 Brings Change

30 Days Later

The earthquake split the people as it did the earth. Many churches boasted pulpits from which preachers were desperate to deny any link between their God and the destruction handed out on San Francisco. Others taught their flock that the time was right to get serious about faith, to expect the latter-day rains to occasionally turn to floods and raging torrents. Newspapers speculated about the next target of the grim reaper, while anxious citizens were left to digest their future for themselves.[1]

Yet the key players in the Azusa Story were barely made to pause for a second by the earthquake. Theirs was a passion and a purpose that surpassed such anxieties. Frank Bartleman, with typical zeal, seized the opportunity to turn the thoughts of the masses to higher things. Within days of San Francisco's tragedy, he had written a tract and commenced the job of distributing the message city-wide. "God must needs make a fearful example at times," was the message.[2] Who was to argue with that?

But if God was in the business of instilling fear as a means of breaking through the apathy of the self-possessed, it would seem pretty clear that there was plenty of awe and joy being served up alongside. With the meetings at the new premises barely out of their first week, people across the city were scared and started to focus on the eternal. As the aftershocks played with Los Angeles on April 18th and sent thousands fleeing in panic, hundreds joined the dots between the frailty of human life and the power of the divine, between the force of nature and the power on display among the dirt and straw at 312 Azusa Street.

While it would be a matter of months before the first edition of the *Apostolic Faith* newspaper would turn up the lights on a new phase of mass communication for Seymour and his co-workers, it is clear from its first edition that the earliest meetings were simply astounding.

> The power of God now has this city agitated as never before. Pentecost has surely come and with it the Bible evidences are following, many being converted and sanctified and filled with the Holy Ghost, speaking in tongues as they did on the day of Pentecost. The scenes that are daily enacted in the building on Azusa street and at Missions and Churches in other parts of the city are beyond description, and the real revival has only started, as God has been working with His children mostly, getting them through to Pentecost, and laying the foundation for a mighty wave of salvation among the unconverted.[3]

Within four weeks the numbers in attendance had risen from one hundred to as many as thirteen hundred. With people crammed into the sixty foot by forty-foot hall—up to eight hundred at the busiest times—another five hundred people would be left straining to hear from the sidewalk.[4] Inside the space, a little over half the size of a basketball court, people were rammed onto the benches, standing three deep up against the rough walls and wedged onto the windowsills. They were, as one journalist pointed out, so full as to be "almost to the point of suffocation," yet such was the intensity of the meetings that the enduring crowds kept on coming.[5]

Whether hungry for God or driven by an appetite for cynical voyeurism, those that turned up were all fair game for the power of the Spirit. As the lead writer explained on the first page of the first house newspaper, it was the change that mattered most:

> The writer attended a few of these meetings and being so different from anything he had seen and not hearing any speaking in tongues, he branded the teaching as third-blessing heresy, and thought that

settled it. It is needless to say the writer was compelled to do a great deal of apologizing and humbling himself to get right with God.⁶

As well as the hall, the windows and the street outside, people at Azusa gathered in the upper room, a long, thin area on the building's first floor. Outside the room was a sign indicating that there was to be no talking louder than a whisper. The reason was simple: The upper room was the place of encounter, where those who wanted prayer for healings or baptism and blessing could do receive prayer. Around the sides of the room were the trophies of lives transformed—crutches, canes, and other unnecessary medical props.⁷

From downstairs would come the sounds of wild abandon, of silence and of singing. One favorite hymn was "The Comforter Has Come." Proclaiming the power of God in the here and now, not just hoping for it to appear in the future, the song typified the approach taken by all involved:

> The long, long night is past, the morning breaks at last,
> And hushed the dreadful wail and fury of the blast,
> As o'er the golden hills the day advances fast!
> The Comforter has come!
>
> O boundless love divine! How shall this tongue of mine
> To wond'ring mortals tell the matchless grace divine—
> That I, a child of hell, should in His image shine!
> The Comforter has come!⁸

Just as it was blatantly clear that the power of God was in effect, so it was clear from even the briefest glance that the meetings in downtown Los Angeles were achieving something truly remarkable—mixing the races. Yes, Los Angeles was a bulging metropolis, a wide-lensed view of the globe's mobile people groups, but it had rarely experienced anything quite like the Azusa Street meetings before. Like much of the country, the highs of reconstruction had worn off long ago, the honeymoon, it would seem, was over. Many would doubt whether it ever really made it away from the reception. As the twentieth century began its awkward, painful life, the separation of races was well established. Migration was the defining rite of passage for countless individuals. Over the next twenty years the flow would increase dramatically— the demographics of the country would shift. With 95 percent of blacks living in rural locations at the end of the nineteenth century, by the 1960s 90 percent of the total black population would be located in urban zones.[9] Back in Los Angeles in 1906, the Jim Crow laws left a bitter aftertaste. Even though by comparison to much of the other parts of the country the place was open minded and forward thinking, Azusa's fine blend was still something of a shock.

What the meetings offered was family. It may sound naïve, trite or simply unsophisticated, but it was true. Once inside—or even once as close as possible on the outside—you were either *Brother* or *Sister*. There was no ostentatious hierarchy, and the breadth of the power contradicted a set of social conventions that prescribed hatred and oppression as a matter of course. Slavery was a memory, but one close enough for the scars to remain and the nightmares to explode in sleep.

Of course, this upside-down way of doing things was precisely what was needed. Again, it was the first edition of the *Apostolic Faith* newspaper that was chosen as the vehicle to make clear the approach to race, prejudice, and the power of equality:

> It has been said of the work in Los Angeles that is was "born in a manger and resurrected in a barn." Many are praising God for the old barn-like building on Azusa Street, and the plain old plank beside which they kneeled in the sawdust when God saved, sanctified and baptized them with the Holy Ghost. Those who know God feel His presence as soon as they cross the threshold. "Can there any good thing come out of Nazareth?" "Come and see." This is the Nazareth of Los Angeles. Some have come from

long distances to this spot, directed of the Lord, and the humble have always been greatly blest. The work began among the colored people. God baptized several sanctified wash women with the Holy Ghost, who have been much used of Him. The first white woman to receive the Pentecost and gift of tongues in Los Angeles was Mrs. Evans who is now in the work in Oakland. Since then, multitudes have come. God makes no difference in nationality, Ethiopians, Chinese, Indians, Mexicans, and other nationalities worship together.[10]

*

Quite what the experience felt like to those approaching is hard to say. Frank Bartleman frequently found himself pausing for breath and prayer on the way to the meetings, struggling under the weight of what he knew would greet his arrival. Not that we're talking about race here. For Bartleman it was the power of God that took his breath away.[11] Yet there were others who found themselves shocked by the color scheme.

Like Gaston Barnabas Cashwell. The premium quality name suited him. Two hundred and fifty pounds of fair-haired, fair-skinned, North Carolinian ex-Methodist minister. This sweating Southerner had jumped the fence some years before, declaring his allegiance to the holiness movement, and leaving Wesley's descendants like so many others. The name and the physique may have marked him out as being born of stock that previously watched from the porch as the profits were harvested, yet this man's passions were for real. Missing an important Southern holiness convention in the process, he was one of the few from his patch that headed to Los Angeles to find out what all the Pentecostal fuss was about.

Three thousand miles later, feeling a little awkward at first, Cashwell considered returning home as soon as he saw the mix of races in the building. Still, North Carolina to Los Angeles is a long way to haul yourself, and he made up his mind to stay. He was challenged still further when, kneeling for prayer and hungry for his own Pentecost, he noticed a black hand place itself upon his own fair head. His reaction? It caused "chills to go down my spine."[12]

Eventually the prejudice began to thaw, and, over a number of meetings, he was able to declare that he had "lost his pride." By the time the year was out, freshly christened as an *Apostle of Pentecost*, Cashwell was back home. On December 31, 1906, he started his own Pentecostal meeting, which would ultimately draw most of the southern holiness movement to the cause. As the *Apostolic Faith* put it a month before, "The sweetest thing is the loving harmony."[13]

Not all white visitors were bound up with the baggage of long-term exposure to a segregated society. English preacher Alexander Boddy arrived at the mission and immediately formed his own thoughts on the scenes played out in front of him: "It was something very extraordinary, that white pastors from the south were eagerly prepared to go to Los Angeles to the Negroes, to have fellowship with them and to receive through their prayers and intercessions the blessings of the spirit. And it was still more wonderful that these white pastors went back to the south and reported to them members of their congregations that they had been together with Negroes, that they had received the same blessings as they."[14]

As Bartleman would later write, "The color line was washed away at Azusa."[15] It is claimed that some have tried to put it back, and today's Pentecostal church continues to wrestle with identical issues and similar problems. Some claim the Azusa Street meetings as a champion of black rights. Others claim them to be the flawed beginnings of a divided church. One thing is clear, however, to the people who showed up and pressed on in, the gatherings were the sweetest taste their souls had ever met.

Chapter 18
We Meet Florence Crawford

No Pride There

"It was not all blessing," wrote Bartleman. "In fact, the fight was terrific. As always, the Devil combed the country for crooked spirits to destroy the work if possible."[1]

There can be little surprise that the meetings were controversial, and few eyebrows will rise at the news that the press ridiculed the events. Such publicity failed to knock their confidence, for as Bartleman explains, it had the benefit of "free advertising. This brought the crowds."[2]

Opposition came from other sources too, less predictable ones. At one point toward the end of the summer, the police were asked to break up meetings that Bartleman was involved with. Meanwhile, back at Azusa Street the venue was a favorite target for spiritualists and even the odd hypnotist, each turning up for a peek and a chance at making off with a little of the power. One incident involving a woman speaking in tongues for the first time causes intrigue still. As she spoke in what sounded like an Asian tongue, a Chinese national looking on had started to blush. Would he translate the words he clearly recognized? He refused, claiming that the words were so offensive as to be wholly inappropriate for any setting, let alone a meeting of God's people. Curious, perhaps, but the controversy failed to develop on the back of the incident, despite Charles Shumway's assertion that it undermined the whole case for glossolalia's validity.[3]

Yet the real opposition, the corner that had to be guarded against most carefully was the one that was closest to home. It was the fellow believers who threatened with the loudest voices. In a curious foreshadowing of what was to come, the chronicler continues: "Then all the religious soreheads, crooks, and cranks came to investigate and to try their influence. We had most to fear from these."[4]

Bartleman had been busy during the early weeks of the mission. His post-earthquake account had set off more than a few tremors of its own, with as many as seventy-five thousand tracts being distributed during the first three weeks of the state's recovery. By the time the deliveries were made it was May, and his return to the meetings allowed him to witness an essential truth—the meetings had undergone a shift in majority from black to white. Gatherings back at 214 Bonnie Brae had often been all black affairs, with the odd inclusion of white members turning up from time to time. Now, though, the message was spreading. Not only had the color line been washed away, it was looking as if it might be permanently erased form the church's future.

What confounded the critics was simple: There was a power about the place that was undeniable and more than a match for those arriving at the squat venue in search of ammunition rather than experience. Ansel Post, a Baptist preacher, was sat at one particular meeting with little expectation of doing anything other than observing the events taking place around him. Without warning— heavenly or otherwise— he was filled instantly. "I began to speak in another language. I could not have been more surprised if at the same moment someone had handed me a million dollars."[5]

Bartleman's descriptions of the meetings create a clear picture of just how remarkable they were. He writes of them being like "holy ground," alluding to the passage in Exodus 3 where Moses is confronted by the burning bush. Azusa Street's hushed silence could give way to chaos at any time, but either way the events appeared to be conducted by an alternative source. Those in attendance knew this and their sense of expectation was high. Upon arriving at the meetings— which, incidentally, appeared to avoid formal structure, merging instead into one another—people would avoid too much human contact. They would quickly find a little space at a bench and get their heads bowed in prayer. A few testimonies might follow, sometimes a dozen, sometimes fewer. Everyone would be able to pray aloud, which they did, until someone stood stand up. In keeping with the open-armed approach, it could have been anyone who spoke—man, woman or child, from front or back. Whoever it was, notes Bartleman, "it made no difference. We rejoiced when God was working."[6] The speaker would deliver the message believed to be from God, signing up to the unwritten rule that this was not a place for grandstanding, but one for genuine pursuit of God.

There were, of course, those who tried to polish their own ego in front of the Pentecostal crowd. Such preachers would come, rise to their feet, and roll out their agenda, but no one would cut them off. People would pray, and Bartleman is clear that God would do the rest: "They generally bit the dust in humility, going through the process we had all gone through. In other words, they died out, and came to see themselves in all their weakness. Then, in childlike humility and confession, they were taken up by God and transformed through the mighty baptism of the spirit. The old man (Romans 6:6) died with all his pride, arrogance and good works."[7]

*

This inversion of hierarchy, this toppling of worldly values is at the very heart of the story, feeding through to very muscle that moved it forward. The unremarkable building in the undesirable location where unimpressive people served unplanned meetings was the vehicle of choice. Despite—or perhaps because of—the decision to avoid advertising, announcing, or preparing meetings, the power increased, and the crowds kept coming. Each time, there, on the floor, taking the lead, was Seymour. He "was recognized as the leader in charge. But we had no pope or hierarchy. We were brethren."[8] Most meetings were carried out with him lost in prayer. The occasional hallelujah or call for people to push on to their own blessing was a rarity. Mostly the leader was just caught up in the moment.

"There was no pride there."[9] Instead it "all came down in humility together at his feet. They all looked alike and had all things in common, in that sense at least. The rafters were low; the tall must come down. By the time they got to Azusa, they were humbled, ready for the blessing. The fodder was thus placed for the lambs, not for giraffes. All could reach it."[10]

The result was a DNA that led to humility and dependence on God. As the scribe put it: "It was a tremendous overhauling process. Pride and self-assertion, self-importance, and self-esteem could not survive there. The religious ego preached its own funeral sermon quickly."[11]

To focus in on Seymour's leadership style is to understand a little more about him as well as the revival with which his name is associated. He has attracted more than his fair share of critics over the century, but it is clear that even the likes of Shumway—the scholar who could not let the glossolalia bone fall from his jaws— remained to be fully convinced of his own critique. Take a look at the end of Shumway's thesis, his critical history written twelve years after the events just described, and the ending comes as something of a shock. His narrative description of the history of the gift of tongues stops at the precise point at which Seymour receives his own blessing there on the floor of 214 Bonnie Brae. There is no hint of the story that followed, a story which, if you hadn't guessed already, contains heroes, villains, and tragic downturns of fortune. Shumway sidesteps the later splits and breakup, avoids the criticisms which would later get rolled out with waspish regularity as accusations laid against Seymour. More than that, though Shumway met and interviewed Seymour (claiming "though of genial heart, his mind cannot be described as robust"[12]) he makes so basic an error as to claim that the man was "born in Indianapolis."[13] Why? It is hard to tell, but one could almost imagine that the faintest glimmer of appreciation had broken through to the cynic. Either way, tongues was a controversial issue long before the spring of 1906, and it continued to be so long after.

Seymour played by a different set of rules than those traditionally adopted by those in his line of work. Although not entirely unheard of,

Seymour made a stand for gender equality within the group, affording what little power and privilege there was in play to women and men alike. Jennie Evans Moore, Clara Lum, Florence Crawford are just three names whose influence on the movement was colossal, thanks initially to the welcome offered by the pastor.

Seymour, it appears, had a rare gift. "No one seemed to get offended at him," wrote Rachel Sizelove. The Springfield, Missouri, native would later play a part in the formation of the Assemblies of God and recalled her time at Azusa Street fondly: "My dear husband used to say the Lord gave Brother Seymour wisdom to rule the people as he did to Moses. No one dared to get up and sing a song or testify unless under the anointing of the spirit."[14]

Others noticed Seymour's integrity. Glen Cook—another future player in the formation of a fresh denomination, and the man whose earlier criticisms soon gave way to appreciation—wrote: "This man…really lived what we had been preaching for years, a sanctified life. It was the wonderful character of this man whom God had chosen that attracted the people to keep coming to this humble meeting."[15]

There were still other indications that things were marching to the beat of a different drum. There was none of the showmanship associated with previous revivals: no hint of Parham's costumes or banners, no well-trained choir, no passionately-prefaced collections and no posters stuck around town. It was precisely the sort of place where "you would hardly expect heavenly visitations…unless you remember the stable of Bethlehem."[16] In all, this unassuming approach may have disarmed a few, but those who were keen for a more profound experience of God than previously tasted had only to follow the lead of the man obscured by the pulpit, face down in prayer and preparation.

Some who praised Seymour's leadership in the early days would later offer different perspectives on their leader. Some, even those who had already shifted from opposition to support of Seymour would later revert to earlier antagonistic stances. Glen Cook's view of "the man whom God had chosen" changed over the years, as did others. Florence Crawford's name is in there too, pushing up towards the top of the list of those whose changing opinion threatened to undermine the Azusa Street story. Still, in the early days—once she warmed to it—she was all smiles and support the Azusa Mission.

"I was a wreck in my body," she said. Crawford was thin, weak, suffering from spinal meningitis and restricted by the presence of a harness, traps and a metal plate, all in the name of medical support. She was "once diseased from the crown of my head to the soles of my feet," until she got to Los Angeles. After that she "was made sound and well through the blood of Jesus."[17]

She had spent much of her life searching for God's power. Like many in the city, she was hungry for more, hungry for the outpouring that had been hinted at. Could the fruit of two thousand years ago return? Like many whites, she first had to humble herself and enter a neighborhood she previously would never have considered visiting save for charity handouts and acts of kindness. To admit that she was in need, and that the source might be found among those at the other end of respectability's scale, was something of a shock. Her first visit clarified her reactions. The Azusa Street singing did not impress. The prayers left her stony. "Finally, a big colored man got up to his feet. He said 'Hallelujah!' It just went through my soul. He waited a minute, and again he said, 'Hallelujah!' I thought, "God, I have heard the voice from heaven. I have heard it at last... He has the thing my heart is reaching after."[18]

In a moment she forgot everything else. Hungry, and in view of the feast, she was determined to satisfy her appetite. She attended more meetings, one of which would change her life forever. Stopping his sermon mid-way, Seymour looked up and said, "Somebody in this place wants something from God."[19] That was all the invitation she needed. Debris was scattered as she made her way to fall on her face in front of the altar. She was in. Years later, although not that many years, she would become one of the leaders in the Pentecostal movement. Other things would happen, too. She would travel. She would leave Los Angeles. Her shift in proximity to Seymour would bring agonizing sorrow. Would his invitation to the front give Seymour cause for regret?

Chapter 19
Lives Are Transformed

Journalists and Sinners

Today's disagreements about William Seymour have much in common with those that were alive with him. There among the questions of influence and ownership, the custody battles over who gets to be called *the Father of the modern Pentecostal movement*, we can find a core controversy that rises above others: What was Seymour's main agenda for his flock? Was it that they should witness and join in the eradication of the color line, or were they to charge headfirst in pursuit of an authentically holy lifestyle? True, Seymour's life today can be seen through a radical, political lens, one where the color contrast is turned up. It is also true that Seymour's legacy reintroduced a spiritual hunger that has touched every nation. But what did it all boil down to? Was it prompted by a passion for racial inclusion or holy living? Whatever your conclusion, in that place, in that time, it appears that the pursuit of holy living and the breaking down of racial oppression had to go hand in hand. The color line was the defining scar across the nation, and to ignore it was to ignore the very essence of the gospel message. Issues of love, forgiveness, unity, and self-sacrifice had particular relevance to all shades of Americans back at the turn of the twentieth century. Uniting races was not limited to being a politically subversive act; it was profoundly spiritual one, too.

It is tempting to look for codes and symbols among the debris of the Azusa Mission. The first convert was the Catholic Mexican construction worker introduced by Osterberg. The first black man saved was Mack E Jonas on April 20th, within a week of the first meetings.[1] Then there were women, children, Jews, Chinese, and even the occasional journalist. The metaphor was as bold as it was simple. Azusa was a patchwork, a fine blend of everything, and everyone united in pursuit of a closer relationship with God. The deal was simple, just as it was back in Acts 2. Described in the verses that swiftly became the poster passage for the group is a state of pure unity in Christ where every race gathered. There were:

> God-fearing Jews from every nation under heaven…Parthians, Medes and Elamites; residents of Mesopotamia, Judea and Cappadocia, Pontus and Asia, Phrygia and Pamphylia, Egypt and the parts of Libya near Cyrene; visitors from Rome (both Jews and converts to Judaism Cretans and Arabs—we hear them declaring the wonders of God in our own tongues!
>
> —ACTS 2:5–11, NIV

Writing later, Seymour made it clear that, in his eyes, there was an unbreakable bond between God's power and racial inclusion. A little under a year after his arrival in Los Angeles, he addressed the topic in print, committing his thoughts on the matter for all to read:

> God…recognizes no flesh, no color, no names. We must not glory in Azusa Mission, nor in anything but the Lord Jesus Christ by whom the world is crucified unto us and we unto the world. Azusa Mission stands for the unity of God's people everywhere. God is uniting his people, baptizing them by one spirit into one body.[2]

Months later he ran with the theme again, underlining the value of relying on God's power to provide the lead out of society's man-made problems:

> It is the blood of Jesus that brings fellowship among the Christian family. The blood of Jesus Christ is the strongest in the world. It makes all races and nations into one common family in the Lord and makes them all satisfied to be one. The Holy Ghost is the leader and He makes all one as Jesus prayed, "that they all may be one."[3]

In the same publication Seymour was clearer still, addressing those critics that reduced the Los Angeles revival to little more than a spiritual indoor fireworks display. Pentecost power was more than entertainment, more than self-indulgent gratification of the senses:

> Pentecost power, when you sum it all up, is just more of God's love. If it does not bring more of God's love it is simply counterfeit. Pentecost means to live right in the 13th chapter of first Corinthians, which is the standard....This is Bible religion. It is not manufactured religion. Pentecost makes us love Jesus more and love our brothers more. It brings us into one common family.[4]

So, these were clearly important times. Social and political problems were bound up in spiritual solutions, and while those at the heart of it were simply following God's moves, the message that something radical was happening on the West coast soon spread far and wide.

Part of the excitement was centered on the fact that here was something truly remarkable that was apparently being led by someone almost wholly unimpressive. According to the manual, Seymour's lack of concern for the signals of success was a mark against him. Without the usual trappings of power and the signifiers of importance the audience would surely fail to listen. Yet in this, as in so many other things, man's wisdom constructed out of self-confidence failed to get it right. Seymour continued to preach in a style that Osterberg described as "slow speaking, humble, unpretentious, Bible loving, God fearing..." Seymour was simply "meek and plain spoken and no orator. He spoke the common language of the uneducated class....The only way to explain the results is this: that his teachings were so simple that people who were opposed to organized religion fell for it. It was the simplicity that attracted them."[5] Simplicity, humility, and a direct appeal to those at the wrong end of the league of success were high on God's agenda, too often too low on our own.

Seymour's mumbles occasionally gave way to passionate outbursts, and at these times his "short" and "fiery" delivery of his message hit the spot.⁶ Hurling challenges out to the gathered masses with all the force and passion of a man who knows his time has come, Seymour would urge people to "let the tongues come forth" to "Be emphatic! Ask for salvation, sanctification, the baptism with the Holy Ghost, or divine healing."⁷

So, what was the reaction? According to Frank Bartleman, the early days of the Azusa Mission were both unique and important. "Opportunity once passed is lost forever," wrote the preacher in June 1906. "There is a time when the tide is sweeping by our door. We may then plunge in and be carried to glorious blessing, success and victory. To stand shivering on the bank, timid or paralyzed with stupor at such a time, is to miss all, and most miserably fail, both for time and for eternity. Oh, our responsibility!"⁸

The weight of that responsibility can only have been intensified by the daily unpacking of fresh pilgrims from trains that had traversed the continent.⁹ Cashwell made the entire three-thousand mile journey by rail, while another family traveled five hundred miles by horse-drawn wagon.¹⁰ Whatever the method, thousands of people were compelled to uproot their lives if only for a short time in order to stand face to face with the powerful blessing that had everyone listening. With coverage in newspapers and church publications across the country, as well as word of mouth started by those who had experienced the events firsthand, the country was soon experiencing an underground buzz about the Azusa Mission revival. Expectation, enthusiasm, and a rapidly improving communication system was all it took to spread the intrigue.

Many who turned up at the doors were critical of what they expected to find on the other side. Some left feeling vindicated, but the majority came back for more. Some felt that the emotionalism was too much, and some holiness churches rejected things outright. However, there were others that shut down their own operations and headed for the Azusa Mission en masse. William Pendleton's congregation did just this, despite the warnings of the Southern California Holiness Association's leader, President Roberts.[11] Even though he had shown earlier interest in Seymour's spiritual journey, Roberts' passions for the nation's greatest move of God in an entire century failed to get beyond lukewarm, rapidly retreating to their default of apathetic ignorance.

For those who spoke out against the events, the focus of attention was drawn to the very facts that pulled many in. The bizarre displays exhibited by people as they responded to God's power left some appalled and others transfixed. The jerks, laughs, cries, twitches, the holy choir... in short it was the same old pandemonium that characterized the very first meeting. Except by now, a couple of months later, there were ten times the number of people involved.

For many it was this "holy choir" that raised the most questions. The cascade of melodies and harmonies was something remarkable. As people sang in tongues, their invisible conductor drawing the focus to the altar and beyond, onlookers were frequently astounded and perplexed. Could it be repeated at will? Not likely, as anything from two to twenty people would spontaneously launch into a cascade of mounting harmonies. "It would sweep over the congregation, no words, just worshipping, intoning in the spirit."[12]

Seymour's message from back then still holds weight today. He urged people to remember the proper perspective: "We all may speak in tongues for a while, but we will not keep it up while preaching service is going on, for we want to be obedient to the word, that everything may be done decently and in order and without confusion."[13] If Seymour could be remembered through one sound bite, then it was on this defining issue that he raised his game and provided a watching world with this gem. Speaking to his congregation, he told them, "Now don't go from this meeting and talk about tongues, try to get people saved."[14]

Without being controlling, Seymour was in control. At least, he managed to keep some kind of order as was appropriate. Yes, people were there to abandon themselves to the power of the Holy Spirit, but practicalities were always considered. If people got too loud, Seymour would calm them down, saying "Brother, that is the flesh."[15] A sense of order underpinned things, both in the downstairs meetings and upstairs among those searching for something deeper. If people downstairs made too much noise and disturbed the upstairs gathering, a good dose of floor banging sent the appropriate signal. For many who came through the doors, the events at 312 Azusa Street might have appeared to given over to raw pandemonium, yet it is clear that Seymour held in mind Paul's advice in 1 Corinthians 14. Seymour was a non-manipulative yet careful steward of the meetings, allowing God space and people freedom at the same time as ensuring that fleshly emotion and human over excitement did not detract from the power of God.

But more than the displays of the Holy Spirit's power, it was inevitably the interracial aspect that concerned many. 1906 holds the dishonor of being the year in which a record number of black men were lynched, and racial tension was clearly affecting many.[16] Alma White's colleague Nettie Harwood arrived at the meetings, and afterward complained of songs, "in a far-away tune that sounded very unnatural and repulsive," as well as of a colored woman's arm draped around a white man's neck while in prayer.[17] That such a sight would be wholly unremarkable today is a clear sign of how divided many in the church were back then. On the one extreme were those who had allowed faith to break through the restrictions of social convention, while at the other end were those whose God was diminished by the fear of society's disapproval.

Many believers found their previously held positions untenable. A missionary from the Philippines once came to "expose the tongue deception." Feeling little more than raw anger as he approached the mission, the people inside soon understood his spiritual state. It is said that he felt angry at their presence, that he wanted to take a whip to the worshipers. Then a woman spoke in tongues, using a little- known dialect belonging to a tribe that was hostile to his work back in Asia. The coincidence was enough to calm his rage and secure his attention. Later, praying in the upper room, he was felled to the floor. The next day another woman spoke in yet another language familiar to him. Again, he was the only person who understood the words. This time they explained that what he was seeing was precisely what was described in Acts 2. He was in.[18]

There are other stories too, like the burglar en route to rob a house. Who knows why, but he ended up stopping off at 321 Azusa Street, found himself at the altar getting saved and leaving his skeleton keys behind.[19] As Bartleman writes, such instances are "too numerous to take space to mention."[20] They are good stories, too, and testimony was an important part of the meetings. But we reduce them to the status of spiritual candy if we feed on them alone. What mattered at the Azusa Mission was participation, not observation.

Of those who came with a critical agenda but left inspired, the story of one nameless foreign-born reporter stands out. While the details are bare, the story is perfectly indicative of the power on hand at Azusa. He arrived with eyes, pencils, and tongue all duly sharpened, ready to test his powers of critique. The shakes, the rolls, the songs, all would have given him the ammunition he craved, yet it was when he heard an illiterate, uneducated woman speak in tongues that his castle began to crumble. This woman, who clearly had never walked his childhood streets, began to speak, mirroring his native tongue perfectly. What's more, she began to tell him secrets about himself that only he could have known. He left convinced, and we know no more than this.[21] Yet what else matters? The road to Damascus seemed to be diverting an awful lot of people through Los Angeles in those days. As for what came next for each one, today's twenty million Pentecostals in America alone are testament to the fact that from such an experience there was no turning back.[22]

Chapter 20
William Seymour Connects with His Widest Audience

The Message

Picture this: Lawrence F. Catley, aged eleven, bent double with a fever as the morning sun rises. His bedclothes remain wet to the touch, the sweat poured into them during the night will take until way past morning to dry. The shortness of breath has been his calling card for weeks, the agonizing cough likewise, but the blood that it now delivers is relatively new. Lawrence, of course, has tuberculosis, one of the major public health concerns of the previous two centuries. Ironically, 1906 is the year that the first successes in immunizing against it have been made, yet for this young black child, the advance came too late—the disease had already found him.

The Catleys moved from San Antonio, Texas, to Los Angeles in the hope that the thirteen-hundred-mile trip would offer an improved climate, life, and future for their son. There was little joy, however. Lawrence still paused before going to sleep to pray, "Lord, don't wake me up." The boy's pain was immense, his future certain. But not quite. A neighbor told his mother of a church nearby. She mentioned that it was a place where "people pray for one another and they get well." Mrs. Catley was skeptical, but she and her son went along. The neighbor was right, too, as the congregation offered to pray for the young boy who was so obviously sick. Mrs. Catley agreed, and the deal was done. Lawrence was healed. End of story.[1]

The Azusa Mission was full of similar tales. Ones like the daughter of Rachel Sizelove—a future founder of one of the Pentecostal movement's largest denominations. The girl in question, Maud, had been suffering for twenty-four hours with a severe kidney stone, "writhing in agony."[2] Seymour was sent for, and on arrival he took out his bottle of anointing oil and addressed the girl directly: "Little girl, do you believe God can heal you?" She did, and after the preacher's prayer she rolled over and slept soundly. Healing complete.

The presence of living, breathing testimonies like Maud and Lawrence, coupled with the high turnover of visitors to the mission, meant that it was only a matter of time before Seymour and his team of fellow leaders felt the need to be able to communicate a little farther than their voices would carry. And so, the *Apostolic Faith* newspaper was born. Comprised of four pages of text only, the publication was to be mailed free to anyone who wanted it. And with five thousand copies of the debut edition printed, it was clear that there were high expectations for the paper.

Like Parham and his hankies, or Paul and his scraps of cloth, the team would lay hands on the copies of the paper and pray before mailing them out. Once at their destination, many would repeat the process, hoping for a transition of spiritual power along with the ink. A word about the team. By now things had progressed rapidly, and change was needed. It was only back in April that the phenomenon started with those "cottage" prayer meetings led by Seymour. By the summer, the thousands who were attending the meetings every week demanded that some sort of formal structure be established to share the load. The newspaper helped crystallize this, drawing on the talents of those who were committed to supporting the spread of the blessing. Warren and Farrow—over from Houston—helped, as did Glenn Cook. An ex-newspaper man, he was the ideal choice to manage the publication. Clara Lum was secretary, stenographer, and editor, and along with Florence Crawford as state director, the two ladies held the power to direct the flow of information. There were others too, people who were involved in the process of praying for others as they came and went to the mission. But either way, the crowd could never have been described as big. Instead, the loose arrangement was a logical and necessary part of drawing together the contacts springing up.

The first issue, published in September 1906 went to great pains to make itself clear. In a bid to correct some common misconceptions, the paper placed great importance on narrating the story so far, and what an opening chapter they had to tell:

> The power of God now has this city agitated as never before. Pentecost has surely come and with it the Bible evidences are following, many being converted and sanctified and filled with the Holy Ghost, speaking in tongues as they did on the day of Pentecost. The scenes that are daily enacted in the building on Azusa Street and at Missions and Churches in other parts of the city are beyond description, and the real revival has only started, as God has been working with His children mostly, getting them through to Pentecost, and laying the foundation for a mighty wave of salvation among the unconverted…
>
> In a short time God began to manifest His power and soon the building could not contain the people. Now the meetings continue all day and into the night and the fire is kindling all over the city and surrounding towns. Proud, well dressed preachers come into "investigate." Soon their high looks are replaced with wonder, then conviction came, and very often you will find them in a short time wallowing on the dirty floor, asking God to forgive them and make them as little children.[3]

The first issue also featured what Brother Seymour had to say "in regard to his call to this city."[4] He explained the past—how he was invited to the city—but it is what he left out that was really interesting. There was no mention of Julia Hutchison. Instead the plot was related as, "One night they locked the door against me."[5] Likewise he mentioned the meeting with Roberts and the rest of the holiness leaders, but there was no mention of his being refused permission to preach. Instead, Seymour emphasized the positive, explaining that "after the president heard me speak of what the true baptism of the Holy Ghost was, he said he wanted it too, and told me that when I had received it to let him know. So, I received it, and let him know."⁶ This simple, placid, non-resentful retelling hints at the heart behind the man.

He went on to relate the earlier adventures and to trace the roots of the current Pentecostal revival. Parham was given due respect, although it is not without intrigue. We have to assume that the story Seymour heard about the birth of things back in Topeka would have come from Parham direct, so we should not be surprised that the section titled "Old Time Pentecost" failed to mention Agnes Ozman's earlier encounter with the Holy Spirit. Instead, it suggested that after much study:

> …when they prayed, the Holy Ghost came in great power and she commenced speaking in an unknown tongue. This made all the Bible school hungry, and three nights afterward, twelve students received the Holy Ghost, and prophesied, and cloven tongues could be seen upon their heads. They then had an experience that measured up with the second chapter of Acts and could understand the first chapter of Ephesians.⁷

Not quite the way Agnes O described it, but close enough. Again, the source of the story told a little about the nature of the storyteller. The narrative then continued to draw the links between the Topeka outpouring, the thirteen thousand souls impacted since its dawn, and the arrival of holy pandemonium in Los Angeles. Like it or not—and later there would be many who would opt for the latter—Parham's influence was there to be seen at the Azusa Mission, even before his first, and only visit. Still, there would be plenty of time for that in the future. In this first edition there was plenty of wholly exciting news to convey, particularly this description of regular events at the mission:

> The meetings begin about ten o'clock in the morning and can hardly stop before ten or twelve at night, and sometimes two or three in

the morning, because so many are seeking, and some are slain under the power of God. People are seeking three times a day at the altar and row after row of seats have to be emptied and filled with seekers. We cannot tell how many people have been saved, and sanctified, and baptized with the Holy Ghost, and healed of all manner of sicknesses. Many are speaking in new tongues, and some are on their way to the foreign fields, with the gift of the language. We are going on to get more of the power of God."[8]

The rest of the first edition makes other important things clear. There is the simple breakdown of the theology that underpinned the approach—written by, or at least credited to Seymour himself—and the explanation of what is titled the "Pentecostal Faith Line." Of course, keeping things going cost money, something which few of the team had in abundance. And with it being a full-time concern, there was little chance of earning a wage. Still, that was never an obstacle. Those that were there remembered seeing how Seymour would wander among the crowds in the mission with five and ten dollar bills wafting out of his pockets, the man having frequently failed to notice as people placed them there.[9]

As the paper explained, "We believe in the faith line for Christian workers, and no collections are taken. During the four months, meetings have been running constantly, and yet with working day and night and without purse or scrip, the workers have all been kept well and provided with food and raiment."[10] Food arrived daily for the workers who lived either above the hall or in a cottage towards the back, and those attending the meetings were encouraged to take personal, private responsibility for the amount of money they felt appropriate to give to the cause. A mailbox was placed in the hall. On it were written the words, "Settle with the Lord."[11] There was little more to say.

Money failed to be an issue for those traveling further afield with the message. There were already a fair number of people who had left, although in the case of A.G. Garr, the first white man to receive the Holy Spirit at the mission, his trip was not as successful as he had hoped. His first destination was India where he expected to be able to preach in tongues with the Holy Spirit taking care of the rest. Parham and others had hoped for similar skills, but all were to be disappointed. Garr was left misunderstood and disappointed. However, he moved to Hong Kong where he adopted more successful conventional methods for spreading the gospel.[12]

Other workers left, supported by an anonymous army of donors who "do not want their names mentioned." After all, as the piece makes clear, "It is a poor time in these last days to hoard up treasures on earth. When the Lord speaks, it is a blessing to those that obey Him, but we covet no man's gold, nor silver, nor apparel. Among those traveling far was Brother Thomas P. Mahler, a young man of German nationality. He has the gift of tongues, besides the knowledge of several. He left here for San Bernardino. He may go by way of Alaska, Russia, Norway, Germany, and to his destination in Africa."[13]

Local information was also featured, with news that "Monrovia, Pasadena, San Pedro, Sawtelle, and Whittier were places about Los Angeles that are catching the Pentecostal fire. Elysian Heights and Hermon, suburbs of Los Angeles have cottage prayer meetings where souls are being baptized with the Holy Ghost."[14]

Alongside the news of people heading off and the explanation of key ideas and principles were the instances of the power of God to heal. Tales of sight and hearing restored sit alongside stories of two decades of asthma, heart, and lung trouble wiped out, of a little girl placed on crutches by TB left skipping about the yard, her crutches resigned to the status of artifacts in the museum of God's grace.[15]

There was also the exciting news of the first round of baptisms to report. Late in the summer, they had held their first baptismal service. Five hundred people had turned up, full of hope and joy, and made the trip to Terminal Island to the southwest of the city. On that one day

Seymour personally baptized 106 new converts while the others worshiped, prayed, and praised in the sun.[16]

Finally, the paper addressed one of the core beliefs—that those were the End Times. The millennium loomed large, and the faithful were convinced that "soon we shall have a rest of a thousand years. We are going to rest from our six thousand years of toil in a reign of one thousand years. That will be the millennial age (Jude 14–15)." Such thoughts have always captivated people, and Seymour and the others were no different. It was all at hand, they felt, and the apparent proximity of the apocalypse surely turned up the heat on the meetings. In fact, such was the intensity that the inevitable attraction of the spiritually "diverse" made for a slight problem for Seymour. The various occultists and hypnotists that had been drawn to the meetings must have presented a serious challenge to the leadership skills of a man whose experience in the role was less than a year. Seymour did the obvious and wrote to his mentor, Parham, asking for advice, as well as asking him to come and oversee the revival.[17]

Parham's reply came in time for inclusion in the first print run. He said he was rejoicing at the news of things in Los Angeles. Later on, he'd be a little less positive about things.

Chapter 21
Charles Parham Delivers His Briefest Sermon

"You know, it is my color."

For William Seymour, the members of the Apostolic Faith Mission, and the ranks of readers who soaked up the news from the *Apostolic Faith* newspaper, Charles Parham was something special. This enigma's influence hovered over the early months of the Azusa experience like the promise of winter's snow in the morning. Yet more than something remarkable they were keen to view; it was a common belief that Parham's arrival would bring with it the key to sparking a city-wide revival. Here was the man with the gifts that assured access to the untouchable power brokers, and as the summer passed, they awaited the arrival with mounting expectation and fast- rising hyperbole. Dubbed the overall leader of choice, he was the man whose mighty influence would prompt the spiritual earthquake they so desperately believed was on its way. For Charles Parham, Azusa Street was also in need of closer inspection. But inspections would have to wait.

Parham was busy building a formidable reputation as a leader with drive and the power to deliver. In his hands, glossolalia was a controversial phenomenon that guaranteed interest. Bold, brave, and often belligerent, Parham used whatever was at his disposal to create a stir. And he did. Prior to arriving in Los Angeles, he led a successful campaign in Zion City, Illinois.

For Charles Parham, success came in many sizes—a well-attended meeting, a well-funded campaign, a well-received sermon. Yet his currency of choice was influence. Zion City swelled that particular bank account nicely, as one newspaper reported:

> People with means and considered among the most influential people of the city have invited Parham into their fine homes, and seem to be showing him every possible attention.[1]

"Seem" to be? The language is bound by the restrictions of outdated formal social convention, yet scratch the surface a little, and Parham's story becomes clearer. The trappings of wealth seduced him, stole his roof-top gaze as they bathed in view of those with an eye for the finer things. Converted before his teens and an experienced preacher well before he started shaving, Parham was always out to prove himself. At the age of nineteen he secured a position working for a prominent Methodist church, from then on choosing to associate himself with those of means and influence. An affluent mine operator sponsored his work in Kansas; a wealthy rancher filled the vacancy when Parham headed for Texas. His Houston campaign, like that in Illinois, found its way into the most prestigious meeting halls and secured favorable reviews in the local press.

Yet if all this sounds like coincidence, sour grapes, or a desire to bend Parham's reputation to fit the role of villain, read on. Parham deliberately made wealth his plumb line for success. In his *Selected Sermons,* he reminisces the days when his Methodist salary was between $500 and $700 per annum.[2] With joy he compares that to his "faith" income of ten times that amount. Money, and particularly a lot of it, was something to be proud of.

Discipline also ranked highly for Parham, or rather, for those who attended his Bible school back at Stone's Folly in Topeka, Kansas. They were, he wrote, "a people thus given up to God, who more fully obeyed the commandments of Jesus, and in a stricter sense had 'all things in common' than any other Bible school in the world."[3]

So, it is not particularly hard to imagine the way Parham would have felt on receipt of unfavorable reports from close followers who had visited Seymour's meetings. News that the meetings—which were being held in the city's slum area—were not the sort of which Parham would approve reached him before he witnessed the meetings personally. So too would the stories that Azusa's leader and Parham's one-time pupil was calling him "God's leader." Seymour had made a key play of the links between himself and Parham, perhaps too big a play. They were both walking similar doctrinal lines, but whether through naivety or a refusal to acknowledge the truth, Seymour's assumptions about Parham's visit were about to be severely challenged.

To say that the meeting was *normal* would be stretching things a little, but, as typical as they were, the meeting into which Parham strode one October night was representative of the many that had gone on before. There may not have been a whole load of shouting, clapping, or jumping, but many were shaking, jerking on an invisible line beyond their control. As the power of the Spirit increased through laying on of hands, many fell to the floor, unable to stand under the weight of so intense an experience. For Seymour, this was all good, as he later wrote:

> The Lord knocked Paul down and he got up trembling and saying "Lord, what wilt thou have me to do?" The Lord knocked all the worldly wisdom out of Paul. That is the reason He knocks so many people down here, to take the worldly wisdom out of them. Paul was a man full of the wisdom and knowledge of this world, but when he got the baptism with the Holy Ghost, he was able to tell us about true wisdom and true knowledge.[4]

Yet Parham was most definitely not on the floor. Full of the wisdom of a world in which racism was permissive, even, he felt, supported by the very sacred text on which he based his life's work, Parham's arrival was a defining moment in the history of Pentecostalism. From the moment he approached the building and heard sounds of people singing their passionate worship, a line in the sand was drawn. On so many levels it was inevitable that he would disapprove—Parham was at the peak of his prestige, yet here was a former pupil creating a monumental stir without him. Parham had spearheaded the drive toward tongues and baptism in the Spirit; Seymour was simply borrowing the script. Finally, Parham was white; Seymour was black.

Years later, with emotions still every bit as raw, Parham committed his recollections of the meeting to paper. "To my utter surprise and astonishment," he wrote, "I found conditions even worse than I had anticipated." Those inside were shaking and "falling under the power," with black catching white and white catching black. One scene in particular appalled him. A wealthy and cultured "white woman" could be found "thrown back in the arms of a big "buck nigger," held tightly while shivering and shaking in what he disparagingly labeled a "freak imitation of Pentecost."[5]

The impact was profound and with a half-life even Parham may have had trouble predicting. In 1914, in his work *Everlasting Gospel*, even the briefest of references to Los Angeles is enough to have the memories flooding back:

> I have seen meetings where all crowded around the altar, and laying across one another like hogs, blacks and whites mingling; this should be enough to bring a blush of shame to devils, let alone angels, and yet all this was charged to the Holy Spirit.[6]

*

So, there he is, walking down to the altar placed at the center of the main meeting room. Parham acknowledges Seymour, turns to the congregation and delivers a verdict which few can misunderstand:

God is sick at his stomach.[7]

Parham spent years in practice, but he never quite managed to come up with a line to rival that first assault. As his life began its fade to black, he did manage to pull a reasonably venomous one out of the bag, claiming that Azusa was "Spiritual power prostituted."[8] Punchy, yes, but nowhere near the quality of the original.

Obvious questions abound at this point: What happened to the meeting? What did Seymour say? What else did Parham say? Did it stun to silence, or was the power of the Spirit too much for the power of Parham's poison? Sadly, speculation is our only source, as reports of the reaction end there. Yet it does not take a great deal of thought to piece things together. At least, from Seymour's side, the reaction was clear.

He said nothing. No response was recorded at the first meeting, and there is no record of him addressing the matter for at least the next two months. While the *Apostolic Faith* had been full of the news of Parham's visit in the issues published in the two months leading up to it, once he touched down there was nothing more said. Although he did allow one defense to creep in, calling for attention to be paid to the hallmarks or humility and racial integration that characterized the Azusa meetings. He also changed the name of the publisher from "The Apostolic Faith Movement of Los Angeles." to "The Pacific Apostolic Faith Movement, Headquarters, Los Angeles."[9] A subtle shift, and one that, depending on your view, either left room for retracing of steps or kept valuable links with a well-known and respected ministry. Either way, Seymour's response places him at the other end of the scale to his now decidedly *former* mentor.

It may be tempting to reduce Parham's list of motivating influences to a handful of sensational headlines, yet his beliefs and prejudices were not nearly so remarkable one hundred years ago. The Jim Crow laws cast a wide blanket under which a colossal range of racial prejudices were covered. To outward appearance, Parham could have been said to be merely playing by the rules of the time, observing the decrees handed down by those in charge. On the question of segregating races while in Texas—the process that left Seymour listening to lectures from the hallway or remaining at the back of a church meeting, unable to approach the altar while the ruling race were in the building—Mrs., Parham defended their actions sweetly:

> In Texas, you know, the colored people are not allowed to mix with the white people as they do in other states.[10]

The implication that the Parhams' hands were tied against their will is a little less than heavyweight. Parham had few qualms about challenging authority, even at a state level. He publicly disagreed with the Kansas City authorities in 1901, refusing them permission to vaccinate him and his family in an attempt to stem a lethal smallpox epidemic at the time. His defense was clear: It was unconstitutional.[11] Add in the fact that he was not shy of supporting the resurgent Ku Klux Klan, and his motivation is pulled into a little sharper focus. To say Parham was an impotent passenger swept unwillingly along by social convention and state law is incorrect. He made that clear himself when he described the Klan as a movement for "reform for man's betterment" made up of "these splendid men who belonged to an organization that has won ten million to its standards in ten years."[12] That he chose the *Apostolic Faith* newspaper as the publication of choice for this final comment is just another measure of how strongly he held onto his views.

As well as racism, the reasons behind the vitriol Parham directed at his former pupil included an intense dislike of demonstrative worship, of the poor, and of those who threatened to reframe the Pentecostal movement as anything other than an extension of his own personal ministry.[13] True, his antipathy toward interracial worship was softened by the claim that he approved of it as long as "colored people kept their place and respected and appreciated the welcome given to them." Quite what that *welcome* would have looked like is open to interpretation. True, he did bend rules to allow Seymour access to study in Houston; he did partner him on missions to evangelize members of black neighborhoods; he did take up the invitation to join the meetings in Los Angeles. But, it is also true that at his core, Parham held on to a belief that the flood that carried Noah and his zoo away was sent as divine punishment for the mixing of the races in Noah's time. According to him, the Anglo-Saxons were the direct descendants of the ten lost tribes of Israel.[14]

The cocktail of slum location, exuberant worship, racial mixing, and the preaching of his message of glossolalia by a black man was too much. Parham's anger of the first night continued, for weeks, months, even years. It accompanied him through feast and famine, it became his constant companion as his appetite for controversy increased. Whether this was the way he had intended the script to play out is one for speculation, but either way his attacks cost him the title he craved so dearly. Once in the running for the *Father of Pentecostalism* slot, he withdrew himself from the race within hours of entering Azusa. The level of antipathy confused onlookers— could a man with so *holy* a reputation really be motivated by such base instincts? Seymour's silence may have ensured dignity, but for many in the congregation, confusion reigned. In private Seymour later allowed himself just one moment of the mildest retaliation, confiding that he understood the true cause of the split: "You know," he said, "it is my color."[15]

With many more months of glorious activity yet to come, the revival at Azusa Street was already doomed. From this moment, this one night, the cancer started to grow.

Chapter 22
The Future Is Glimpsed

The Forest Fire Dream

Another night; another dream. This time the dreamer finds himself outdoors, watching as a preacher stands in the half light, surrounded by dry scrub land, an empty grain sack at his feet. The man looks uncomfortable. He can feel heat—direct heat, specific, coming from behind him. He turns to see that the brush scattered about the ground has caught fire. More heat, again behind him. This time turning around reveals two more fires, sprung from nowhere. More fires in less time, and as Seymour watches, he sees the man spinning around, too slow to keep up with the flames. Soon they no longer appear as individual fires, but combine to form one solid wall of flames. The wall moves forward, too close for the preacher, who notices the sack at his feet. Suddenly the sack is wet, and Seymour watches as the preacher uses it to try and put the fire out. He fails, the fire too strong for his efforts. The fire grows and more fuel is consumed. Eventually, all is flames.

The dream was not hard to interpret. As Seymour shared it with fellow Azusa Mission member Frank Cummings, the meaning became clear. "Frankie, son," declared the pastor, "this teaching is meant to spread over the entire earth."[1] Against his natural instincts, Seymour was persuaded by the young man to share the dream with the congregation, and, in the edition of the *Apostolic Faith* that followed Parham's arrival at Azusa, the story made final draft of the paper. Tagged to the end were the words: "Our God is marching on. Hallelujah. The man with the wet gunny sack is here also, but his efforts only call attention to the fire."[2] Was Parham the preacher in the dream, desperate to quash the move of God? If so, was this one of those passive-aggressive retaliations, a thinly veiled threat that implied doom for anyone who got in the way of things? Was this a prophetic sign that God was wholly on the side of those whom Parham had decried?

Possibly. Yet perhaps there was something *fleshly* about the timing. The dream itself was one that had played out in Seymour's subconscious one night before the Azusa Mission started, months before Parham's arrival. Knowing Parham's abilities as a charismatic preacher, having explained through the paper just how influential the movement had been since its Kansas dawn back in 1900, it is understandable that Seymour would have wondered whether his one-time mentor was about to take charge of the mission. He may well have felt threatened—who wouldn't? But Seymour's self-restraint was fully functional. In the two months following Parham's declaration of God's nausea, the retelling of the dream was the only public comment that Seymour made on a subject approaching the Parham situation.

The others at the mission were less restrained. Many in the congregation did not accept Parham's claims to leadership, and Osterberg put it bluntly when he explained: "We didn't like it that he told us he was above us."[3] Having preached just two or three times at the mission, it was Parham's turn to be locked out in the city of Angels. This time, however, the padlock was verbal and the chains invisible. Still, Parham got the message and decided to do what any self-respecting teenager would do—he took his ball away. Charles Parham, evangelist and self-titled *Projector of the Pentecostal Movement*, turned his back on the meetings and headed off to the Women's Christian Temperance Union Building on the corner of Broadway and Temple streets, an altogether smarter, more fashionable locale that today plays host to the big boys of the city's administration. Back toward the end of 1906, the WCTU housed the Kansas preacher's aspirations as he claimed to fill the building with two hundred to three hundred ex-Azusa's who had signed up for his rival meetings.[4] Nothing permanent ever happened; no rival revival ever broke out there, although Parham did maintain a degree of consistency by condemning the Azusa Mission strongly at every available opportunity for the rest of his life.[5]

Seymour, on the other hand, never spoke of it. Correction, he allowed himself the one comment given in private to a friend, and one small article in the paper. Beyond that, the pupil took a wholly different path than the master.

The public comments themselves were slow in coming forward. It was two months before the *Apostolic Faith* would mention Parham's name again. In the December 1906 issue the lead article had this to say:

> Many are asking how the work in Azusa Mission started and who was the founder. The Lord was the founder, and He is the Projector of this movement. A band of humble people in Los Angeles had been praying for a year or more for more power with God for the salvation of lost and suffering humanity. They did not know just what they needed, but one thing they knew, people were not getting saved and healed as they desired to see...
>
> Some are asking if Dr. Chas. F. Parham is the leader of this movement. We can answer, no he is not the leader of this movement of Azusa Mission. We thought of having him to be our leader and so stated in our paper, before waiting on the Lord. We can be rather hasty, especially when we are young in the power of the Holy Spirit. We are just like a baby—full of love—and are willing to accept anyone that had the baptism with the Holy Spirit as our leader. But the Lord commenced settling us down, and we saw that the Lord should be our leader. So, we honor Jesus as the great shepherd of the sheep. He is our model."[6]

This appraisal of the situation is typical of Seymour. The hallmarks are easy to spot: the inclusive language, the self-deprecation, the emphasis on the lessons learned, and the final focus shift toward a positive statement about pursuing a closer relationship with Jesus.

The December edition of the paper retold the story of how the revival began, although somehow this time around the words chosen appear to have a little more resonance. The collection of believers at Bonnie Brae are "a band of humble people" who happened to encounter "a great deal of opposition" while "Bro. Seymour is simply a humble pastor of the flock over which the Holy Ghost has made him overseer." Later in the paper there is a warning about "counterfeits," those who claim to have the baptism but who have failed to receive it. Importantly there is also a focus on Christ's sacrifice, on suffering, on opposition, as well as on the Year of Jubilee, the Levitical doctrine never once acted out, but that offered the prospect of freedom to slaves and justice for all.

While it was almost fifty years since the Emancipation Proclamation, the sense of oppression was clearly still felt. If this was criticism, it was all very indirect and followed the strict policy that Seymour had laid down—the Azusa Mission would never allow unkind words to be spoken of critics.[7] They had plenty of opportunity to practice over the years, too, never failing to maintain the standard of dignified silence.

Seymour's only comment about his color being the spur for Parham's anger leads us back to the question of racism. Parham was clearly no abolitionist, yet was racism his primary driver in causing the first-ever split in the Pentecostal movement? For a man with such a fine palette for self-promotion, surely the sight of power being handed out without his direct involvement must have been intensely frustrating. Then there was the matter of theology: Parham was a big believer in the potential that the gift of tongues represented for the mission field. According to him, the outpouring of the Holy Spirit in this way would enable missionaries to preach to foreign heathens without having to learn the language (or the sermon). What he was therefore keen on was *xenoglossia*, the God-given gift of speaking in or writing an authentic language unknown to the speaker. While there are some stories of this happening at the mission—remember the Pilipino preacher?—what Parham saw more of at Azusa was *glossolalia*, the uttering of incomprehensible sounds that some call the language of the angels. Whatever it was, Parham didn't like it.

Race, power, theology—all three combined to leave an unpleasant taste in the visitor's mouth. Other leaders—other white leaders—had managed to humble themselves and learn at the Azusa Mission, but not Charles Parham. Cashwell, Osterberg, Garr, Bartleman, Pendelton, even George, the brother of English missionary C. T. Studd, joined with the rest of the races and spent time on the dirt floor, down there among the babbling, twitching social undesirables. But not Parham. True, there were other leaders, other white leaders, who were offended by the events and failed to sign up to the racially inclusive blessing—Roberts, for one, never managed to overcome his aversion to the scenes—but when it comes to influential objectors, Parham found himself at the top of the pile. Perhaps he liked it that way.

In his subtle way, Seymour backed up his assertion that Parham's anger was racially motivated. Writing in the *Apostolic Faith* he set out more positive statements about what defined the mission:

> We believe in old time repentance, old time conversion, old time sanctification, healing of our bodies and the baptism with the Holy Ghost. We believe that God made Adam in His own image, according to Gen. 5 1; Ps. 8 4; and Matt. 19 4. We do not believe in any eighth day creation, as some have taught.[8]

No prizes for guessing who the "some" are. What "they" taught was that while God created a race of men on the sixth day, he followed it up with a superior, whiter, range on the eighth day. Even without the split, such heresies deserved to be kicked fully into touch.

In a bizarre way, Parham did get to lead some of the Azusa Pentecost. He did enough to assure his name's inclusion in the story. Sadly, however, it tended to be the white leaders who bought into the Pied Piper routine. For those who followed the music, the Pentecostal blessing was at best a pale, monotone imitation of that described in Acts 2.

So, was it race or was it power or was it theology that prompted the split? In truth it must be seen as all three. Parham never really got over the sense of personal injury at the Azusa Mission's audacity to do things differently than his original blueprint. Later he would repent of all manner of sins yet to come, but he would never let go of the sense of personal injustice at the swiftly closed chapter. And while this was to be the beginning of the end for Parham, there was far longer left to run for those soaking up the blessing in Los Angeles and around the world.

Yet the cancer had started to grow. Despite the fact that Parham's physical presence at the Azusa Mission could be counted in minutes rather than weeks or even days, his leaving was a blow. It cut him off from the movement to which he had been the titular leader and left him in the cold. It also split the movement and threatened to damage future hopes of moving from an influential local mission with national contacts to a national drive that fed into local churches. For this they needed power, and power came in only one color. Without whites to back it, Azusa Mission would remain on Azusa Street. It was a devastating blow, but one which would lie dormant, benign for some time. Meanwhile there was another year to enjoy, one of unprecedented growth, one in which it was easy for Seymour to remain quiet about his former mentor's outburst. The white man's influence dropped off so rapidly that his accusations and rantings lacked the power to carry them all the way to the West coast. Besides, Seymour had better things to do than worry about the racist bile and self-indulgent backstabbing of a man he barely knew. For one thing, Seymour had a fire to stoke.

Chapter 23
Charles Parham's Story Is Told

Scars and Rubble

Wisconsin is able to boast of many things, yet as well as being the milk, snowmobile, and bratwurst capital of the world, Wisconsin can lay claim to being a part in the Azusa Street story. Turn the clock back one hundred years, and the badger state was home to a unique—if a little ill-tempered—church publication. Published by the Metropolitan Church Association, *The Burning Bush* newspaper had a chip on its shoulder. However, it served its faithful readers with a dedicated diet of gossip, back-stabbing, and satirical cartoons. Each edition of their paper started with a full front-page image that dealt with the editors' concerns of the day. Take March 14, 1907, for instance. A square-jawed, powerfully dressed man with clenched fists stands above two slain, rather haggish-looking women, a stake driven through their hearts. Emblazoned across the chest of the victorious man are the words *Burning Bush Editor*, while the unfortunate women are labeled *God's Revivalist* and *Christian Science*. The stake, incidentally, gets the tag *Cartoon*. Beneath are the scriptures Numbers 25:7–8 and Psalm 106.31, proclaiming that there will be given "righteousness unto all generations in the slaying of the opposition." Forget debate or reasoned discourse, Burning Bush took the short cut to getting the message across loud and clear.[1] Then there's the cover of May 9, 1907. A band of earnest-looking portraits of the greats—John Wesley, Martin Luther, St Paul, St James, and John the Baptist—sits above the line, "We believe in hard work." Caricatures of various individuals are placed beneath, with the words, "We don't," screaming out around them. Among them can be seen our old friend Alma White along with her rather bedraggled-looking husband.[2]

Yet best of all has to be the cover on January 24, 1907. The image depicts the scene in Azusa Street, showing William Seymour inside holding shut the door to the mission as Charles Parham remains locked outside. Seymour appears without his beard, the illustrator instead choosing to depict him as an archetypal black slave, all big lips and bald head. Parham, on the other hand, is out on the road, where his fine features are presumably suffering in the snow. Seymour is surrounded by whites, all staring at him with shocked disapproval while Parham holds at his side a copy of the *Apostolic Faith*. One more thing, Seymour's body has been replaced by a boot, while Parham has an enlarged head and a tiny body. Beneath the image is the line, "The foot cannot say to the head, I have no need of thee. Schism in the 'tongues' body."[3]

It gets better inside. Criticizing the movement for claiming to follow Parham in September, but ditching him in December, the editorial also says, "From all we can learn, either wing of this mongrel body is scooping in anything that comes…feeding on the backsliders and floaters from all over the country."[4]

Whether it was paranoia, genuine dislike, or a twisted concept of fairness, the editors went on to heap criticism upon Parham and, somewhere among the bile and insecurity, is a seed of truth. Catching up with the ex-leader on his return to the mission in Zion City, Illinois, which had diverted him en route to California, the editorial relates:

> Mr. Parham spent much of his time in all the services denouncing the work of the Tongues movement in Los Angeles, California and declared repeatedly that the jerks, fits, and spasms, such as he saw when there, were not the work of the Holy Ghost, but that he "when He (the Holy Ghost) comes, He will make a person dignified and proper in his demeanor."[5]

It seems that Parham had the bit between his teeth, as the report continues:

Parham publicly declared that two thirds of the Los Angeles work was of the flesh and the devil....Privately he told us that many of the works outside of Los Angeles on the Pacific coast where they were reporting great work going on were sending out false and exaggerated reports of their meetings.[6]

However, if Parham hoped that his private interviews would secure the favor of *The Burning Bush* staff, he was wrong. "Of all the religious meetings we have ever seen," they wrote in conclusion, "this was the deadest."[7]

Of course, the criticism from the Wisconsin group failed to throw Parham off course. By now the feelings were running deep, and his rejection of Seymour, as well as his failed attempt to return to the previous levels of success in Zion City, meant that things were about to change. The paternalistic racism that he had practiced before—the very sort that had allowed Lucy Farrow to lay hands-on people in prayer—soon gave way to a more blatant, far harsher kind.[8]

Theology remained a contentious issue too. At first glance it appears as though Parham changed his mind about the gift of tongues, having previously advocated it, and then criticizing what he heard coming from mouths at the Azusa Mission. These sounds he described as "babbling" and the result of those wishing to trick others by "the working of the chin, or the massaging of the throat."[9] With hindsight it is clear that Seymour and Parham's disagreement had roots that went down further than shallow bitterness and resentment. It was the old *glossolalia/xenoglossia* disagreement, which Parham settled with a simple formula—if it didn't sound like a proper foreign language, it was worthless.

His bid to set up a rival mission in Los Angeles never really worked. By the end of 1906, a mere two months after his arrival, Charles Parham left California, placing his Texan friend Carothers in charge of the declining gathering of the well-heeled at the WCTU.[10] Carothers, the feisty right winger whose racist views made Parham's look like that of an open-armed liberal, declared that it was racial hatred, not tongues that was a true gift of the spirit.

While Carothers was left in charge in Los Angeles, Parham took a decisive, yet confusing step. He resigned as leader of his own Apostolic Faith Movement. For some this was perhaps a bid to counter the accusation that he was power hungry.[11] His open letter in January 1907 certainly revolves around the theme of power:

> In resigning my position as projector of the Apostolic Faith Movement, I simply followed a well-considered plan of mine, made years ago, never to receive honor of men, or to establish a church. I was called a pope, a Dowie, etc., and everywhere looked upon as a leader or a would-be leader and proselyter. These designations have always been an abomination to me.[12]

Yet perhaps there was another reason for his decision. As early as January 1907, rumors were circulating about some serious sin issues below the surface in Charles Parham's life. There was talk, gossip even. One story had it that someone had witnessed detectives turning up to question Parham while he was in the middle of a northeastern tour. But, rumors being rumors, it was not until July 19th that Parham had anything really serious to worry about. When it all broke out, however, it was bad, the press announcing:

> Evangelist Arrested! C.F. Parham, who has been prominent in meeting here, taken into custody.[13]

The *San Antonio Light* had the story of the forty-something evangelist and the twenty-two-year-old man, arrested for "an unnatural offense." Bail was set at $1,000. Everybody knew that such charges related to sexual acts, and the story was spiced up further when it became clear that the young man in question—J. J. Jourdan—was known to the police already. Two months previously he had been charged for the theft of $50 from an upmarket hotel.[14]

Despite the scandalous ingredients, the case with Parham never made it to trial. While he and his wife assumed that this was all the vindication they needed, the lack of evidence turned out to be anything but a blessing. By failing to secure a clear statement of innocence in front of the public, Parham was to be forever tarred with the scandal.

While the *San Antonio Light* had limited itself to retelling the story simply and without much in the way of speculation or judgment, the Christian press was to be far less kind. Their reports appeared with far more detail and poetry than the original short piece in the *Light*. The word "sodomy" took pride of place in the reports, and proved to be far more damaging to his career than the locked doors at Azusa. Parham blamed a range of people, mainly rival groups, but nothing helped ease the acute sense of embarrassment for him and his wife.

The experience changed him, hardened him, made him a far harsher man than before. If the Azusa Mission had turned up the heat on his racist fires, this poured even more fuel on them. He lambasted other Pentecostals as often as he spoke, becoming less of a flamboyant showman and more of an embittered fairground attraction. There were other damaging incidents too, although the next was hardly his fault. September 1907 was the month when a little-known Pentecostal group formed by Howard Mitchell, a man who had been along to a few of Parham's meetings in Zion City, Illinois. Mitchell had conducted a barbaric healing ritual that resulted in the death of Letitia Greenhaulgh. Telling two of her adult children to remove the "demon of rheumatism," Mitchell watched as the woman's limbs were wrenched out of place, breaking her bones in the process. Mitchell then suffocated her with a pillow, broke her neck and tried to convince the Greenhaulgh children than their mother was simply sleeping. Although there was no reason to connect the two other than scandal, Parham's name was dragged into the story. The press outrage that followed called for justice and "the extermination of the most vicious and brutalized religious sect on the face of the earth, the Parhamites."[15]

There was to be one final blow to be endured before Parham essentially gave up and retreated. In order to rescue his name, he knew that he would have to pull off something truly remarkable. So, he returned to his original Big Idea. Dusting off his grand plan to trek out to the Holy Lands and dig up the Ark of the Covenant required significant fundraising, which he duly began early in 1908. As part of his bid to raise funds and profile, Parham suggested that while he was out there, he'd also make a point of digging up Noah's Ark.[16] Strange as it may sound today, Parham's sales pitch worked, and people handed over the cash to support his two-for-one rescue mission. Money in hand and with certain elements of the press won over yet again, he headed to New York City in December 1908 to board the ship to Jerusalem. Sadly, January 1909 saw him back in Kansas. He had, so he said, been mugged and never got to buy the ticket.[17] The end was nigh.

His life still had two decades left to run, but the final years barely contained enough variety to outlast a page. In March 1909 he and his family headed back to Baxter Springs, Kansas. It was safe there, with good memories and a bunch of people who respected him. They also gave him a building free of charge, which helped tremendously. Through this act and others, it was clear that affection for him had not vanished completely, despite his checkered past and uncertain future. Every year on his June 4th birthday, hundreds of Followers would show up for a religious meeting in Baxter Springs.[18]

In his final racist attack, he praised the resurgent Ku Klux Klan, considering them admirable but ultimately futile since, in his opinion, they lacked a spiritual purpose. In 1927 he urged all members of the "invisible empire" to work together on their "high ideals for the betterment of mankind." How? Through the glories of Pentecostal "old time religion."[19]

Eventually Parham did in fact make a trip to the Holy Land, but he returned without either the Ark of the Covenant or the grid reference for Noah's boat. Instead, he limped back to Kansas weak and with failing health. A year later he was dead. On January 29, 1929, his chest pains signaled heart failure, and he was gone.[26] Later, much later, people would turn back and consider his relatively obscure death to be at odds with his position as key player in the story of the modern-day Pentecostal movement. It could, of course, have all been so different.

Chapter 24
William Seymour's Faith Rises Even Higher

The Greatest Miracle the World has Ever Seen

Los Angeles 1907 was a long way from Baxter Springs, Kansas, 1929. Between them were decades, developments, and a story that was far from over. And yet, in a way, the two poles are closer than first appear. United by ambivalence and awkwardness, Parham's ending was set in motion when he turned his back on Seymour in October 1906. While his own decline would take in some of the same sights that Parham viewed, Seymour was sufficiently aware of the significance of the times to make perhaps his boldest declaration. These were the days in which something remarkable was beginning, and the quiet-spoken preacher broke with convention, unflinchingly stating, [w]e are on the verge of the greatest miracle ever seen.[1]

He had plenty of evidence to support his claim, too. The paper's print run went from the initial five thousand to fifty thousand within just two years.[2] The building became something of a spiritual distribution center, with people hungry for more pouring in and missionaries pouring out. Page one of the February-March edition of the paper mentions by name connections with London, Sweden, Hawaii, India, and Norway. Within three years of the humble beginnings at Bonnie Brae, over fifty countries were in receipt of missionaries from the Azusa Mission.

Of the people who came on a quest and left feeling inspired and envisioned, it only took a handful of them to transform the face of Christianity: Farrow and Hutchins were personally responsible for the African export, tearing up New York on the way. Durham took it to Chicago and from there to South America. It was left to Cashwell and Mason to sow the seeds of Southern Pentecostalism.

Charles Mason's story took a vital turn when, aged forty, he arrived at the Azusa Mission, a long way from his Memphis,

Tennessee, roots. He had met Seymour years earlier, as Seymour had traveled through Tennessee, fired up by his experiences in Cincinnati, Like Seymour, Mason's childhood included Baptist teaching and personal visions, although Mason's were of both heaven *and* hell. Holiness teaching had also made a profound impact on him, and once at Azusa Mission he was "hungry and thirsty."[3] He soaked up his first meeting, sitting alone afterward, weighing things up, praying. Eventually he was to be found thanking God and going with the flow, when, just five weeks later, he was off, taking the message and the blessing back to the hardlands of his childhood.[4] Like so many for whom the Azusa Mission was a pit stop, a crash course, or whatever other energizing metaphor you with to use, Mason was propelled out, back to where it all mattered, being part of the spread that was rapidly transforming the face of church. Mason followed Glenn Cook to Tennessee where the "fire had fallen."[5] While there he also met up with old friend C. P. Jones. The two men had previously founded the Church of God in Christ together, but the returning traveler's newfound belief in the importance of tongues caused a rift between the two men. Mason continued to lead the Church of God In Christ, until his death, and today the church's meetings still throb to the Azusa Mission heartbeat.

Traveling parallel to Mason was Cashwell, who reported back of "hundreds baptized in the South." From 1906 to 1909, he and Mason made the American South "the first region in the world where Pentecostalism put down deep roots and significantly changed the spiritual landscape."[6] Finding a host of impoverished people from all races, Pentecostalism took root. Later the region would shape Pentecostalism itself, but for the time it was Los Angeles that was the heart of the action.

Back in 1907, the year of extraordinary blessing, it was not at all unusual for the mission to receive as many as fifty letters each day.[7] These contained requests for prayer or copies of the paper as well as much appreciated notification of yet another breakthrough. News of this kind could come from anywhere, national or international, and with as many as fifty other Pentecostal papers and periodicals springing up in the first six years of the movement.[8] The network for gathering and dispersing information was becoming highly developed and incredibly effective.

Local growth was significant too, resulting in some unprecedented steps being taken. As well as the spread throughout the city and its suburbs, Los Angeles area pastors met weekly on Mondays at the Azusa Mission.[9] This unity led to a summer mission in 1907 hosted and run by a collective of all the local groups. This first Pentecostal camp meeting was held close to the city in Arroyo Seco, a beautiful location where eucalyptus trees offered shade from the burning sun. It was Rachel Sizelove's idea, and a good one too.[10] Thousands attended. Blacks and whites had separate accommodations but worshiped together. More than a hundred converts were baptized in a nearby stream.

Growth equated stability, and in the middle of the year of increase their rented building came up for sale. Having discussed it with the congregation, the group agreed to begin the three-year process of raising the money to purchase the building. Quickly they were able to put down $4,000 toward the $15,000 total price, and it took no more than another year before they had the remaining $11,000 to hand over, way ahead of schedule.[11]

It is almost impossible to convey the sense of energy that emanated from the place, but the pages of the *Apostolic Faith* do a good job of it. Cascading across the columns is a flow of information about new people moving on to take the gospel wherever their God-given passions led them:

- "Sister Rees from Oakland visited Azusa Mission recently."

- "A number from Winnipeg, Canada, have come to Los Angeles and are now rejoicing in the baptism with the Holy

Ghost. Others have come from the Atlantic coast and from Colorado and different states."

- "Bro. and Sister H. McLain have gone to San Jose, Cal."

- "Bro. Turney and wife who were at San Jose are now in Honolulu."

- "Bro. and sister E. W. Vinton from near Boston, Mass., 322 Brown Ave., McKeeaport, Pa., Feb. 8. The Holy Ghost has fallen on about a dozen here and they are speaking in tongues and we do not know where the work will stop."

- "There have been two who received their call to China."

- "Davis Ave. and Ann St., Mobile, Ala., Feb. 1. —After a hard battle in this wicked place, the Lord gave me a tent in answer to prayer. We give God all the glory for victory. Five have been sanctified and three received Pentecost."

- "Spokane, Wash., Mar. 21. Thank God, the work of the Holy Spirit is reaching into the remotest places of the earth....Upwards of thirty have received their Pentecost right here in Spokane."

- "Burgess, S.C. March 16…We are having a wonderful meeting in our midst.

- Several are being baptized with the Holy Ghost. Pentecost has fallen in Santa Cruz."

- "The Lord is blessing in Long Beach, Cal. We cannot tell just how many at this date have received their Pentecost and speak in tongues."

- "Hungry souls are seeking 1624 Oakland Ave., Des Moines, Ia., Feb. 21. —God is working here. Seven or eight are speaking in tongues and others awakened to the truth."

- "215 Locust Ave., San Francisco, Cal., Mar. 3——The Lord is working mightily in San Francisco. Many souls have been converted, sanctified, and baptized with the Holy Ghost and fire, and healed by the power of God."

- "924 N. Kansas Ave., Topeka, Kans., Feb. 21. —Glory to Jesus for the real Pentecostal power that is coming back to His people. About three months ago, Bro. and Sister Batman stopped off here for a few days on their way to Africa and told of the wonderful work of God going on in the West, and it made us real hungry for more of God, and we began to seek earnestly for the Baptism with the Holy Ghost. Soon afterwards a band of workers came from Denver and were with us ten days."

- "In 8th and Maple Ave. Mission, Los Angeles. The old time Pentecostal power returned to us during the four days and nights tarrying meeting we had beginning Dec. 28 and went over New Years to 5:30 A.M."

- "A poor lost woman, a victim of the cocaine habit, come into the meetings, was convinced of sin, and as a second definite work was sanctified and has obeyed God confessing Christ in baptism. This is a wonderful case."[12]

So many stories. The energy broke with convention; the revival was clearly in force, moving on even from the hands of those ordained at the altar in Los Angeles, springing up instead through the loosest of connections.

Of course, the dissenting voices still shouted from the sidelines. Racial intermingling remained the key bone of contention, with one newspaper echoing the shared sentiment of horror at the "disgraceful intermingling of races, they cry and make howling noises all day and into the night."[13] The troubles were not just lived out at the editors' desks either, as Henry Prentice found out. Back in June 1906, he was arrested for having pointed his black hand at a white woman and told her she was a sinner. She happened to be a preacher's daughter, and the police were called to calm those in the congregation who were calling for him to be hung. Prentice was sentenced to thirty days hard labor on a chain gang.[14]

W. M. Collins, a Baptist preacher, summed up the weight of the controversy surrounding the mission at the time: "What has it meant to me? On the one hand it has meant loss—loss of friends, loss of money, loss of position, loss of reputation. On the other hand, gain. Here I fail. I cannot tell the heights, the depths, the lengths, the breadths of the riches which this blessing has brought into my experience."[15]

Seymour had his say too, making it clear again and again that retaliation was off the menu. There were to be no personal attacks of critics, no matter how false their claims:

> You cannot win people by abusing their church or pastor. As long as you preach Christ, you feed souls; but as soon as you jump on the preacher, you grieve the Spirit. Preach Christ, and you will feed the flock and have fat sheep; but if you get to preaching against churches, you will find that sweet spirit of Christ that envieth not, vaunteth not itself, is not puffed up, thinketh no evil, suffereth long and is kind, is lacking and a harsh judging spirit takes its place. If

you feed them from Christ, you will find the same Spirit burning in their hearts.

When people run out of the love of God, they get to preaching dress, and meats, and doctrines of men, and preaching against churches. All these denominations are our brethren. The Spirit is not going to drive them out and send them to hell. We are to recognize every man that honors the Blood. So, let us seek peace and not confusion. We that have the truth should handle it very carefully. The moment we feel we have all the truth or more than anyone else, we will drop.[16]

One religious publication picked up on Seymour's words, giving its reply in May 1907:

…he says, "The churches are not to blame for the divisions." This is untrue, as the different creeds and doctrines are the very foundation for the so-called churches and the sects that divide and scatter the people who profess to be the people of God. He further says that people have not the love of God when they preach against the churches and against dress….This betrays a real compromise with all the worldly dress of sect professors, their sect, and all, betrays the spirit of the thing…we warn all who may be getting their poisonous sheet, called "The Apostolic Faith", to beware it, consign it to the flames as there is where its followers will land unless they see the error of their way and repent.[17]

Along with their insular approach to the Christian faith, the *Gospel Trumpet*'s calls for separation from the world and the burning of "controversial" items typified a church stance that has been adopted by believers for generations, tracing a heritage right back to the Pharisees. With opposition like this around Seymour, eventually gave in to sense and took steps to protect the Azusa Mission. Trustees were appointed—interracial of course—among them Richard Asberry and Louis Osterberg, mother of Arthur. Articles of incorporation were drawn up and stated that the organization was formed "to do evangelistic work; conduct, maintain and control missions, revivals, camp meetings, street and prison work."[18]

The formal structure may have felt a little uncomfortable at the time. After all, the group had only ever been at most a "group." Building a new denomination was never on the agenda—with revival in the air, the faithful were aiming for something of far greater significance. This was, after all, the season of the latter day rains, the time when God's blessing was being poured out ahead of the final tying up of the story that started way back with a garden, a man, a woman, and some rather tempting fruit. For Seymour and the others, 1907 had been a truly remarkable year, and all signs pointed to the assumption that something phenomenal was around the corner. Being involved, seeing it explode still further in 1908, was surely just a matter of remaining faithful and obedient to the plan.

Chapter 25
William Seymour Is Deceived

The Greatest Betrayal

If 1907 was all about success, phenomenal growth, and the expectation of an imminent global revival, 1908 was scripted by a different hand. Within just five months the Azusa Mission had undergone a radical shift, one that changed the tone from one of pure and optimism and hope to one of mistrust, sorrow, and frustration. On the surface things remained normal, but as the months trudged by, it became ever easier for the casual observer to notice that something was seriously wrong.

It could all have been so different. Cashwell and Mason were experiencing phenomenal success in the South, with holiness leaders readily accepting the Pentecostal experience despite initial reservations. A formerly disgraced Baptist minister by the name of H. Irwin had found both his integrity and his own Holy Spirit baptism at the mission and was now leading Pentecostal services up the Western seaboard from California to Oregon.[1] At Portland his work was handed over to Florence Crawford, whose efforts there were promoting a radical revival in the city. Others fanned the flames in different sites like Indiana, Ohio, North Carolina, Georgia, Minnesota, New York, Massachusetts, Virginia... the list went on and on. The revival was spreading, crossing state lines, borders, and oceans as if they were little more than garden fences.

There were other reasons for joy too, particularly for those who made up the core family of team leaders back at the Azusa Mission. In May the group's leader, their own Brother Seymour, decided to marry. For his bride he chose Jennie Evans Moore, the beauty whose own Pentecost had played such a key role in the birth of others.

Yet the harmony that should have followed on from such events failed to materialize. With things going this well, spreading this far, this fast, bystanders could have been forgiven for thinking that 1908 was bound to be a gold-plated version of its predecessor. Not so. Instead by the time the happy couple were ready to move in together, the days of the Azusa Street revival were numbered. With nothing more than the inertia of the previous two years to keep things moving, the end was already in sight.

What happened was both sickeningly simple and confoundingly ambiguous. Prior to 1908 the movement had been remarkably free from discord. Apart from the purging of Charles Parham's bitterness, there had been only one moment of conflict within the camp. One of the trustees—Professor Carpenter—wanted Seymour to give account for all the funds given to the mission. There can be little surprise at the fact that Seymour was unable to provide the required information, after all, this was a man who largely left giving as a matter for individuals to settle between themselves and God. This was the same man who wandered the room unaware of the fact that his pockets erupted dollar bills placed there by well-meaning members of the congregation. When it came to the subject of money at the Azusa Mission it had simply come in as it had and been given out as it was needed, with no formal books being kept.[2]

These were days of faith and miracles, of people putting their lives on hold as they uprooted and traveled the world to preach the gospel. Missionaries were supported financially by the church, as was the monumental task of printing and mailing fifty thousand copies of the *Apostolic Faith* newspaper. These were the type of days when balance sheets seemed perhaps somewhat irrelevant. Still, Seymour was perhaps a little naïve to believe that questions would not end up being asked about the significant cash flows. Not that there was ever any hint of financial impropriety: Seymour was and always remained a man who never owned property, and one who spent his life within breathing distance of poverty.[3] Professor Carpenter admonished him for his errors, and from then on full accounting was the order of the day. The bullish methods that Carpenter used caused a "different spirit" to gain a foothold, one that was "destructive to the place."⁴ If Seymour thought his time of internal opposition was over, he was wrong.

The breakdown occurred around the time of his marriage. On paper, the facts about the union appear innocent enough: Jennie Evans Moore believed that their matrimony was a divine appointment. Seymour agreed.[5] She was both beautiful and intelligent, a trusted member of the team who had previously traveled to Chicago to establish missions in the city. Proud of her roots and not afraid of causing a murmur of intrigue, Mrs. Seymour gave her race as Ethiopian on the marriage certificate, which was issued on May 13, 1908.[6] Edward Lee performed the ceremony, his wife and Richard Asberry stepping up as witnesses. Seymour even managed to allow a little humor to escape when asked how many times he had been married previously. "Just this once."[7]

There was nothing particularly remarkable about the marriage. He was thirty-eight, she was a little younger. After the ceremony she moved into the apartment above 312, leaving the family with whom she had worked back at 217 Bonnie Brae. Just one generation had passed, but it seemed a world away from the day when Seymour's parents had tied the knot. Then, with Southern laws—both written and secret—dictating affairs, Seymour's parents were still bound to their past as slaves. Carlin, the plantation owner who had previously owned Seymour's mother offered them hospitality back at his place, their presence there a reminder of just how far that had not come from the days before the war.

But for William and Jennie Seymour it was different. There were no reminders of a cruel past one had, no limitations on a future that all could tell was bound to be a glorious one. Sadly, this is not true. Even before the happy couple moved in together the damage had been done. In fact, some suggest that it was the act of marriage—or the choice of bride—that caused the split that proved fatal to the Azusa Street revival.

*

Central players in the saga are Clara Lum and Florence Crawford. Crawford had left Los Angeles some months earlier and had met with typical success as she established a thriving mission up the coast in Portland, Oregon. Back in the ninth edition of the *Apostolic Faith* newspaper, tagged June to September 1907, she had sent glowing reports of high opposition and even higher success:

The Revival in Portland

One of the mightiest revivals that Portland ever knew has taken place in that city. The devil raged, shots were fired, some were arrested and brought up before the judges, but the Lord worked on and healed all manner of diseases that were brought baptized and saved many precious souls.

In June a camp meeting was opened up there, where 100 souls were baptized with the Holy Ghost. Ministers were brought into the work. The Christian and Missionary Alliance in Portland came into the work in a body. God is working there in mighty power today.[8]

There had been physical healings, overcrowded meetings, and long journeys for those hungry for more of God. The report closed with a note in praise of "such a humble people, such love and unity I never saw."[9]

Writing later, this time in the October to January 1908 edition of the paper, Crawford was ready to take a more personal line, delivering her testimony to the legions of readers around the world. She recalls how she "sat and listened to dear Brother Seymour expound the Word of God" and how it impacted her "in my innermost being." With all the insight of one who knew the movement well, she got to the heart of the success that confounded critics of the day:

It's clean hands and pure hearts and a walk blameless before God, in holiness, in fear, meditating day and night in the law of God that keep this wonderful anointing. Few will pay the price to get that that Joel should come, and few will continue to pay the price to keep it; but by His grace and power, I mean to keep it if all hell should shake and conspire to make me fall or step for one moment aside. I've taken the narrow way. O I love it. I mean to go through with the despised few.[10]

When she wrote that she meant "to keep it all" did Seymour wonder? Crawford had been one of those prickly customers at first, the sort who was never slow to air her doubts or criticisms. Yet she was remarkable too, taking on the male-dominated church scene of Portland and drawing the masses together. But if there was something that was not quite right about her self-promotion, her high-level humility, did it raise Seymour's suspicions? Had he wondered whether things might turn sour with Florence Crawford? Opening the paper in January, Seymour was greeted with another installment in The Florence Crawford Story, this time featuring the leader's personal opinion on the current state of play:

O how I love Jesus. I never loved Him as I do now. His word never was so sweet. It's my meat and drink day and night. How can I ever praise Him enough or do enough or suffer enough for what He's done for me!... How it thrills my heart to think of the dear blessed saints that are standing true. As never before we are going to see the mighty signs follow the preaching of the Word; as we keep in line with the truth and in no way compromise, preach the word and let the Holy Ghost magnify Jesus....O I want to be spotless and have every thought brought into subjection. This Gospel is going like wildfire. It shall sweep everything before it, compromisers and all.[11]

Good words. The passion is high, and the sense of purpose is tangible. These are the words of a woman fired up, a woman whose mission is clear. The repetition of the allusion to those that "compromise" makes it clear that she is keen to position herself as one who is holding fast to a true and authentic faith. While it all might seem innocent enough, at the same time the piece was published, Crawford had welcomed in a visitor from Los Angeles. And there, in the bags of Clara Lum—acting managing editor of the *Apostolic Faith* newspaper—were two documents that spelt death to Seymour's hopes for worldwide revival.

Clara Lum had taken, stolen, or borrowed without permission—the differences are irrelevant in the face of the outcome—two of the twenty-two mailing lists containing the addresses of those to whom the *Apostolic Faith* was mailed.[12] While it might not sound so bad— after all, Seymour and the others back in Los Angeles were left with the other twenty—the truth was brutal. Lum had taken with her the lists of national and international supporters, leaving Seymour with only the names of those in the Southern California region. With two swift hands and a train ticket, Clara Lum castrated the Azusa Mission. End of story.

The theft—for that surely is what it was—came to light quickly. The Azusa Mission trustees objected. Lum remained silent. The paper continued to be published, and Seymour and others were forced to watch as the ink and power and contacts slowly trickled away from them, snaking their way up north. The May 1908 edition gave the mailing address as Portland, Oregon, while in June 1908 the mailing address had shifted back to Los Angeles. But the *Apostolic Faith* banner was missing. So too was any article from Seymour. By the time the next edition was out, there was no mistaking Lum's intentions. The July/August 1908 edition contained no reference at all to anything happening in Los Angeles. More importantly the paper made another break with tradition:

Some have asked how to send money offerings. Stamps are very acceptable. If necessary to get a money order, it can be made payable to the APOSTOLIC FAITH, PORTLAND ORE."[13]

Seymour had never let this happen before. But things were different now, as the paper hinted:

We have moved the paper, which the Lord lain on us to begin at Los Angeles to Portland, Oregon, which will now be its headquarters.[14]

Without the two vital mailing lists the Azusa Mission was cut off from its global contacts. While Seymour had never used the paper to solicit donations, yet the paper had been a vehicle through which they had come. More importantly, the national and international addresses represented the opportunity to connect and collate the experiences as Pentecost spread. With Lum's move up North went any possibility of the Pentecostal movement sticking to its original course as a racially inclusive move of God. The two white, middle-class women, taking their message away from the urban mix of the coastal city and restricting their new audience to the more mobile members of society, effectively redrew the color line. Instead of one glorious mix of wealth and race and background and culture, the Pentecostal movement was divided into territories. The beginning had ended, and what followed was, for many, a pale imitation of those twenty-four months of passion and chaos.

Chapter 26
The Doors Are Closed

When "Please" is no Longer Enough

A year on and Clara Lum and Florence Crawford apologized. Sort of. Having failed to fully inform the readers of the shifts that had taken place for twelve months, they decided to offer an explanation of their side of the story, their words covered in self- protection and evasive excuses. Judge for yourself:

> This paper would be no.21 from the beginning in Los Angeles, but it is no.7 of Portland. We said it was moved from Los Angeles when we should have stated we were starting a new *Apostolic Faith* of Portland, as nothing was moved except two lists of subscribers, leaving 20 complete lists of all subscribers in Los Angeles. We ask the forgiveness of any souls that have been grieved over the mistake.[1]

Had souls been grieved? Of course, they had. Within a couple of months of their marriage, Seymour and his wife traveled to Portland to ask for the return of the mailing lists. Their request was refused. One story has it that, leaving the meeting with the two ladies and making his way down the stairs, Seymour bumped into Ernest Swing Williams—an earlier member of the Azusa Mission. Williams had been profoundly impacted by what he had seen there, pursuing his own powerful experience of God with integrity and perseverance. Described as a gentle yet determined man, Williams traveled as an evangelist having been ordained at the Azusa Mission, much as Seymour had been by the Evening Light Saints in Cincinnati.[2] Back on the stairway in Portland, Seymour asked Williams: "Are you going to continue to preach here?" Yes, was the reply. Seymour ended the conversation there and then, saying "I'll have the railroad take away your clergy book."³ This was not an empty threat, as the black pastor revoked the white preacher's privileges. The pain was real, the reactions natural.

With face-to-face diplomacy failing, Seymour published just one more edition of the *Apostolic Faith* newspaper from his Los Angeles base. Dated October/November 1908, the words betray Seymour's true feelings:

> I must for the salvation of souls let it be known that the editor is still in Los Angeles…and will not remove 'The Apostolic Faith' from Los Angeles without letting subscribers and field workers know.…This was a sad thing to our hearts for a worker to attempt to take the paper which is the property of the Azusa Street Mission to another city without consent, after being warned by the elders not to do so.⁴

Typically, he held back from naming or directly criticizing those who stood in opposition to the mission. Instead, the focus is returned to the sense of pain experienced by those left behind.

The fact that Seymour only attempted one further mailing after Lum absconded with the two key lists is a clear indication of the precise value of those lists. Despite the fact that Seymour was still able to contact local supporters in Anaheim, Long Beach, and Pasadena, without the two key lists all was lost.

While there is no doubt about who did it, the reasons why Lum took the lists are a little more complex. The proximity of the event to Seymour's marriage brings up the inevitable set of questions: Was Lum jealous? Did she disapprove of the pastor's choice of bride, or did she simply object to the whole idea of marriage at such a time as this, what with the apocalypse being just around the corner?

Crawford's earlier article offers some insight. Her repeated accusations against those who "compromise" would have been significant to readers with a background in the holiness movement.

For them, as well as those pursuing the fire of God in step with the Azusa Mission, the very notion of compromise was abhorrent. Yet such a serious charge was delivered without specific evidence or direct accusation.[5] Apart from Seymour's decision a little later on in life to start wearing neckties, Seymour was never considered a controversial figure. Though people tried, no dirt has ever been uncovered with which his reputation can be tarnished. The truth is that Seymour was always stricter than the rest, raising the holiness bar way above the others.

What is more likely is that it was Seymour's decision to marry that Crawford considered so unwise. Throughout her earlier years in Portland, this "strong minded woman" (according to E. S. Williams[6]) was publicly critical of the institution. In fact, marriage had clearly been a controversial topic for some, contentious enough for Seymour to address it himself. Writing in the January 1907 edition of the paper he claimed: "It is no sin to marry."[7]

While this may explain Crawford's accusations that Seymour had gone soft on personal integrity, it still fails to answer the question of Lum's original theft. Was she working under Crawford's orders? Of that there is no evidence, but perhaps there was another, more personal reason for Lum inflicting such a wound on Brother Seymour. According to Ithiel Clemmons, one time president of the Society for Pentecostal Studies, Seymour had been in touch with his old friend Charles Mason earlier in 1908.[8] He had asked the Church of God in Christ leader whether he felt it was wise for him to marry someone of a different race. Mason advised against it, suggesting that an interracial marriage by Seymour could have sparked the discord. Seymour obviously took Mason's advice and decided to wed within his own race, and relatively quickly, too. With Lum's exit and theft taking place in the weeks before the marriage of the Seymours, it seems reasonable to conclude that she was the subject of the discussion of hypotheticals with Mason. Jealous, hurt, angry, and perhaps a little embarrassed, Lum retaliated. No wonder

Seymour took Jennie with him when he confronted Lum in Portland later that summer.

*

Meanwhile, back at the Azusa Mission, subtle changes were taking place. As George Studd's diary explains, the meetings maintained their passion and quality throughout the first five months of the year. Often describing them as "pretty good," "splendid," or "excellent."[9] However, Seymour had shifted his position on the structure of the services and started to allow more people to preach. Studd's interest and attendance started to drop off, and by August when he next returned, he commented that the meetings were "entirely controlled (humanly speaking) by blacks."[10] Deliberate or not, the balance of power and representation was shifting.

1908 was a difficult year for race relations in the United States, and the summer months were colored by events in Springfield, the state capital of Illinois. There on the evening of August 14, a white mob started a series of riots that would lead to attacks on black people, businesses, and homes throughout August and September. While initially focused on the crimes of two black prisoners, the mob's venom soon turned toward less obvious targets as successful middle-class black residents became the victims. One black woman who was a little girl in a middle-class family in 1908 recalled: "See, the people that they harmed, and hurt were not really the no-gooders. They were very busy hurting the prominent, and so, of course we were frightened. We owned property; many poor whites didn't. There was a great deal of animosity toward any well-established Negro who owned his house and had a good job."[11]

Lynchings, lootings and all the rest followed. While commentators hinted at rising levels of black crime as the cause of the unrest, the economic stability of the location, as well as the identity of the attackers' victims suggested otherwise. What was going wrong as Lincoln's promises started to fade was simple: As former slaves gained success and started to acquire wealth, certain whites lashed out, unable to contain their displeasure.

Was this the case in Portland? Had Lum and Crawford taken the lists out of a jealousy with roots as racial as they were romantic? What about down in Los Angeles…were things changing there in response to the more widespread reports of racial tension? Was Seymour moving away from his earlier vision of a racially inclusive response to God's sovereign power in an attempt to protect what was left of the mission? The formation of the NAACP in February 1909 was clearly a response to the palpable sense of tension, yet Seymour remained quiet on the matter. Unlike his admission that color was the reason for Parham's actions, word of his feelings about Lum and Crawford was never made public. Instead, only time would tell how Seymour felt.

One last point. Looking at the history of Crawford's Apostolic Faith Church up in Oregon, a small denomination that still exists today with fifty churches across America, there is no attempt made to hide the roots of the organization. Or, at least, Azusa Street is mentioned. As for stolen lists, there is a curious absence of information. As far as today's church goes, the Azusa Mission *became* the Apostolic Faith Church in Portland. Finally, the photos reveal more than any autobiography. From the early days it is clear that the members of Crawford's new congregation were almost exclusively white.[12]

Chapter 27
William Seymour Is Forced to the Edge

The Centrifuge

If 1906 had been the year of birth, 1907 the year of growth, and 1908 the year of betrayal, one could be forgiven for thinking that 1909 would offer little more than a direct route back to minimal activity and maximum obscurity. Yet it did not. What the following twelve months offered was the opportunity for the meetings to continue, for the faithful to gather at the mission, and for the Holy Spirit to continue to turn lives upside down in all His glorious power. Crippled, neutered, or simply hamstrung by the loss of the lists, the Azusa Mission continued, refusing to be beaten.

Arriving in Los Angeles in 1909 was one Reverend William Baxter Godbey. A prolific author, traveler, evangelist, scholar, and possessor of some notable eccentricities, Godbey was credited with being the holiness movement's foremost Greek scholar and Bible commentator. Circling the globe five times during his seven-decade period of ministry, it was inevitable that he should spend a little time in Los Angeles. His reactions, recorded by Alma White, give a clear picture of a city still fizzing with the excitement emanating from 312 Azusa Street:

> I found the city on tip toe, all electrified with the movement, the meetings running without intermission day and night. Messengers watched all the trains to receive the holiness people who arrived from every point of the compass at all hours, and escorted them at once to the… meeting."[1]

Azusa was far from over, as Godbey's sketch easily proves. But there is more to his testimony, too. His reactions after his arrival—having made his initial assessment of the continuing popularity of the mission—offer a deeper insight into one of the reasons for the mission's ability to sustain life in the face of betrayal. Holding back a little, Godbey chose not to join the masses as they flocked to the meetings. Instead, he remained away from the hub until a personal invite from Seymour drew him in. Seymour would have known Godbey from his time in Cincinnati where the scholar worked closely with Martin Wells Knapp—the influential ex-Methodist turned holiness man and newspaper guru. Godbey did not approve of the Pentecostal movement, that much was clear, yet he was asked to preach and was met by a large audience. The inevitable question of the hour came after the service: Did he speak in tongues? Godbey replied with trademark sarcasm, rolling out a little ancient Greek. The congregation did not appreciate Godbey's rather unique humor, nor did the visitor appreciate his audience.[2]

Godbey got his money's worth out of his experience at the mission, reveling in telling others of his low opinions of the gathered masses. Yet despite his reaction, it is important to note that not only did he acknowledge the meetings to still be thriving in 1909, but that William Seymour, the man whose fingers had been well and truly burnt by domineering white churchmen and women, still offered his pulpit to one of these textbook opponents of the mission. This, surely, is one of the answers to the great questions about the success of the Azusa Street revival. In William Seymour, God had not only a safe pair of hands—the kind that would not attempt to mold and sculpt according to his own personal agenda—but a gracious and humble soul. After everything he had gone through, after Hutchins and padlocks and Parham and psychics and Lum and great loss— William Seymour still opened up the pulpit to someone he *knew* was bound to challenge his authority. At best such a challenge from Godbey would take the form of gossip and backstabbing. At worst it could have led to a split within the mission as the congregation followed another Pied Piper out of the building. In the end Seymour only had to put up with Godbey's egocentric grandstanding from the pulpit as well as his slating of the entire revival to Alma White. Godbey's comments were fuel for her criticisms, with the man claiming that those to whom he had preached were, "Satan's preachers, jugglers, necromancers, enchanters, magicians, and all sorts of mendicants" with their roots in nothing more weighty than spiritualism.³ Whatever the outcome had been, Seymour's attitude remained on track, his small steps of humble service taking him toward a glorious destination.

There were other observers in 1909 who offer insight into the workings of the mission, men like Pastor George N. Eldridge.⁴ On paper he may have been like Parham and Godbey, but in practice Eldridge turned out to be altogether different. His Anglo-Saxon Methodist/holiness background was typical, but his sixty-three years of age may have given him a tendency to look long and hard before asking questions. Having moved to Pasadena in 1908 where he was West Coast leader of the Christian and Missionary Alliance, he was able to examine the mission as it staggered from the Lum crisis. Fifteen miles out, elevated above the city's chaos, the pastor drew his own conclusions, eventually joining the mission in 1910, his wife by his side:

> She was enabled to yield herself more fully than ever before, to praise and adore her Lord so wholeheartedly that the blessed spirit came upon her as he did upon the early disciples, and she, too, magnified the Lord Jesus in other tongues and was filled to overflowing.
>
> Later on, as I was communing with the Lord during the night watches, the Spirit spoke through me in other tongues. It was like the outflowing of water from my inmost being according to Jesus words in John 7:37, 38.⁵

Later Eldridge took his freshly delivered experience and established Bethel Temple, one of the city's leading Pentecostal congregations. Again, Seymour's strength of character and integrity had placed him in the potential firing line. This time, however, his generosity was not abused.

While Eldridge observed for two years before getting involved and supporting the work, Frank Bartleman's role within the Azusa Mission gently shifted over the years. Initially he was a source of encouragement to Seymour, a dynamo whose passion for saving souls saw him delivering tens of thousands of tracts and ably assisting in the representation of the events in the city to a curious media. In later years, however, he became a critic. First of all, Bartleman attacked the mission's decision to paint a sign on its front wall. By calling itself the "Apostolic Faith Mission" Bartleman felt that Seymour had allowed the movement to become self-centered. It may seem like a slight overreaction, and Bartleman's criticisms are not supported by an army of similar critiques, yet the preacher was convinced that the three words spelled the beginning of the end. "The truth must be told," he wrote. "Azusa began to fail the Lord also early in her history…sure enough, the very next day after I had spoken this warning in the meeting, I found a sign outside the building reading "Apostolic Faith Mission."…From that time the trouble and division began."[6] Vehemently opposed to the imposition of any form of structure on the Azusa Street revival, Bartleman's next step was a curious one—he set up a rival mission at 8th and Maple. This, he claimed, was to go "even deeper" than Azusa's blessing.

As well as his ideas on structure, Bartleman's opinions on the interracial aspect of the revival were also different to others. While Studd claimed that the majority of the congregation were black, Bartleman claimed them as mainly white.[7] Whatever the reasons though, Bartleman was right in one thing—he knew that "there can be no divisions in a true Pentecost."[8] Sadly, Bartleman's criticisms of Seymour and the mission increase in regularity as his memoirs progress. They read as if Seymour can do nothing right while Bartleman is left alone to walk the path to glory. He claims too that the meetings lost their sense of spontaneity. The next page, however, contains news that when he was fundraising for a global trip, the Azusa mission was the only group in the city to give him any financial support.⁹ He may not have given them much in the way of support since their sign went up, but the cash certainly helped.

In truth, Bartleman's opinion of the Azusa Mission was not always negative after the early days. In 1909 he attended a meeting at which "the Lord met me in great power," although this was clearly in his mind little more than a momentary blip.¹⁰ The seeds of division had been sown, and, in his mind at least, there could be little to change it.

Strangely the Azusa Mission had one more surprise in store for Frank Bartleman. He would, in turn, find himself back beneath its low ceiling and prostrate across its humble floors. He would claim that once more the fire was there, that the revival was in full flow again despite the errors he had noticed in the past. Ironically, at these times, Seymour would be many miles away. As Bartleman and others would once more crowd into the mission, it would not signify a renewed hope for the future. Instead, it would be proof that, finally, the glory days of the Azusa Mission were well and truly over.

Chapter 28
William Durham Wrestles for Control

Them and Us

When A. W. Frodsham—an Englishman abroad in Fort William, Ontario—visited Los Angeles sometime in late 1910 or early 1911, he wanted to visit a church. Once there he found crowds of hundreds of people, many having traveled great distances, soaking up the blessing as the power of the Holy Spirit caused gentle chaos to flood the building. But this was not Azusa Street. Instead, he had made his way to the Upper Room on Spring Street where George Studd and Elmer Fisher were enjoying a taste of the revival that had been hovering over the city for the previous five years. He enjoyed his time there too, but, out of curiosity, had a natural urge to extend his tour a little:

> Of course, we had to visit Azusa Street Mission, the place where the fire first fell....The mission has not been flourishing of late, but now there are signs of abundance of rain and many are being blessed. Colored and white folk worship freely together in this meeting place.[1]

At the time A. W. Frodsham was not the only person intent on making a trip down to what he called "a poor locality...and an old building."[2] Azusa Street still had a substantial reputation that drew the crowds in. Even though the revolving fortunes appeared to be a little less than predictable, with numbers sometimes being up, sometimes being down, at the start of 1911 there was enough energy about the place for its name to still count for something. Seymour, for example, was off around the country preaching and spreading the Word. It might have seemed like a good idea at the time—a chance to reconnect with some of the people and churches with whom contact had been lost since Lum's earlier departure—but it was not long before he was being called back to the mission as a matter of urgency.

William H. Durham was another man who felt the pull to Los Angeles. Like A. W. Frodsham, he headed first to the Upper Room when he arrived in the city. Later he followed in the Brit's footsteps and made his way to the Azusa Mission. However, Durham was after more than a postcard from "the place where the fire first fell." Durham wanted to take it over.

Like so many others in the story, Durham had Chicago connections. The former pastor at the North Avenue mission there first visited Los Angeles back in February 1907 when Mr. and Mrs. Louis Osterberg, former members of his congregation, sent the train fare to travel south and join with them as they marveled at the power of God. The trip did not disappoint, as Durham was powerfully affected by his experiences at the Azusa Mission, leaving with a passion for this new Pentecost and a cast-iron admiration for Seymour. Calling him "the leader of the movement of God," the feeling was, apparently, mutual—Seymour had also been impressed with the Chicago man, prophesying that he would become an apostle of the new movement.[3]

With the two leaders publicly proclaiming their confidence in each other, Durham headed back to Chicago and got on with the job of spreading the latter-day rain. Before long, his church, the North Avenue Mission, had become a hub for Pentecostal revival in both the Midwest and Canada.[4] With the loss of the lists in 1908, it was only a matter of time (specifically it only took until 1910) before Durham's own paper—*The Pentecostal Testimony*—became the international journal of choice for those interested in the global spread of the phenomenon. Along with the dissemination of information came great influence, as for the next decade the church became the effective center for Pentecostal training and theology. Besides both these great responsibilities, the man and his church were also responsible for the spread of Pentecostalism as far as Canada, Italy and South America. Without Durham the spiritual landscape of such places would be considerably different today.

But this is moving too far, too fast. Back in 1911, Chicago may have been the hub, but Los Angeles still had plenty of appeal, as the presence of the Godbeys, Frodshams, and Durhams all makes perfectly clear. Four years after his initial visit, Durham returned. This time the move was permanent, with the Chicago preacher accompanied by five workers and a fresh slab of theology he was determined to display and have others digest.

This controversial new doctrine went by the title "The Finished Work of Calvary."[5] While most Pentecostals with a holiness background believed in the three-staged approach—starting with salvation, moving on to sanctification, and then tongues as a sign of God's blessing—Durham took a different line. According to his new theology, sanctification took place at the moment of conversion, not at a later date. Sin would need to be dealt with continually, and the believer would gradually grow in stature, but, crucially, Durham saw no need for a second crisis, which was vital to Seymour and his fellow Pentecostals.[6]

Keen to raise the profile of his new theology, Durham went first to the Upper Room, the largest congregation in the city at the time. There he was refused permission to preach, leaving him to take the next logical step of heading down to Azusa Street.[7] Whether he expected to find Seymour there, or whether he knew he was away, we cannot be sure. However, Seymour's absence opened up an immediate opportunity that Durham could not resist taking.

Perhaps Durham felt as though he had no choice but to make an impact in Los Angeles. In fact, there is a hint that he had left Chicago under a cloud, or at least there is a suspicion that he could not go back. The first edition of *The Pentecostal Testimony* to go to press after his exit from the city made it perfectly clear that he had 'severed all connections' with the church.[8] Such information could explain why Durham's style at the mission was clearly quite aggressive, way beyond the limits of boisterous enthusiasm. Passionately he made it clear that, in his mind at least, the "Finished Work" was the defining issue of the day. Either you were in or you were out. Put simply, he said, "There is no other gospel."⁹

Durham was certainly aware of the potential conflict that would follow on from his message:

> The Finished Work is by far the most important teaching in the Bible. What could we expect but that the enemy would oppose with all his power.... [we] knew it would mean loss of friendship of all who did not see it, and who would still cling to the second work theory.¹⁰

Realizing that his message was bound to split the church, Durham made a gross error in how he presented it. As if he was intent of causing the maximum amount of damage, he essentially staged a coup at the Azusa Mission. Along with his five supporters, Durham refused to flinch in his pursuit of the prize. For ten weeks he took over the meetings at Azusa Street, refusing to step down or alter the message that conflicted so drastically with that on which much of the work had already been built.¹¹

Things went well for him too, as even by the very first Sunday meeting the mission was overfilled to the extent that some five hundred people had to be turned away. The Upper Room, on the other hand, suddenly found that it had more than enough space, as the exodus had followed Durham's shift.

Eventually the Azusa Mission trustees called Seymour back, who by then was in New York. Having been wired the money for the return journey, Seymour reentered the building, undoubtedly surprised by the sight of an all-white team stirring up controversy in his absence. He and Durham—the man who he had last seen at the mission declaring his loyalty and bathing in the power of the Holy Spirit—went to talk. Seymour asked him to stop preaching. Durham refused. Seymour asked him to alter his message. Durham refused. Then Durham made Seymour an offer—he would go back and preach the next day, a

Sunday morning, and ask the congregation to vote. Whether Seymour agreed or not is beside the point, as by now Durham not only held all the cards but was delighting in showing off a few power tricks at the same time. So, the two men duly went to church. Durham preached, introduced the vote, and later claimed that fewer than ten members went along with Seymour's three-stage theology.

There was surely only one way left to deal with such audacious behavior. Seymour gathered the trustees, sought, and gained permission from the majority to have the hijacker locked out. And so, on May 2nd, William Seymour found himself involved for the second time in the padlocking of a church.[12] This time, however, he held the keys. Yet despite being forced to take such drastic action, the process inflicted immediate wounds.

Not all the trustees agreed that locking Durham out was the best solution. Osterberg, for one, opposed the move and resigned in protest. Reflecting on the incident later on in life, Osterberg remembered it as an entirely racial issue—the black members of the congregation felt that they were being taken over. He said that "Seymour himself was very humble about it." Instead, it was Mrs. Seymour who "antagonized all the colored people. The colored folks believed in an inter-racial church as long as they had a Negro pastor."[13] For a generation whose parents and grandparents wore irons, whose scarred black flesh was the result of weapons held by white hands, surely this seems fair enough. In the absence of a white person championing the cause of equality, it was surely natural for those fighting oppression to look to their own for a leader. After all, the same formula worked well enough at the other end of the century as Nelson Mandela led his rainbow nation toward a new dawn. Was it so wrong of Jennie Seymour, proud of her African roots, to defend the cause of integration this way?

Sadly, the stance in defense of the black community coincided with a split straight down the color line. Frank Bartleman helped Durham move on to a new mission in the city, and while hundreds of predominantly white churchgoers joined, the cracks in Durham's leadership were there. Even Bartleman, whose enthusiasm had been high at first, claiming that Durham's arrival at Azusa had brought back the fire, soon tired of Durham's abrasive style. Durham took it as his "unpleasant duty" to launch a full-scale character assassination of Seymour through *The Pentecostal Testimony*, pointing out his "failures and blunders" and making clear his opinion that "the power of God had entirely left him."[14] In his defense, however, Bartleman called Durham's words "retaliation" to great provocation. Still, Bartleman's heart was clearly not in it, and he went on to call his rebuffs a "carnal controversy."[15]

With as many as one thousand turning up to Durham's meetings in Los Angeles, Azusa Mission was left "deserted."[16] Satisfied with his job, or simply hungry for more, Durham then made his way to Portland, Oregon. Asked for permission to preach from her pulpit, Crawford refused. The argument was far from over, as Durham resorted to his usual strong-arm tactics, threatening to "take all her members away from her." Florence Crawford stood firm. After all, she was getting used to refusing requests from male preachers who had traveled up from Los Angeles. "You are welcome to every member you can get," was her reply.[17] The battle lost before it even began, Durham promptly left, heading back to Chicago.

Rapidly he got ill, and left the city again, this time leaving for the warmth of California on July 2, 1912. Arriving back in Los Angeles on July 5, by mid-morning on the 7th he was dead. Pulmonary tuberculosis had carried him off, but not without warning. Six months earlier Charles Parham had ploughed into the Durham controversy, praying that God alone would settle the issue of the Finished Work by taking the life of whichever teacher had got it wrong. Of course, any satisfaction for Parham would be relatively short-lived—the three-stage approach would never last. Instead, it was Durham's concept of the power of the cross that would become the default setting for the modern Pentecostal movement.

Chapter 29
The Splits Start to Split

A View from the Crowd

While the local churches fought among themselves in Los Angeles, and starker divisions established themselves across the country, the Pentecostal movement was continuing to have a significant influence worldwide. This move of God had always had an international feel to it, with early believers packing up and moving on across the continents. Even before everything happened in Los Angeles, events across the Atlantic caused a stir that created a unique link between the United Kingdom and the United States. The Welsh Revival, which started in 1904, resulted in thirty thousand conversions, twenty thousand new church members, and a mass of anticipation on the Californian coast.[1] Back in Wales, Joseph Smale had met Evan Roberts and returned to tell the Angelenos of the massive potential available to them.[2] With Bartleman signing up for the excitement prior to Seymour's arrival in the city, people were already talking of an imminent global revival. The first drops of the latter-day rains were surely about to fall.

Later on, things would spread, with the Pentecostal message that found so loud a voice and so clear a form at the Apostolic Faith Mission igniting all over Europe, in South Africa, and Russia. There, in the early days of the Soviet Union, the work of Ivan Efimovich Voronaev offered lasting transformation. For Voronaev it all started on receipt of a prophecy from the lips of Pentecostals in Manhattan. Baptized in the Holy Spirit and ready to return to his native land, the former Baptist preacher faced trial and difficulty as he worked across the region. Fewer than twenty years later he had founded the first Russian Pentecostal movement with more than three hundred and fifty churches across the Slavic territory. Yet communist sympathies were not with him, and after numerous arrests he met with inevitable imprisonment in one of the infamous Gulags. In 1943 Voronaev attempted escape, was shot, and his body ripped apart by dogs—a martyr, a founder and a Pentecostal to the last.³

Korea was also impacted by the Azusa Mission, with Mary Rumsey having soaked up the experiences at Azusa Street in 1907. When she eventually arrived in Korea in 1928, she had to work under the restrictions of Japanese occupation, accompanied by a trademark lack of religious tolerance. What started as quiet, charismatic meetings within a local Methodist hospital became, a decade later, a handful of Pentecostal congregations. Handing over her work to the Assemblies of God in 1952, the first project of the new Korean church was the opening of a Bible school. In that first class was one Paul Yonggi Cho, converted from Buddhism and on the way to establishing the world's largest Christian congregation.⁴

The story of Nigeria's largest church also has roots in the Azusa story, with Florence Crawford's Apostolic Faith Church providing the missionaries who introduced future leaders to the Christian life.⁵ Such a crossing of international borders is a key theme in the Azusa Mission's influence over the years, as is the growth of positive change out of the soil of Azusa's earlier troubles. Crawford's influence was capable of causing great pain as well as fulfilling great potential. Similarly, the formation of the Assemblies of God movement signaled the end of the interracial aspect of the Pentecostal movement. Its birth in 1914 was marked by a deliberate move by white churchmen loosely linked to Mason's Church of God in Christ to form their own group. Theology was used to draw the dividing lines, and despite the presence of Mason as a guest speaker at the inaugural meeting, there were few doubts about the future. Church of God in Christ served the black population, while the Assemblies of God served the white.⁶ Yet both, of course, enjoyed massive growth, with the latter becoming the largest Pentecostal denomination in the world today.

*

Back in August 1912, William Seymour was again traveling in the east of the country. It had become customary for him to be away for long periods of time, spending several weeks at centers for ministry ranging from Indianapolis, Chicago, and Cincinnati to New York, Washington, Baltimore, and Houston.

Just like before, his absence coincided with the arrival at the mission of a white male, a pastor who was drawn to the history represented by the squat building's name. Yet unlike Durham, Englishman A. A. Boddy's idea of receiving a blessing at the Azusa Mission did not include walking off with the majority of the congregation.

Boddy was an Anglican vicar from Sunderland, England's mirror image of Cleveland. He was also a keen follower of revivals and was clearly intrigued by the rapid growth of the worldwide Pentecostal movement. Like so many others, Boddy saw the pilgrimage to Azusa Street as an essential part of his trip to California, and on arrival he found Jennie Seymour and another worker willing to talk.[7]

The Durham controversy may have ceased ripping the Azusa Mission apart in 1912, but it remained a local and national issue that few involved in the Pentecostal movement could ignore. Yet any wariness of the visitor was clearly quickly overcome as Boddy's reaction told of his genuine respect for the place:

> It was good to look into the bright, dark face of this intelligent negro sister....We descended at length into the large lower room, now with a boarded floor and nicely furnished (out of debt by the kindness of a visitor whom, they will not soon forget). We knelt, three of us, in prayer near the altar, in that place where so many had received their blessing. Two colored friends and a white brother from Sunderland praying together in Azusa Street Mission!"[8]

His exit was accompanied by a promise that he would, if time allowed, return the following week to preach. It ended up being a

Thursday evening. His description in the November 1912 edition of the newspaper *Confidence* paints a picture of a congregation of mixed race, by no means deserted as Frank Bartleman suggested, but "though the regular gatherings are not what they were, yet "Azusa Street" is a sort of "Mecca" still to Pentecostal travelers."[9]

Jennie Seymour welcomed Boddy and turned the meeting over to him. He preached, cast a demon out of a drunk, and left feeling encouraged by the faith on display.[10] Like most white English people, he had a soft spot for the passionate singing, strangely alien to the Anglican tongue. It is a fond picture that he paints, one of warmth in which "it seemed like meeting old acquaintances as one looked into their faces and heard how they valued our paper, and I received a warm embrace from one brother."[11]

Boddy's arrival in the city ended up being more than a quick round of spiritual tourism as the preacher began to wonder whether he might be needed there. It did not take a genius to perceive the problems within the church throughout Los Angeles, and Boddy was clear that he had a task ahead of him. Throughout his time in the city, he banged the drum for unity among believers, drawing together those who had been split by the Durham legacy—like the previously inseparable Studd and Fisher whose work at the Upper Room mission had been gathering real pace prior to Durham's arrival. The two were now divided, a bitter taste left in the mouth. Wherever Boddy preached he urged others to soak up a "Baptism of Love"[12]:

> I pleaded with them also to bear when spoken against, to be silent and not to answer back again, and to pray for the other side lovingly, whichever side they belonged to. [13]

His efforts to join the "Finished Work" brigade with those of the "Second Grace" persuasion ultimately failed. There was division right through the movement, and it was seemingly impossible to heal. In both Los Angeles and Chicago, the split was wide, a gaping, open sore that bled hurt and bitter resentment. As another observer noted, "Perhaps the very zeal that consumes some hearts along certain lines hinders them from seeing and recognizing the perfect law and liberty of Christ....Whatever doctrine they may hold there are vital things lacking in the hearts of many dear Pentecostal people...we must cease foolish striving about words (and, I might add, works)."[14]

There was no doubt about the cause of the problems. It was said that Durham "created an issue all over the country....The result was that division occurred in many of the newly formed Pentecostal Assemblies....The issue was a hot one all over the country."[15]

Yet the momentum was with Durham's followers, and they showed no sign of backing down. In 1913 they announced plans for a worldwide camp meeting at Los Angeles. The venue was the old Arroyo Seco where the first Pentecostal mass gathering had taken place in 1907. This time, Studd and R. J. Scott were in charge. The results were a perfect microcosm of the troubles that afflicted the Pentecostal movement at the time.

Studd and Scott gave headline billing to Mrs. Mary B. Woodworth-Etter, a sixty-eight-year-old with a reputation for a healing ministry and international stripes earned as an evangelist. With a thousand people turning up and the program running from April 15th to June 1st—two weeks longer than planned, it was, on paper, a true success, particularly as Woodworth-Etter claimed it was "no doubt the largest gathering of baptized saints in the last days."[16]

However, it was also a chance for certain members of the Pentecostal movement to fight among themselves for scraps of power. Like a particularly fractious children's pageant, as many as two hundred ministers would crowd onto the platform at any one time, hungry for the limelight.[17] Much like Boddy, Woodworth- Etter was keen to promote unity, but the other leaders had different thoughts. Some of them saw the meetings as representative only of those who had signed up for Durham's sanctification theology. Clergy rebelled, got huffy about the amount of healings, and grumbled for more theological debate.

And where was William Seymour in all of this? He was there all right, but remained just one of the crowd, since nobody invited him to the platform or asked him to be involved in any way.[18]

The message to Seymour was clear, and he could do little more than observe as the splits and schisms arose with alarming regularity. The Durham group itself started to divide over the issue of how important it was for water baptisms to be carried out in Jesus' name. Others felt that the Trinity should have great emphasis, rather than being separated so. Within three years, the issue had become so contentious that it had taken a third of the people away, a third who, incidentally, happened to be the majority of the black members. What started in 1906 as an interracial pursuit of power and holy living had quickly become a segregated selection of in- fighting and backstabbing. As Boddy noted, the country's racial divisions were "increasingly acute" due to the fact that "the whites are determined to keep their position as a dominant race."[19]

So, there it was. Divided. Segregated. It all may have appeared to be about the theology, but there was an air of sorry inevitability about the groups that ended up being formed. Each group tended to share the same skin tone, the same social values, and same social backgrounds. Inclusion, so it seems, had had its day.

Chapter 30
William Seymour Considers the Future

A Man of Color

The Apostolic Faith Mission was not the only church to experience racial tension at the time. Back in Indianapolis the Evening Light Saints—the group that had first offered Seymour his credentials as a minister of God—were waking up to the fact that "a radical change came over the movement." According to Massey, the black theologian of the movement, by 1916 "the segregation system had become openly advised and displayed even in the North....The case for interracial fellowship in its full manifestation...seemed hopeless."[1]

Sadly, predictably, it was not only the church that saw division. Away from the missions and the assemblies and the churches and the tent meetings there were clear indications that the heat was most certainly on the rise again. Lynchings were becoming increasingly popular, and for those unfortunate enough to be the wrong face in the wrong place at the wrong time, stabbings, clubbings, floggings, and brandings with acid were par for the course.[2]

As Europe descended into its own race wars in 1914, Hollywood set up the projectors for screenings of *Birth of a Nation*. Based on Thomas Dixon's 1905 anti-black, bigoted play *The Clansman*, the film made no attempt to disguise its racist retelling of life in the South during reconstruction. It played to big crowds too, including a special showing in the White House, and turned out to be the most profitable film for two decades.[3] It would take a white maiden and her seven stunted friends to beat the white supremacist at the box office.

Meanwhile, returning from Europe, black soldiers were routinely abused, beaten, and even murdered, all in the name of keeping them aware of their true place. America was well and truly divided.

All the hatred, the violence, the burnings, and abuse came to a head in 1915 when the so-called Red Summer introduced "the greatest period of interracial strife the nation has ever witnessed."[4] Chicago experienced the death of fifteen white and twenty-three black people, plus the burning of the homes of a thousand mainly black residents. Why? All because a young black boy swam into a part of Lake Michigan reserved for white swimmers. He paid for his mistake with his life.

Then there was the Ku Klux Klan, reviving itself in 1915 and gaining one hundred thousand members within twelve months. Its popularity increased dramatically, as within a decade there were four million members across the country.[5] Tolerated by the powers that could have made a difference, blind eyes were the order of the day.

And in the midst of all this public strife and hatred, one has to ask what the church was doing. Instead of picking up the baton of Wesley, Wilberforce, Lincoln, and other men of God who fought for reform, the collective of believers found themselves possessed by a new obsession. Churches for once found a cause over which they could unite—Prohibition. Due in part to constant lobbying from church-backed groups, 1919's contribution to social justice from the bride of Christ saw a nationwide ban on alcohol, enshrined in the 18th amendment. Black citizens, meanwhile, seemed to have lost the power of the 13th and 14th amendments.

Seymour's response amidst the chaos was predictable. He remained on course, refusing to follow anything other than his original plan of uniting races in pursuit of a deeper, more powerful relationship with God. Back at Azusa Street the crowds may have gone, turned away in part by rhetoric that had become increasingly ugly over the years, but William Seymour refused to shift from his position.

While determination and integrity were in abundance, resources, however, were limited. Durham had escorted two-thirds of Seymour's staff off the premises, and the 24/7 gatherings were by now a thing of the past. Meetings were generally limited to all-day affairs on Sundays, despite Seymour's attempts to get things up and running through mid-week services.[6] The interest just wasn't there, a fact that still seems strange today. After all, this was the man to whom tens of thousands listened just a decade earlier, one whose Apostolic Faith Mission was a prize worth stealing. Now, with just twenty or so members—most of them women, most of them black, most of them from the original days back on Bonnie Brae Street— church became an often unremarkable affair. Occasional all-night prayer meetings were held in various homes, but the joy only really kicked in when old faces from earlier times showed up.

Of course, just as much of an issue as enthusiasm or motivation was the lack of money available. This was a dramatic change for the group who previously were able to raise the required cash for the purchase of the building two years ahead of schedule. Now, when required, Jennie Seymour would take her culinary skills out to work in an effort to support the couple. As the glory days became a distant memory, Seymour was forced to ask for offerings, rather than let people "settle with the Lord" of their own accord. At times the collection would barely reach seventy-five cents. Looking down at the coins, Seymour would have to ask for a second offering to be taken, saying, "Expenses, please, at least."[7]

Despite the warning signs that the life of the mission was in poor condition, Seymour was determined to continue work with its future in mind. In May 1914 he took a bold step in securing that future. While racial tension increased, and the church fought about doctrine but remained quiet about social injustice, he revised the mission's constitution, making two key changes:

> The Apostolic Faith Mission shall be carried on in the interest of and for the benefit of the colored people of the state of California, but the people of all countries, climes, and nations shall be welcome.[8]

The legal wording reinforced the reality that had been in play ever since the Bonnie Brae days—this was a collection of predominantly black believers, but one which was open to all. Hutchins and her original group had been all black, the Bonnie Brae meetings were the same, and ever since the core had welcomed those who were different to join in as they chased after God together.

Second, the revisions made it clear that the mission should be run by a Bishop, Vice Bishop, and trustees, all of whom were to be "people of color." A controversial move? Considering the past and the present, Seymour's move was surely sensible. In fact it proved to be absolutely essential in later years.

A year later, writing his Doctrines and Discipline of the Azusa Street Apostolic Faith Mission, Seymour expanded his vision:

> Our colored brethren must love our white brethren and respect them in truth so that the word of God can have its free course, and our white brethren must love their colored brethren and respect them in the truth so that the Holy Spirit won't be grieved. I hope we won't have any more trouble and division spirit.[9]

> W. J. SEYMOUR

There really is no room for painting Seymour as a defensive, anti-white reactionary. If anything, he was guilty of being overly optimistic, of being too trusting of those who were, as Boddy had rightly said, "…determined to keep their position as the dominant race."[10] Seymour never gave up on unity, and merely acted in this way to protect his own flock from those who threatened to abuse privilege for their own purposes. Seymour's actions in 1917 or 1918 proved both his desires and his misplaced optimism—he set up one last attempt at restoring the damage that had been inflicted on the churches throughout Los Angeles over the years. Calling a meeting of all the leaders in the city, he hoped to restore Pentecostal unity. Only two leaders showed up. Wounded and hurt by the rejection, Seymour was reaching the end of his resources. Finally, he was feeling the strain of a too-long journey over too-hard ground. Confiding in those closest to him, he allowed himself a rare moment where his true feelings made their way to the surface. He talked about the failure of the local leaders to follow his rallying cry and finally admitted that he had done all he could to help the movement.[11]

But Seymour could not let that be the end of the story. The message meant too much to leave it alone. He wanted to do more, and in 1920 held the "14th Anniversary of the Out-pouring of the Holy Spirit in Los Angeles."[12] Drawing on spirituals and more, the meeting focused on repentance, conversion, sanctification, and baptism in the Holy Spirit. The fact that there is little or no information about it available today is a clear sign—the time had gone. Success as measured by public support was now a stranger.

Again, he refused to end it there. Seymour continued with one last missionary trip, this time to Columbus, Ohio. In what may well have been a bittersweet case of symmetry, the well-attended meetings brought back some familiar sights as black and white met together, united in worship. As one observer noted, Seymour thrived on it:

> The glow would be on that man's face. He looked like an angel from heaven. So many wanted to hear him, they had heard of him. Brother Seymour did not want the offering. Sometimes they made him take it. He was no man to exalt himself, but a humble man.
>
> He did not believe in a lot of emotion. One lady stood up and started shouting, going around touching others. He looked at her and said, "Will you please sit down? It's the flesh, you can tell it right away." She sat down too.
>
> Brother Seymour believed in true emotion. He had good discernment. You could look at his face and if what was going on was real or not. He only had one eye—you could hardly tell it— but he saw a lot with that one.[13]

Years later, in 1922 this time, there was another convention of the great and the good in Los Angeles, organized by those who saw the Azusa Mission as, at best, an aging curiosity that they would rather leave alone. As before, Seymour attended, yet again he had not officially been asked to take part but found a seat in the congregation, nevertheless. Again, he sat, this time looking more tired than before. Again, he returned home, unacknowledged from the platform. There could be little more left to do. There was nothing left to give.

Chapter 31
The Story Ends and Repeats

Coffins and Padlocks

September 28, 1922. A man runs through the Thursday morning crowds that punctuate the downtown streets, making his way to South Spring Street and the offices of Dr. Walter M. Boyd. The doctor is needed, urgently. Rushing back to the fifty-two-year-old patient, the doctor hears snatches of the story: the sudden attack, the severe pain, the ailing heart.

After examining the patient, Boyd left him resting. Later that same day, at 5 PM, the patient was awake, sitting up, dictating a letter. He had spent the previous hours with his wife, singing, praying, praising God, and planning the work which they, or rather she, would carry out in the coming months. He made a plea "for love among the brethren everywhere."[1] Then the pain returned—this time with more force; this time with less warning. Breath escaped, unable to be clawed back. The last words were held on the faintest breeze that hovered between the walls of the Azusa Street mission: "I love my Jesus so."[2] William Seymour was dead.

*

On October 2, 1922, a crowd of two hundred people, mainly black, gathered to watch the redwood casket as it was lowered into plot number 3332 in the city's Evergreen Cemetery.[3] There were many stories to be told by people whose lives had been affected by this humble, gracious, and truly godly man. Eventually his widow arose, and the ceremony was finished.

At the end of the month, someone, somewhere had decided that a redwood casket simply would not do for the man whose life had impacted so many. The coffin was dug up, replaced with a concrete vault and a granite headstone bearing the simplest message:

> Our Pastor
> Rev. William J Seymour
> May 2, 1870 -Sep. 28, 1922

Jennie Seymour carried on as leader of the Apostolic Faith Mission, although without the title *Bishop*. Perhaps she knew the end was closing in; perhaps she simply preferred to lower her profile. Either way, she remained there, holding meetings and carrying on the traditions carved out of an unwilling culture by her husband.

For eight years the life of the mission continued, without problem. It was, in a way, the longest period without controversy that the place had ever experienced. For the forty or so members— some of whom were white, some of whom were black—there was little that changed during the time.[4]

At least, that was how things were until 1930. One day, while leading midday prayers, Jennie Seymour's eyes lifted to the door. There she saw a white stranger asking to join them. He was welcomed, of course, and his eloquence and enthusiasm raised the interest of those attending considerably. At the close of the meeting people circled him, probed him with questions, and asked him to return. He was, he said, R. C. Griffith, a Coptic priest and bishop, and, yes, he would be delighted to return. His Orthodox background, his sense of mystery, his prayers, all marked him out as something remarkable.[5]

Every day he visited, melding with the members, becoming part of the very fabric of the building. Months passed, and then it happened—the inevitable, the familiar, the dreaded conflict. Announcing to Mrs. Seymour that he had discussed it with the members of the church, Griffith proclaimed that the Apostolic Faith Mission was now his church. Since, he claimed, that most of the people preferred him, she was out.

In a way he was right. While some of the older members from the Bonnie Brae days stayed loyal to Jennie Seymour and the legacy of her husband, some of the more recent members were swayed by the visitor's fine words and purposeful approach. Sadly, they happened to be the white members, too.[6] Griffith made such a fuss, pursued his claim so vigorously, that the matter of who owned the mission went to court. Under orders to place an enforced pause on the dispute until the courts had a chance to resolve it, the Los Angeles Police Department took action on January 16, 1931. For the third time in the story the padlocks came out.

Finally, the judge threw the petition out and found in favor of Jennie Seymour. If it had not been for her husband's foresight in tightening up the constitution, her defense would have been significantly weaker. Yet the victory was not the yellow brick road that some may have hoped for. It demanded a high price, and legal expenses were extensive. The trustees of the Apostolic Faith Mission were forced to borrow $2,000 from Jennie Seymour, who had taken out a six-year mortgage on the building in the final days of 1930.[7] With just twenty-seven members remaining, outnumbered by too many debts, the local authorities were now fully aware of the tenuous grasp that the mission had on life. The passing of days and weeks counted out the final heartbeats of the mission.

Soon after the case was over, the city launched proceedings to have the building condemned as an alleged fire hazard. There was little chance of defending the building that shared its birth year with her dead husband. Later in 1931 the wooden structure was torn down. In its final hours, Frank Bartleman returned, drawn by loyalty or nostalgia, and took down the numbers "312" from the building and returned them to his home, where they remained on display. It is alleged that the Assemblies of God were offered the building, but they refused. They were uninterested in "relics."[8] Years later that would change, but as the timbers were torn down and the building turned to dust, most believed that the memories of the Apostolic Faith Mission would not be far behind. Obscurity seemed like the building's only lasting legacy.

Jennie Seymour may have displayed considerable self-assurance at earlier points in her life, but by now there was little more that could be done. Along with the Asberrys and a handful of others, she returned the meetings to Bonnie Brae, but these lost ones could do nothing to avoid the inescapable outcome. In fact, the moment had already gone, the mission was over. All that was left were the remaining twitches of life as the air escaped.

The vacant lot that held the ground where so many thousands had worshiped remained in the possession of the trustees, but as the Great Depression settled across the country, there was no chance of paying the interest on the mortgage or annual city taxes. By March 30, 1933, it was all too much. Jennie Seymour was forced to hand over the mortgage on the invisible Apostolic Faith Mission as well as on her own property to the Security-First National Bank.[9]

What followed was worse. Her health deteriorated, and by 1935 there was no chance of her being able to look after herself, let alone lead services. At the end of the year the bank moved to sell her home, and two weeks later began foreclosure proceedings on the Azusa Street property. The faithful—Jennie and the trustees led by Richard Asberry—fought with all they had. It could never be enough. On February 3, 1936, Jennie Seymour was admitted to Ranchos Los Amigos, an oddly jolly title for the place in which she, like so many others, would eventually die. The county hospital for the terminally ill took care of her until July 2nd, when at age sixty-two she died. The heart of the widow, like that of her husband, was unable to keep going. Her body made its way to lie, unmarked, beside the man with whom she had served.[10]

Just three weeks before she died, Jennie Seymour had heard that a judge had ruled in favor of the mission, allowing them to retain ownership. However, two years later on June 10, 1938, the bank finally won, taking possession of the lot. Later the property passed to the city, under whose ownership it remained as a car parking lot for some time.[11] Today it is Little Tokyo. Tomorrow it could be something different altogether.

*

The speed of history outpaces most rivals with ease. The story of the Azusa Street revival slotted in its place, its influence spreading in two different directions. First was the theological. As the visible birth of Pentecostalism, Azusa's influence has been immense and virtually immeasurable. In many countries today the charismatic tradition, which is so securely rooted in the events of 1906 to 1909, is the sole area in which significant church growth can be seen. It has renewed the church, and breathed life into a body less vibrant than it would like to admit.

With estimates at worldwide Pentecostal membership ranging from 115 million to 400 million, and growth at 19 million per year, it is clear that Azusa's influence remains.[12] Preaching conversion, baptism in the power of the Holy Spirit, and dedicated pursuit of a lifestyle marked by devotion and integrity, Seymour's core beliefs are shared with an estimated eleven thousand Pentecostal or charismatic denominations worldwide.[13]

The other path down which the influence of the Azusa Street mission moved has been less well traveled. What separated Seymour from Parham, and what continues to give the former the edge in the awarding of the title of *Father of Pentecostalism* (a title that Seymour would, of course, have hated), is race. Parham's generosity of spirit extended to a chair in the hallway. Seymour's determined pursuit of racial integration left the platform open to all. Against a backdrop of increasing racial tension, with slavery feeling close behind, and the Civil Rights movement appearing too far off in the distance, the Azusa Street meetings were truly remarkable. Within years the movement had split along racial lines, remaining largely so to this day.

In a century marked by bigotry and racial oppression, Seymour's integrated mission was yet another victim. Seymour's death came while he pastored an integrated church, one with fewer members than an average classroom. Today's colossal membership of the Pentecostal movement marks its greatest success. The limits to its racial integration mark our greatest failing.

When did things on Azusa Street end? Was it with the death of Jennie Seymour or the lashings of the wrecking ball? Was it the Coptic priest and police padlocks, or perhaps the last breath of the man whose life had come so far from his first steps in Louisiana? Was it the snub from the platform as the great and the good decided to fight things out among themselves, or was it Durham's unleashing of controversy and his ten-week hostile takeover? Could Lum and the lists carry the blame for ending it all, or maybe it is Parham's vitriol that brought down the pillars?

Then there is the question of when it all started. Was it with the Mexican builders and the African American cleaners? Or was it Jennie Evans Moore and the spontaneous melodies? Was it Edward Lee or Agnes Ozman who started it all, or do the roots go back further within the city of Angels to the faithful prayers of those hungry for a sign from heaven?

The answer to both questions is simple: The Azusa Street revival neither started nor finished with William Seymour. It belonged, of course, to a greater power, scripted by a larger hand, seen within a wider context. The prayers of saints join across the generations, making it as impossible as it is inadvisable to attribute glory to any one man or group of people.

Yet William Seymour's story deserves to be told. Reflecting on the frailty of life and the passing into death, William Seymour found comfort in the Psalms:

> I will keep my mouth with a bridle, while the wicked is before me.
> I was dumb with silence, I held my peace, even from good; and my

sorrow was stirred. My heart was hot within me, while I was musing the fire burned: Then spake I with my tongue, LORD, make me to know mine end, and the measure of my days, what it is; that I may know how frail I am.

—PSALM 39:1–4, KJV

The words could so easily have been written by Seymour himself. Holding his tongue, refusing to join with those who descended into abuse of others, William Seymour maintained his dignity and integrity in equal measure. The sorrow, the pain, the fire that burned—he knew them all. And after the oppression and the betrayal and the struggles came the question of God, the willingness to serve no matter what the cost. For William Seymour, the glorious and ultimate destiny was to be reached after death, not before. The sparkling trappings of power held little appeal for him. Similarly, the abuses against him were no indication of personal failure. The journey of William Seymour was made up of a multitude of small steps—obedience, sacrifice, forgiveness, devotion. At the ride's end, there were no material jewels, little in the way of public recognition, but the ultimate prize of all—the smile of God.

Notes

Chapter 1: William Seymour Gains His Vision
1. John Pitcairn, "The Fallacy of Vaccination," From Both Sides of the Vaccination Question, The Anti-Vaccination League of America, Philadelphia, 1911, as viewed at http://www.alternativehealth.co.nz/vacines/fallacie.htm on September 1, 2005.

2. David A. Koplow, Smallpox: The Fight to Eradicate a Global Scourge (University of California, 2003), chapter 1, accessed via www.ucpress.edu/books/pages/9968/9968.ch01.html.

3. Ibid.

4. Ibid.

5. Douglas Nelson, "For Such a Time as This: The Story of Bishop William J. Seymour and the Azusa Street Revival," unpublished Ph.D. dissertation (Birmingham, UK: University of Birmingham, UK, 1981).

6. Ibid., 158.

Chapter 2: The State of Louisiana is Formed and Raised
1. "Louisiana History, State of Louisiana Official Website, http://www.doa.louisiana.gov/about_history2.htm, as viewed September 1, 2005.

2. "The French Empire in North America: From Canada to Louisiana, a Shared History," The Historic New Orleans Collection Quarterly, Vol. XIX, Num. 4, Fall 2001, as viewed at http://www.hnoc.org/HNOC_Q4_01.pdf, on September 1, 2005.

3. Interview with Fielding Lewis, May 1, 2005.

4. Joseph Holt Ingraham, The Southwest, by a Yankee, 2 vols., 1835 (Ann Arbor, MI: reprint 1966), accessed via www.education.nsula.edu/ historicaldemo/historical%20site%20educators/plantation_back_2.htm.

5. "Explore Louisiana," Louisiana, Work, Live, Play, as viewed at http://www.crt.state.la.us/ crt/ocd/hp/STUDYUNIT/hpsuplif.htm,on September 1, 2005.

6. Alcee Fortier, Louisiana Studies (New Orleans: F. F. Hartsell & Bro., 1894), 126, 129, 175, 267, 300, accessed via www.loyno.edu/history/journal/1985-6/doherty.htm.

7. Ibid.

Chapter 3: Seymour's Life Begins
1. "Toward Racial Equality," Harper's Weekly Reports on Black America 1857–1874, Humor Item, March 13, 1858, 175, as viewed at http://www.blackhistory.harpweek.com/2Slavery/SlaveryLevelOne.htm on September 6, 2005.

2. Larry Martin, *The Life and Ministry of William J. Seymour*, (Joplin, MO: Christian Life Books, 1999), 34.

3. Ibid.

4. "Instrument of Torture Used by Slave-holders," Harper's Weekly Reports on Black Slavery 1857–1874, as viewed at blackhistory.harpweek.com/2Slavery/SlaveryLevelOne.htm on September 6, 2005.

5. "Secession Crisis: Nat Turner, 'the Prophet,' The War for States Rights, as viewed at http://civilwar.bluegrass.net/secessioncrisis/natturner.html on September 6, 2005. See also Africans in America, accessed via www.pbs.org/wgbh/

aia/part3/3p1518.html.

6. "John Brown (1800–1859)," Civil War Biographies, as viewed at http://www.civilwarhome.com/johnbrownbio.htm on September 6, 2005.

7. Ibid.

8. Africans in America, accessed via www.pbs.org/wgbh/aia/part3/3p1518.html

9. "Cost of the American Civil War," Civil War Potpourri, as viewed at http://www.civilwarhome.com/ warcosts.htm on September 6, 2005. See also Shotgun's Home of the American Civil War, accessed via www.civilwarhome.com/warcosts.htm.

10. Ibid.

11. John A Garraty, *The American Nation: A History of the United States Since 1865* (New York: Addison Wesley Publishing Company, 1983).

12. Joe Gray Taylor, *Louisiana Reconstructed: 1863-1877* (Baton Rouge: Louisiana State University Press, 1974).

13. Martin, *The Life and Ministry of William J. Seymour*, 36; see also Rebecca Brooks Gruver, An American History, Vol. 1: to 1877 (Reading, MA, Random House, 1981).

14. Martin, *The Life and Ministry of William J. Seymour*, 36.

15. University of Louisiana, Center for Louisiana Studies, accessed via www.louisiana.edu/Academic/LiberalArts/CLS/Teacher_Resources_Pages/health_in_st_mary.htm.

16. Ibid.

17. Samuel H. Lockett, Louisiana *As It Is: A Geographical and Topographical Description of the State* (Baton Rouge, LA: Louisiana State University Press, 1969).

18. Ibid.

19. Peyton McCary, *Abraham Lincoln and Reconstruction* (Princeton: Princeton University Press, 1979).

20. "The Freedman's Bureau," Harper's Weekly Reports on Black America 1857–1874, July 25, 1868, 467, as viewed at http://blackhistory.harpweek.com/4Reconstruction/467TheFreedmensBurea u.htm on September 6, 2005.

21. "The Ku Klux Klan Hearings," Harpers Weekly Reports on Black America 1857–1874, August 22, 1868, 531.

22. Ibid.

23. The African American Registry, accessed via www.aaregistry.com/african_american_history/1871/Hiram_Revels_pioneered_southern_Black_politics.

24. Ibid.

25. Martin, The Life and Ministry of William J. Seymour, 50; see also www.itd.nps.gov/cwss/ Personz_Detail.cfm?PER_NBR=152186.

26. Ibid.

27. Ibid.

28. Ibid.

29. Timothy Hebert, "Methodism Along the Bayou," as viewed at http://www.iscuo.org/hist4.htm on September 6, 2005.

30. Martin, *The Life and Ministry of William J. Seymour*, .53; see also Planter's Banner, December 28, 1867.

31. Ibid.

32. Ibid.

33. American Experience, accessed via www.pbs.org/wgbh/amex/grant/peopleevents/e_colfax.html.
34. Ibid.
35. "A History of Grant Parish," *The Town Talk*, Monday, May 9, 2005, as viewed at http://www.thetowntalk.com/apps/pbcs.dll/article?AID=/20050509/COMM UNITIES/50228009/1079 on September 7, 2005; see also Martin, *The Life and Ministry of William J. Seymour*, 40; and "The Louisiana Murders', *Harper's Weekly*, 10 May 1873.

Chapter 4: William Seymour Learns His Lessons

1. This story is told by Bernard Broussard in A History of St Mary Parish (1955).
2. Ibid.
3. Interview with Fielding Lewis, May 1, 2005.
4. Broussard A History of St. Mary Parish (1955), 70; see also Benjamin La Bree, The Confederate Soldier in the Civil War, 1861–1865 (New Jersey: Prentice Press, 1897).

The Confederate Soldier in the Civil War, 1861–1865 (New Jersey: Prentice Press, 1897), 67.

5. Ibid., 142.
6. Broussard A History of St Mary Parish (1955), 72.
7. Ibid., 31.
8. Ibid., 70.
9. Ibid., 71.
10. Ibid., 72.
11. Ibid.
12. Ibid., 73.
13. Martin, *The Life and Ministry of William J. Seymour*, 55.
14. Charles William Shumway, A Critical Study of 'the Gift of Tongues, dissertation for University of Southern California, 1914.
15. Broussard *A History of St Mary Parish*, 76–81.
16. Ibid., 21; see also Jewell Lynn Delaune, "A Social History of St Mary Parish, 1845–1860", *Louisiana Historical Quarterly*, (1948), 62.
17. Broussard A History of St Mary Parish, 25.
18. Ibid.
19. Planter's Banner (Franklin, Louisiana), Saturday 24 March 1900
20. Nelson, "For Such a Time as This,"158; see also Donald G. Matthews and Martin E. Marty, *Religion in the Old South*, (Chicago: University of Chicago Press, 1977), 228.

Chapter 5: Poverty Strikes and Prophecy Inspires

1. Martin, *The Life and Ministry of William J. Seymour*, 56.
2. Ibid., 57.
3. Ibid., see also Phillis Seymour, General Affidavit, 10 February 1896; and Simon Seymour Pension Files, National Archives and Records Administration.
4. Martin, *The Life and Ministry of William J. Seymour*, 58; see also Widow's Pension, 577, 804, Simon Seymour Pension Files, National Archives and Records Administration.
5. Ibid.

6. Reconstruction, The Second Civil War, accessed via http://www.pbs.org/wgbh/amex/reconstruction/schools/index.html.

7. See "Plessy v. Ferguson" at http://library.thinkquest.org/J0112391/plessy_v_ferguson.htm, and http://www.answers.com/topic/ plessy-v-ferguson, as viewed on September 8, 2005.

8. "Creation of the Jim Crow South," accessed via afroamhistory.about.com/library/weekly/aa010201a.htm.

9. Mac McLean, staff writer, "Who was Charles Lynch?", Danville Register & Bee, August 1, 2005, as viewed at http://www.registerbee.com/servlet/Satellite?pagename=Common%2FMGArticle%2FPrintVersion&c=MGArticle&cid=1031784177595&image=drb80x60.gif&oasDN=registerbee.com&oasPN=%21news on September 8, 2005.

10. Robert L. Zangrando, "Lynching," The Reader's Companion to American History, (Boston: Houghton Mifflin, 1991).

11. Ibid.

12. Richard M. Perloff, "The Press and Lynchings of African Americans," Journal of Black Studies, January 2000, 315–330, accessed via academic.csuohio.edu/perloffr/lynching.

13. A 1910 statement by Mississippi Senator James K. Vardaman that illustrates the extreme racist sentiments common in the South in the first half of the 20th century, propelling many African Americans to the North. Viewed at http://www.pbs.org/gointochicago/migrations/southern1.html on September 8, 2005.

14. Thomas Wentworth Higginson, "Negro Spirituals," African American History, as viewed at http://afroamhistory.about.com/library/blthomas _higginson_ spirituals.htm on September 8, 2005.

15. Ibid.

16. Ibid.

17. Ibid.

Chapter 6: Opposition and Opportunity Are Found

1. Martin, The Life and Ministry of William J. Seymour, 5.

2. New Perspectives on the West, accessed via www.pbs.org/weta/thewest/people/s_z/singleton.htm.

3. Bobby L. Lovett, "Benjamin 'Pap' Singleton," A Profile of African Americans in Tennessee History, as viewed at http://www.tnstate.edu/library/digital/single.htm onSeptember 8, 2005.

4. Larry Martin's research suggests this route as a possibility but recognizes that it cannot be proven beyond doubt. See, *The Life and Ministry of William J. Seymour*, 66.

5. Carolyn M. Brady, *Black History News & Notes,* No. 65, August 1996, a newsletter of the Indiana Historical Society, as viewed at http://www.indianahistory.org/ihs_press/periodicals.html on September 8, 2005.

6. Emma Lou Thornbrough, *The Negro in Indiana Before 1900: A Study of a Minority* (Indianapolis, IN: Indiana Historical Bureau, 1957; reprint, Bloomington, IN: Indiana University Press, 1993), 229n, 265.

7. Nelson, "For Such a Time as This," 159.

8. Ibid.

9. Ray Stannard Baker, *Following the Color Line: American Negro Citizenship in the Progressive Era* (New York: Doubleday, Page & Co., 1908; reprint, New York: Harper

and Row, 1964).
    10. Thornbrough, Negro in Indiana Before 1900, 395–396.
    11. Ibid., 260, 264n.
    12. Ibid., 160.
    13. Ibid.

Chapter 7: William Seymour Finds Unexpected Inspiration
    1. Nelson, "For Such a Time as This," 162.
    2. Martin, *The Life and Ministry of William J. Seymour*, 74.
    3. Ibid., 75; see also The Leaves of Healing, periodical, 11 June 1904.
    4. Martin, *The Life and Ministry of William J. Seymour*, 75; see also Cincinnati City Directory, Cincinnati, Ohio, 1901, 1902.
    5. Nelson, "For Such a Time as This," 164.
    6. Charles Carroll, *The Negro a Beast*, (St. Louis, MO: American Book and Bible House, 1900), 23.
    7. Ibid, 23.
    8. Ibid, 3.
    9. Ibid. 73
    10. Nelson, "For Such a Time as This," 164.
    11. Martin, *The Life and Ministry of William J. Seymour*, 79.
    12. Ibid.
    13. Nelson, "For Such a Time as This," 164.
    14. Ibid.

Chapter 8: Agnes Ozman Is Introduced
    1. Shumway, "A Critical History of Glossolalia", dissertation for for Boston University, 1918, chapter 7.
    2. Christian History Institute, accessed via chi.gospelcom.net/DAILYF/2003/05/daily-05-03-2003.shtml.
    3. James R. Goff Jr., *Fields White unto Harvest: Charles F Parham and the Missionary Origins of Pentecostalism* (Fayetteville, AR: University of Arkansas Press, 1988), 67.
    4. Ibid., 68.
    5. Vinson Synan, *The Holiness-Pentecostal Tradition: Charismatic Movements in the Twentieth Century* (Grand Rapids, MI: Wm. B. Eerdmans Publishing, 1971), 92.
    6. Ibid.
    7. Goff Jr., *Fields White unto Harvest: Charles F Parham and the Missionary Origins of Pentecostalism*, 72.
    8. Ibid., 64.
    9. Ibid., 65.
    10. Harold D. Hunter, Beniah at the Apostolic Crossroads: Little Noticed Crosscurrents of B.H. Irwin, Charles Fox Parham, Frank Sandford, A.J. Tomlinson, accessed via www.pctii.org/cyberj/cyberj1/hunter.html.
    11. Unity Publishing, What Spirit?, accessed via www.unitypublishing.com/NewReligiousMovements/WhatSpirtPart6.html.
    12. For information on Sandford's arrests and conviction for manslaughter and his ten-year prison sentence, see "Frank Sandford and Shiloh," at http://www.unitypublishing.com/ NewReligiousMovements/WhatSpirtPart6. html, as viewed September 8, 2005.

13. Editorial opinion in the *Rome, (New York) Sentinel*, Tuesday, November 21, 1978, in an article reporting the links between Shiloh and the Jonestown Massacre, as viewed at http://www.unitypublishing.com/NewReligiousMovements/WhatSpirtPart6. html on September 8, 2005.

14. Ibid.

15. The Rome, New York Sentinel, Tuesday, November 21, 1978.

16. Tongues of Fire, July 1 & 15, 1900, 111 and 115.

17. Martin, *The Life and Ministry of William J. Seymour*, 80.

18. Nelson, "For Such a Time as This," 166.

Chapter 9: Charles Parham Becomes Better Known

1. Sarah E. Parham, *The Life of Charles F. Parham: Founder of the Apostolic Faith Movement* (New York: Garland Publishing, Inc, 1930, 1980.

2. James R. Goff Jr., *Fields White unto Harvest*, 70.

3. Ibid. 71.

4. Ibid., 71; see also *Apostolic Faith* (Houston, Texas) October 1908.

5. Ibid.; see also Agnes La Berge, A History of the Pentecostal Movement from January 1, 1901, manuscript, *Pentecostal Evangel* editorial files, February 1922.

6. Ibid.

7. James R. Goff Jr., *Fields White unto Harvest*, 39.

8. *Topeka Daily Capital* (Topeka, Kansas), 6 January 1901, Goff Jr., Fields White unto Harvest, 79.

9. James R. Goff Jr., Fields White unto Harvest, 79–81.

10. Ibid., 83.

11. Ibid. 85.

12. Ibid.

13. Ibid., 86.

14. Ibid., 87.

15. Ibid., 88.

16. Ibid., 90.

17. Ibid., 93.

18. Ibid., 95. 19.

19. Ibid., 96–97.

20. Howard Goss, "The Winds of God: The Story of the Early Pentecostal Days (1901–1914)" in the *Life of Howard A. Goss* (New York: Comet Press Books, 1958).

21. Ibid.

22. Ibid., 97–105.

23. *Houston Daily Post*, August 13 1905; see also Goff Jr., *Fields White unto Harvest*, 104.

Chapter 10: Charles Parham Remains Cloaked

1. James R. Goff Jr., *Fields White unto Harvest*, 107

2. James R. Goff, *Charles F. Parham and His Role in the Development of the Pentecostal Movement*, 104.

3. Ibid., 106.

4. Goff, Charles F. *Parham and His Role in the Development of the Pentecostal Movement*, 107

5. Nelson, "For Such a Time as This," 167, 187.

6. *Apostolic Faith*, (Azusa Street) 1906.

7. Rufus Sanders, *William Joseph Seymour: Black Father of the 20th Century Pentecostal/Charismatic Movement* (Sandusky, Ohio, Alexandria Publications, 2003), 72.
8. Ibid.
9. Nelson, "For Such a Time as This," 167.
10. Ibid.
11. Goff, *Charles F. Parham and His Role in the Development of the Pentecostal Movement*.
12. Ibid., 108
13. *The Apostolic Faith Newsletter*, Melrose-Houston, March 1906; and Goff, *Charles F. Parham and His Role in the Development of the Pentecostal Movement*, 109.
14. Martin, *The Life and Ministry of William J. Seymour*, 93.
15. Ibid.

Chapter 11: William Seymour Meets Alma White

1. "Alma Bridwell White, Women in American History, viewed at search.eb.com/women/articles/White_Alma_Bridwell.html.
2. Ibid.
3. Ibid.
4. General Commission on Archives and History, The United Methodist Church, accessed via www.gcah.org/Museum/Women_Preaching/page_4.htm.
5. Bishop Alma White, *The Ku Klux Klan in Prophecy* (Zarapath, NJ: Pillar of Fire 1925.)
6. "Alma Bridwell White, Women in American History, viewed at search.eb.com/women/articles/White_Alma_Bridwell.html.
7. Nelson, "For Such a Time as This," 83
8. Ibid.

Chapter 12: William Seymour Delivers His Message to His Hosts

1. Nelson, "For Such a Time as This," 187.
2. Ibid.
3. Martin, *The Life and Ministry of William J. Seymour*, 102.
4. Accessed via "Los Angeles: Past, Present & Future," http://www.usc.edu/isd/archives/la
5. Larry Martin, The Life and Ministry of William J. Seymour, 105; see also "Population of this City," *Los Angeles Express* (14 April 1906).
6. Martin, *The Life and Ministry of William J. Seymour*, 125.
7. Ibid., 123.
8. Ibid., 128.
9. Ibid., 128; see also Nelson, "For Such a Time as This," 186.
10. Martin, *The Life and Ministry of William J. Seymour*, 129.
11. Nelson, "For Such a Time as This," 187; see also Martin, *The Life and Ministry of William J. Seymour*, 131.
12. Nelson, "For Such a Time as This," 187.
13. Ibid.

Chapter 13: William Seymour Receives His First Job Appraisal

1. Nelson, "For Such a Time as This," 187.
2. William Seymour, *The Words That Changed the World: Azusa Street Sermons*, ed.

Larry Martin (Joplin, MO: Christian Life Books, 1999), 54.
   3. Clara Davis, *Azusa Street Till Now: Eyewitness Accounts of the Move of God*, (Springdale, PA: Christian Publishing Service, 1993). 15.
   4 Sanders, *William Joseph Seymour*, 86.
   5. Ibid.
   6. Nelson, "For Such a Time as This,"188.
   7. Ibid., 189.

Chapter 14: Passions Are Unleashed
   1. Nelson, "For Such a Time as This," 188.
   2. Ibid., 225.
   3. Ibid., 188.
   4. *The Apostolic Faith,* (Azusa Street) 1906.
   5. Frank Bartleman, *Azusa Street* (New Kensington, PA: Whitaker House, 1982), 7.
   6. Nelson, "For Such a Time as This," 189.
   7. Ibid.
   8. Ibid.

Chapter 15: William Seymour Presses Forward
   1. Shumway, "A Critical Study of 'The Gift of Tongues'" 174; see also Nelson, "For Such a Time as This," 190.
   2. Ibid., 190.
   3. Shumway, "A Critical Study of 'The Gift of Tongues'", 44.
   4. Nelson, "For Such a Time as This," 190.
   5. Ibid.
   6. Ibid.
   7. Ibid., 191.
   8. Ibid.; see also *The Apostolic Faith*, (Azusa Street), May, 1907.
   9. Shumway, "A Critical History of Glossolalia", 1.
   10. Ibid., 45.
   11. Nelson, "For Such a Time as This," 191.
   12. Martin, *The Life and Ministry of William J. Seymour*, 168.
   13. Nelson, "For Such a Time as This," 191.
   14. Ibid., 227; see also Mother Emma Cotton, "Inside Story of the Outpouring of the Holy Spirit, Azusa Street, April 1906," *Message of the Apostolic Faith* newsletter, Vol. 1, No. 1, April 1939, Los Angeles, 3.
   15. Douglas Nelson, "For Such a Time as This," 192.
   16. Ibid.

Chapter 16: The Church Delivers a Message
   1. Bartleman, *Azusa Street*, 41.
   2. Ibid., 44.
   3. Nelson, "For Such a Time as This," 192.
   4. Ibid., 193.
   5. Martin, *The Life and Ministry of William J. Seymour*, 159; see also Clara Lum, "Miss Clara Lum Writes Wonders," *The Missionary World* (August 1906), 2.
   6. Nelson, "For Such a Time as This," 229; see also Arthur G Osterberg, "Tears—

The Secret of the Azusa Revival," *Voice of Healing* (July 1954), 12.

7. Martin, *The Life and Ministry of William J. Seymour*, 159.

8. Nelson, "For Such a Time as This," 229; see also Osterberg, "Tears—The Secret of the Azusa Revival," 12–13.

9. Nelson, "For Such a Time as This," 230.

10. Though this translation is common knowledge, it is interesting to note how significant the name has become. Even motorcyclists are keen to align themselves with the history. See www.azuzastreetriders.com/azuza_ more.html.

11. Bartleman, Azusa Street, 160.

12. Nelson, "For Such a Time as This," 195.

13. Richard J. Foster, *Streams of Living Water; Celebrating the Great Traditions of Christian Faith* (San Francisco, New York: Harper, 1998), accessed via www.prmi.org/gateways9.pdf.

14. Nelson, "For Such a Time as This," 231.

15. Ibid., 195.

16. Sanders, *William Joseph Seymour*, 96.

17. *Los Angeles Daily Times*, April 18, 1906.

18. Gladys Hansen, Chronology of the Great Earthquake, and the 1906-7 Graft Investigations, accessed via www.sfmuseum.org/ alm/quakes2.html.

Chapter 17: April 1906 Brings Change

1. Martin, *The Life and Ministry of William J. Seymour*, 167.

2. Ibid., 173.

3. *The Apostolic Faith* (Azusa Street), September 1906.

4. Nelson, "For Such a Time as This," 196.

5. Martin, *The Life and Ministry of William J. Seymour*, 177.

6. *The Apostolic Faith* (Azusa Street), September 1906.

7. Martin, *The Life and Ministry of William J. Seymour*, 190.

8. Words by Frank Bottome, 1890, Public Domain; as used in Martin, *The Life and Ministry of William J. Seymour*, 354.

9. "Black Experience in America" accessed via www.rit.edu/~rrcgsh/bx/bx09a.html.

10. *The Apostolic Faith* (Azusa Street), September 1906.

11. Bartleman, *Azusa Street*, 51.

12. Synan, *The Holiness-Pentecostal Tradition*, 114.

13. *The Apostolic Faith* (Azusa Street), November 1906.

14. Walter J. Hollenweger, *The Pentecostals* (London: Hendrickson, 1972), 24; see also Nelson, "For Such a Time as This," 198.

15. Bartleman, *Azusa Street*, 51.

Chapter 18: We Meet Florence Crawford

1. Bartleman, *Azusa Street*, 45.

2. Ibid., 46.

3. Shumway, "A Critical History of Glossolalia", 59.

4. Bartleman, *Azusa Street*, 46.

5. Ibid., 60.

6. Ibid., 58.

7. Ibid., 59.

8. Ibid., 55.
9. Ibid., 56.
10. Ibid., 57.
11. Ibid., 56.
12. Shumway, "A Critical History of Glossolalia", 112.
13. Ibid., 115.
14. Nelson, "For Such a Time as This," 200.
15. Ibid.
16. *The Apostolic Faith* (Azusa Street), November 1906.
17. Martin, *The Life and Ministry of William J. Seymour*, 191.
18. Nelson, "For Such a Time as This," 200. 19. Ibid., 201.

Chapter 19: Lives Are Transformed
1. Martin, *The Life and Ministry of William J. Seymour*, 183.
2. *The Apostolic Faith* (Azusa Street), January 1907.
3. Ibid., May 1908.
4. Ibid.
5. Martin, *The Life and Ministry of William J. Seymour*, 185.
6. Ibid., 184.
7. Synan, *The Holiness-Pentecostal Tradition*, 99.
8. Bartleman, *Azusa Street*, 66.
9. Synan, *The Holiness-Pentecostal Tradition*, 98.
10. *The Apostolic Faith* (Azusa Street), December 1906.
11. Martin, *The Life and Ministry of William J. Seymour*, 257.
12. Ibid., 187.
13. Ibid., 189; see also *The Apostolic Faith* (Azusa Street), January 1907.
14. Martin, *The Life and Ministry of William J. Seymour*, 189.
15. Ibid.
16. Ibid., 197.
17. Reve M Pete, "The Outpouring of the Holy Ghost at the Azusa Street Mission," accessed via members.aol.com/ revepete/HolinessCh9.html.
18. Martin, *The Life and Ministry of William J. Seymour*, 182.
19. Ibid., 184; see also *The Apostolic Faith* (Azusa Street), May 1908.
20. Martin, *The Life and Ministry of William J. Seymour*, 182; see also Frank Bartleman, "Letter From Los Angeles" *Triumphs of Faith*, (December 1906).
21. Synan, *The Holiness-Pentecostal Tradition*, 101.
22. Patrick Johnstone and Jason Mandryk, Operation World (2000) accessed via en.wikipedia.org/wiki/Pentecostalism.

Chapter 20: William Seymour Connects with His Widest Audience
1. Nelson, "For Such a Time as This," 206.
2. Larry Martin, *The Life and Ministry of William J. Seymour*, 192.
3. The *Apostolic Faith* (Azusa Street), September 1906.
4. Ibid.
5. Ibid.
6. Ibid.
7. Ibid.
8. Ibid.

9. Synan, *The Holiness-Pentecostal Tradition*, 99.
10. *The Apostolic Faith* (Azusa Street), September 1906.
11. Ibid.; see also Nelson, "For Such a Time as This," 262.
12. Synan, *The Holiness-Pentecostal Tradition*, 102.
13. *The Apostolic Faith* (Azusa Street), September 1906.
14. Ibid.
15. Ibid.
16. Martin, *The Life and Ministry of William J. Seymour*, 184; see also *The Apostolic Faith* (Azusa Street), September 1906.
17. Synan, *The Holiness-Pentecostal Tradition*, 100.

Chapter 21: Charles Parham Delivers His Briefest Sermon
1. Nelson, "For Such a Time as This," 209.
2. Goff Jr., *Fields White unto Harvest*, 151.
3. Nelson, "For Such a Time as This," 239.
4. *The Apostolic Faith* (Azusa Street), April 1907.
5. James R. Goff Jr., *Fields White unto Harvest*, 130–135.
6. Reve' M. Pete, "The Outpouring of the Holy Ghost at Azusa Street," *The Impact of Holiness Preaching as Taught by John Wesley and the Outpouring of the Holy Ghost on Racism*, accessed via members.aol.com/revepete/HolinessCh9.html.
7. Nelson, "For Such a Time as This," 209.
8. David W. Cloud, "Azusa Street Mission," as viewed at www.tribwatch.com/azusa.htm on September 27, 2005.
9. Nelson, "For Such a Time as This," 211.
10. Martin, *The Life and Ministry of William J. Seymour*, 93.
11. Goff Jr., *Fields White unto Harvest*, 83.
12. Ibid., 157; see also Douglas Nelson, "For Such a Time as This," 146.
13. Nelson, "For Such a Time as This," 97.
14. Goff Jr., *Fields White unto Harvest*, 102.
15. Martin, *The Life and Ministry of William J. Seymour*, 270.

Chapter 22: The Future is Glimpsed
1. Nelson, "For Such a Time as This," 213.
2. *The Apostolic Faith* (Azusa Street), November 1906.
3. Martin, *The Life and Ministry of William J. Seymour*, 270.
4. Nelson, "For Such a Time as This," 210.
5. Ibid.
6. *The Apostolic Faith* (Azusa Street), December 1906.
7. Nelson, "For Such a Time as This," 212.
8. *The Apostolic Faith* (Azusa Street), December 1906.

Chapter 23: Charles Parham's Story is Told
1. *The Burning Bush*, Wisconsin, March 14, 1907.
2. Ibid., May 9, 1907.
3. Ibid., January 24, 1907.
4. Ibid.
5. Ibid.

6. Ibid.
7. Ibid.
8. James R. Goff Jr., *Fields White unto Harvest*, 132.
9. Ibid., 133.
10. Nelson, "For Such a Time as This," 211.
11. James R. Goff Jr., *Fields White unto Harvest*, 134.
12. Ibid.
13. Ibid., 136.
14. Ibid., 137.
15. Ibid., 143; see also the *Waukegan Daily Sun*, September 1907.
16. James R. Goff Jr., *Fields White unto Harvest*, 144.
17. Ibid., 145.
18. Ibid., 149.
19. Ibid., 157; see also *Apostolic Faith* (Baxter), January, March 1927. 20. Ibid., 159.

Chapter 24: William Seymour's Faith Rises Even Higher
1. *The Apostolic Faith* (Azusa Street), October-January 1908.
2. Nelson, "For Such a Time as This," 213.
3. Martin, *The Life and Ministry of William J. Seymour*, 215.
4. Ibid., 216.
5. Ibid., 217.
6. Synan, *The Holiness-Pentecostal Tradition*, 129.
7. Nelson, "For Such a Time as This," 213.
8. Ibid., 214; see also Shumway, "A Critical Study of the Gift of Tongues."
9. Nelson, "For Such a Time as This," 216.
10. Martin, *The Life and Ministry of William J. Seymour*, 276.
11. Nelson, "For Such a Time as This," 216.
12. *The Apostolic Faith* (Azusa Street), February 1907.
13. Martin, *The Life and Ministry of William J. Seymour*, 249.
14. Ibid., 253.
15. Ibid., 59.
16. *The Apostolic Faith* (Azusa Street), January 1907.
17. Nelson, "For Such a Time as This," 215.
18. Martin, *The Life and Ministry of William J. Seymour*, 271.

Chapter 25: William Seymour Is Deceived
1. Synan, *The Holiness-Pentecostal Tradition*, 127–8.
2. Martin, The Life and Ministry of William J. Seymour, 275.
3. Ibid.
4. Ibid.
5. Nelson, "For Such a Time as This," 216.
6. Ibid., 217.
7. Ibid.
8. *The Apostolic Faith* (Azusa Street), June-September 1907.
9. Ibid.
10. Ibid., October-January 1908.
11. Ibid., January 1908.
12. Nelson, "For Such a Time as This," 217.

13. *The Apostolic Faith* (Portland, Oregon), July/August 1908.
14. Ibid.

Chapter 26: The Doors Are Closed
1. The Apostolic Faith (Portland, Oregon) May-June 1909.
2. Martin, *The Life and Ministry of William J. Seymour*, 213.
3. Ibid., 281.
4. Nelson, "For Such a Time as This," 218.
5. Ibid., 78.
6. Martin, *The Life and Ministry of William J. Seymour*, 278.
7. The *Apostolic Faith* (Azusa Street), January 1907.
8. Martin, *The Life and Ministry of William J. Seymour*, 278.
9. Ibid., 282.
10. G. B. Studd, "Los Angeles" *Confidence*, 15 August 1908; see also Martin, The *Life and Ministry of William J. Seymour*, 283.
11. Roberta Senechal, Historical Research and Narrative, accessed via www.lib.niu.edu/ipo/iht329622.html.
12. "The History of Our Church," The Apostolic Faith Church, as viewed at http://www.apostolicfaith.org/aboutus/history.asp.

Chapter 27: William Seymour is Forced to the Edge
1. Nelson, "For Such a Time as This," 218.
2. Ibid., 219.
3. Michael L. Brown, *From Holy Laughter to Holy Fire* (Shippensburg, PA: Destiny Image, 1997), 197–198.
4. Nelson, "For Such a Time as This," 219.
5. Ibid
6. Bartleman, *Azusa Street*, 7.
7. Ibid., 51.
8. Ibid., 68.
9. Nelson, "For Such a Time as This," 92.
10. Bartleman, *Azusa Street*, 143; see also Martin, *The Life and Ministry of William J. Seymour, 283*.

Chapter 28: William Durham Wrestles for Control
1. "Skeptics and Scoffers: The Religious World Looks at Azusa Street: 1906-1907," ed. Larry Martin, (Joplin, Missouri, 2004), 144–145.
2. Ibid.
3. Nelson, "For Such a Time as This," 246; 216.
4. Synan, *The Holiness-Pentecostal Tradition,* 104.
5. Ibid., 248.
6. Ibid., 247.
7. Ibid.
8. Ibid.
9. Ibid.
10. Ibid., 248.
11. Ibid.

12. Ibid.
13. Martin, *The Life and Ministry of William J. Seymour*, 288.
14. Ibid., 289.
15. Bartleman, *Azusa Street*, 122.
16. Ibid., 7.
17. Nelson, "For Such a Time as This." 249.

Chapter 29: The Splits Start to Split
1. Synan, *The Holiness-Pentecostal Tradition*, 86.
2. Martin, *The Life and Ministry of William J. Seymour*, 125.
3. Synan, *The Holiness-Pentecostal Tradition*, 138-139.
4. Ibid., 140–141.
5. Ibid., 141.
6. Ibid., 155.
7. Nelson, "For Such a Time as This," 252.
8. Ibid., 253.
9. A. A Boddy, *Confidence*, November 1912.
10. Martin, *The Life and Ministry of William J. Seymour*, 324.
11. A. A Boddy, *Confidence*, November 1912.
12. Nelson, "For Such a Time as This," 253.
13. A. A. Boddy, *Confidence*, November 1912.
14. *Confidence*, April 1913.
15. J. Roswell Flower, "Letter to Richard Crayne" in Richard Crayne, *Pentecostal Handbook: A Reference Guide to the Origins, Personalities, and Doctrines of the Pentecostal People in the United States of America.* (Morristown, TN: The Author, 1986), 202. see also Nelson, "For Such a Time as This," 282.
16. Nelson, "For Such a Time as This," 254.
17. Ibid.
18. Ibid.
19. Ibid., 255; see also *Confidence*, November 1912.

Chapter 30: William Seymour Considers the Future
1. Nelson, "For Such a Time as This," 256.
2. Ibid.
3. Ibid., 257.
4. Ibid., 258.
5. Encyclopedia Britannica, accessed via: www.africanamericans.com/KuKluxKlan.htm.
6. Nelson, "For Such a Time as This," 261.
7. Ibid., 262.
8. Ibid., 264.
9. William Seymour, *Doctrines and Discipline of the Azusa Street Apostolic Faith Mission*, ed. Larry Martin (Joplin, MO: Christian Life Books, 2000).
10. Harold Hunter, International Pentecostal Holiness Church, accessed via: www.pctii.org/arc/iphc.html.
11. Nelson, "For Such a Time as This," 41.
12. Ibid., 268.

13. Ibid., 269.

Chapter 31: The Story Ends and Repeats
1. Larry Martin, *The Life and Ministry of William J. Seymour*, 330.
2. Ibid.
3. Ibid.
4. Nelson, "For Such a Time as This," 272.
5. Ibid., 273.
6. Ibid.
7. Martin, *The Life and Ministry of William J. Seymour*, 332.
8. Ibid., 333.
9. Nelson, "For Such a Time as This," 274.
10. Ibid.
11. Ibid.
12. Patrick Johnstone and Jason Mandryk, *Operation World (2009)* accessed via en.wikipedia.org/ wiki/Pentecostalism; see also Christianity Today, November 16, 1998.
13. Christian History, Spring 1998.

Bibliography

Baker, Ray Stannard. *Following the Color Line: American Negro Citizenship in the Progressive Era* (New York: Doubleday, Page & Co., 1908; reprint, New York: Harper and Row, 1964).

Bartleman, Frank. *Azusa Street* (New Kensington, PA: Whitaker House, 1982).

Boddy, A. A *Confidence*, November 1912.

Brady, Carolyn M. Black History News & Notes, No. 65, August 1996, a newsletter of the Indiana Historical Society, as viewed at http://www.indianahistory.org/ihs_press/ periodicals.html on September 8, 2005.

Broussard, Bernard. *A History of St Mary Parish* ([Franklin, LA: the author, 1955).

Brown, Michael L. *From Holy Laughter to Holy Fire* (Shippensburg, PA: Destiny Image, 1997).

Carroll, Charles. *The Negro a Beast*, (St. Louis, MO: American Book and Bible House, 1900).

Cloud, David W. "Azusa Street Mission," as viewed at www.tribwatch.com/azusa.htm on September 27, 2005.

Davis, Clara. *Azusa Street Till Now: Eyewitness Accounts of the Move of God*, (Springdale, PA: Christian Publishing Service, 1993).

Delaune, Jewell Lynn. "A Social History of St Mary Parish, 1845–1860, *Louisiana Historical Quarterly*, 32 (1948), 17-102.

Foster, Richard J. *Streams of Living Water; Celebrating the Great Traditions of Christian Faith* (San Francisco, New York: Harper, 1998).

Garraty, John A. *The American Nation: A History of the United States Since 1865*. (New York: Addison Wesley Publishing Company, 1983).

Goff, James R. Jr. *Fields White unto Harvest: Charles F Parham and the Missionary Origins of Pentecostalism* (Fayetteville, AR: University of Arkansas Press, 1988).

Goss, Howard. *The Winds of God: the Story of the Early Pentecostal Days (1901–1914) in the Life of Howard A. Goss* (New York: Comet Press Books, 1958).

Gruver, Rebecca Brooks. *An American History, Volume 1: to 1877* (Reading, MA, Random House, 1981).

Hunter, Harold D. "Beniah at the Apostolic Crossroads: Little Noticed

Crosscurrents of B.H. Irwin, Charles Fox Parham, Frank Sandford, A.J. Tomlinson" *Cyberjournal for Pentecostal-Charismatic Research*, accessed via http://www.pctii.org/cyberj/cyberj1/hunter.html.

La Berge, Agnes. *A History of the Pentecostal Movement from January 1, 1901*, manuscript, *Pentecostal Evangel* editorial files, February 1922.

La Bree, Benjamin. *The Confederate Soldier in the Civil War, 1861–1865* (New Jersey: Prentice Press, 1897).

Lockett, Samuel H. *Louisiana as It Is: A Geographical and Topographical Description of the State* (Baton Rouge, LA: Louisiana State University Press, 1969).

Lovett, Bobby L. "Benjamin 'Pap' Singleton," *A Profile of African Americans in Tennessee History,* as viewed at http://www.tnstate.edu/library/digital/single.htm on September 8, 2005.

Marty, Martin E. *Religion in the Old South*, (Chicago: University of Chicago Press, 1977.

Martin, Larry, ed. *"Skeptics and Scoffers: The Religious World Looks at Azusa Street: 1906-1907,"* (Joplin, Missouri, 2004.

Martin, Larry. *The Life and Ministry of William J. Seymour,* (Joplin, MO: Christian Life Books, 1999.

McCary, Peyton. *Abraham Lincoln and Reconstruction* (Princeton: Princeton University Press, 1979).

McLean, Mac. "Who was Charles Lynch?" [Danville] *Register & Bee*, August 1, 2005.

Osterberg, Arthur G. "Tears—The Secret of the Azusa Revival," *Voice of Healing* (July 1954).

Parham, Sarah E. *The Life of Charles F. Parham: Founder of the Apostolic Faith Movement* (New York: Garland Publishing, Inc, 1930, 1980).

Pete, Reve M. "The Outpouring of the Holy Ghost at the Azusa Street Mission," accessed via members.aol.com/revepete/HolinessCh9.html.

_Pete, Reve M. "The Impact of Holiness Preaching as Taught by John Wesley and the Outpouring of the Holy Ghost on Racism," accessed via members.aol.com/revepete/HolinessCh9.html.

Perloff, Richard M. "The Press and Lynchings of African Americans," *Journal of Black Studies*, January 2000, 315–330, accessed via academic.csuohio.

edu/perloffr/lynching.

Sanders, Rufus. *William Joseph Seymour: Black Father of the 20th Century Pentecostal/Charismatic Movement* (Sandusky, OH: Alexandria Publications, 2003).

Seymour, William. *Doctrines and Discipline of the Azusa Street Apostolic Faith Mission*, ed. Larry Martin (Joplin, MO: Christian Life Books, 2000).

Seymour, William. *The Words that Changed the World: Azusa Street Sermons*, ed. Larry Martin (Joplin, MO: Christian Life Books, 1999.

Shotgun's Home of the American Civil War, accessed via www.civilwarhome.com/warcosts.htm.

Shumway, Charles William. "A Critical History of Glossolalia," dissertation Boston University, 1918.

Shumway, Charles William. *A Critical Study of 'the Gift of Tongues*, Ph.D. dissertation for University of Southern California, 1914.

Synan, Vinson. *The Holiness-Pentecostal Tradition: Charismatic Movements in the Twentieth Century* (Grand Rapids, MI: Wm. B. Eerdmans Publishing Co., 1971).

Taylor, Joe Gray. *Louisiana Reconstructed: 1863-1877*. (Baton Rouge: Louisiana State University Press, 1974).

Thornbrough, Emma Lou. *The Negro in Indiana Before 1900: A Study of a Minority* (Indianapolis, IN: Indiana Historical Bureau, 1957; reprint, Bloomington, IN: Indiana University Press, 1993).

White, Alma. *The Ku Klux Klan in Prophecy*. (Zarapath, NJ: Pillar of Fire, 1925).

Zangrando, Robert L. "Lynching" in Eric Foner and John A. Garraty, eds, *The Reader's Companion to American History*. (Boston: Houghton Mifflin, 1991).

Articles

"Cost of the American Civil War," *Civil War Potpourri*, viewed at http://www.civilwarhome.com/warcosts.htm on September 6, 2005.

"A History of Grant Parish," *The Town Talk*, Monday, May 9, 2005, as viewed at "Alma Bridwell White, Women in American History, viewed at search.eb.com/women/articles/White_Alma_Bridwell.ht ml.

"Instrument of Torture Used by Slave-holders," *Harper's Weekly* Reports on Black Slavery 1857–1874, as viewed at blackhistory.harpweek.com/

2Slavery/SlaveryLevelOne. htm viewed on September 6, 2005.

"The Freedman's Bureau," *Harper's Weekly* Reports on Black America 1857–1874, July 25, 1868, as viewed at http://blackhistory.harpweek.com/4Reconstruction/467T heFreedmensBureau.htm on September 6, 2005.

"The History of Our Church," *The Apostolic Faith Church*, as viewed at http://www.apostolicfaith.org/aboutus/history.asp.

"The Ku Klux Klan Hearings," Harpers Weekly Reports on Black America 1857–1874, August 22, 1868, 531.

The Louisiana Murders, Harper's Weekly, 10 May 1873. "Toward Racial Equality," *Harper's Weekly* Reports on Black America 1857–1874, Humor Item, March 13, 1858.

"Widow's Pension" Los Angeles Daily Times, April 18, 1906.

Bartleman, Frank. "Letter from Los Angeles" *Triumphs of Faith*, (December 1906).

Cotton, Emma. "Inside Story of the Outpouring of the Holy Spirit, Azusa Street, April 1906," *Message of the Apostolic Faith*, 1, 1, April 1939, Los Angeles, 3.

Goff, James R. "Charles F. Parham and His Role in the Development of the Pentecostal Movement", Kansas State Historical Society, *Kansas History* 7: 3 (Autumn, 1984), 226-237.

Hebert, Timothy. "Methodism Along the Bayou," as viewed at http://www.iscuo.org/hist4.htm on September 6, 2005.

"Atlantic Monthly; Negro Spirituals (Reprint); 1867." *Buffalo Quarters Historical Society Papers. Digital Collections.* http://digitalcommons.buffalostate.edu/magazines-books/9.

Lum, Clara. "Miss Clara Lum Writes Wonders," *The Missionary World* (August 1906.

Studd, G. B. "Los Angeles" *Confidence*, 15 August 1908.

Periodicals

Apostolic Faith (Baxter), January, March 1927.
Apostolic Faith (Houston, Texas) October 1908.

Confidence

Christian History, Spring 1998.

The Apostolic Faith (Azusa Street),
- November 1906. T
- December 1906.
- February 1907.

The Apostolic Faith (Portland, Oregon) May-June 1909.

The Apostolic Faith Newsletter (Melrose-Houston) March 1906;

The Burning Bush, March 14, 1907.

The Leaves of Healing, 11 June 1904.

Tongues of Fire